Buffalo
Nation

*American Indian Efforts
to Restore the Bison*

KEN ZONTEK

UNIVERSITY OF NEBRASKA PRESS
LINCOLN AND LONDON

Library of Congress
Cataloging-in-Publication
Data

Zontek, Ken.
Buffalo nation : American
Indian efforts to restore the
bison / Ken Zontek.
p. cm.
Includes bibliographical
references and index.
ISBN-13: 978-0-8032-9922-1
(pbk. : alk. paper)
ISBN-10: 0-8032-9922-2
(pbk. : alk. paper)
1. Indians of North America—
Domestic animals—Great
Plains. 2. American bison—
Great Plains. 3. Cultural
property—Protection—Great
Plains. 4. Human-animal
relationships—Great Plains.
I. Title.
E78.G73Z66 2007
333.95'96430978—dc22
2006018311

Set in Quadraat by
Kim Essman.
Designed by R. W. Boeche.

For Native America

Contents

Illustrations

Maps

Acknowledgments

Numerous individuals contributed to the completion of this work, and all warrant gratitude to varying degrees. First and foremost, I would like to thank the many Native people who assisted me in telling the remarkable story of bison restoration. Most notably, Jim Garrett, who embodies the focus of this study in Native American bison landscape stewardship, provided keen insight. Fred DuBray and Louis LaRose shared their vision and enabled me to conduct a thorough examination of the efforts of the Intertribal Bison Cooperative. Garrett, DuBray, and LaRose also helped review my original manuscript. Dennis Rousseau provided access to the Cheyenne River Reservation bison herd and staff so a focused study of a single herd emerges in the photo essay. Throughout Indian Country in the United States and Canada, Native people welcomed me and assisted me in my quest to describe their relationship to the bison. I forever will remain indebted to all of them. This work is dedicated to them and their home landscape.

This book emerges from my doctoral dissertation at the University of Idaho. Bill Swagerty, who served as my advisor, both professionalized and personalized my historical study. He will remain a lifelong mentor. Kathy Aiken, history department chairwoman, kept me attuned to the value of telling a good story in the presentation of history. Ethnohistorian Dale Graden enhanced my cultural sensitivity. Meanwhile, Gerry Wright from the department of wildlife resources helped me construct a more scientific approach for my historical analysis. Also, interim committee member Carlos Schwantes helped me learn how to view history through the lens of landscape. Office manager Nancy Dafoe guided me through the administrative procedures necessary to complete a work of this nature. Colleague John Whitmer offered me a model of graduate work. As well, the John Calhoun Smith Fund at the University of Idaho supported much of my travel and research costs, enabling me to cover thousands of miles in my fieldwork.

Perhaps no single individual contributed more to the development of this work than Mary Meagher. Her work with bison in general and particularly in Yellowstone for more than forty years led me to consult her expertise. She helped me every step of the way as I sought to understand the bison, its landscape, and its stewardship. Valerius Geist, the eminent conservation biologist of Canada, thoroughly examined my original manuscript as well and provided important direction. Karen Stock took time from her own doctoral work at the University of Manitoba on Canadian bison restoration to offer helpful suggestions. Bill Campbell of Homefire Productions, Inc. most graciously donated several key photographs. Chris Thorsen of Cascade Graphics provided the maps. Mary Radeke conducted "eleventh-hour" edits. Jessica Sutterlict helped with title selection. Jamie Chipman helped me administer surveys of tribes committed to bison restoration. Sona Skarkova provided insight into the analysis of animals. My friends and colleagues at Yakima Valley Community College, including Mary Lou Rozdilsky, Kelley Chase, Monty Walker, and Tim Jeske, gave me sanctuary to complete my work in the waning months of its production. Ken Stewart, Chelle Somsen, and Carol Jennings offered special assistance in acquiring photographs at the South Dakota State Historical Society archives, and Rebecca Kohl did the same at the archives of the Montana Historical Society. Gary Dunham and Gretchen Albers at the University of Nebraska Press proved invaluable in working toward the publication of this manuscript and confirmed my long-held belief that the friendliest folks in America live in Nebraska.

My family played a paramount role in the making of this work. My parents always encouraged me and fostered a love of learning. My father joined my sister in thorough editing of initial manuscripts. My brother helped with maps and tables and provided computer assistance. Tricia Valdez-Zontek provided technical and administrative assistance. My son, Zachary, gave me perhaps the best reinforcement when he adopted "kanka" (*tatanka*) as one of his first distinguishable vocabulary words, which he repeated while holding his index fingers alongside his head.

Ultimately, I thank God for enabling me to persevere in this endeavor and for putting such supportive people in my life. I bear full responsibility for any errors, omissions, or misinterpretations. In the final acknowledgment, however, and in the spirit of many traditional Native Americans, I must thank the buffalo nation for returning and giving us a second chance to improve our relationship with our natural environment.

Introduction

Over the past century and a quarter, a phenomenal story of cultural perseverance has unraveled in Indian Country, as Native Americans have sought
to preserve the bison as an extension of preserving themselves and their
culture.[1] Many variables, including questions over the very survival of some
tribes, were formed in Native America as a result of the dislocation of the
past half millennium. However, one constant for a significant number of
Indian people has been the desire for a landscape where the buffalo can
roam. In the roaming of the bison, dreams could also then materialize for
Native people to retain their cultural autonomy. This book attempts to tell
the story of Native Americans working to save bison to keep alive the possibilities bestowed on them as residents in the North American landscape.
In a fashion perhaps quite peculiar to many Euro-Americans, prominent
Native leaders in the bison restoration movement provided a milestone event
when, in the early 1990s, using a traditional ceremony, the leaders "asked"
the bison if they wanted to return.[2] The leaders received an affirmative answer, validating their efforts past, present, and future.

The story of the Native American restoration of the buffalo nation warrants telling.[3] More importantly, the story requires a Native voice. Hence,
this author drove fifteen thousand miles through Indian Country, from
New Mexico in the south to the Northwest Territories in the north and from
Washington in the west to South Dakota in the east. Dozens of interviews
with Native North Americans and observations of Indian people interacting
with bison emerged from these travels. The common threads in this research
remained the bison and the land, which provided a rich environment both for
the Native American discourse and the reflection offered here. The results
of the fieldwork and archival labor spawned one journal article, a master's
thesis, and a doctoral dissertation that evolved into the present work.[4]

Several key topics of discourse emerge from the story of Native American bison restoration. Broad categorization of these salient features separates them into cultural, ecological, contemporary, and comparative considerations. Evaluating the story through the cultural, or ethnohistorical, lens leads to several conclusions. In analyzing these summations, we must understand that Native Americans developed diverse, vibrant cultures that defy stereotype. However, the relationship Natives developed with bison offers one homogenizing aspect of North American indigenous culture: wherever buffalo roamed, they impacted Native Americans, who sought to interact with bison as much as possible. Arguably, Native Americans established a virtually unprecedented human-animal relationship with the bison, in which buffalo country became Indian Country.[5]

It's difficult to think of another group of humans who have become so intertwined with a wild animal species that it pervaded their culture. Bison permeate virtually everything material for Native Americans as well as the spiritual, as exemplified by many of the plains groups and to a lesser extent groups located farther from the heart of the bison landscape. Moreover, Native people did not lose their physical relationship with the bison after the demise of the great herds. They retained access to smaller groups, or later captive herds, even after their alienation from their lands, which culminated in the late nineteenth and early twentieth centuries. Native Americans never lost a spiritual relationship with their kindred mammal. Unsurprisingly for many students of Native American culture, the last steward of bison prior to the loss of physical contact was a woman, Sarah (Laribee) Philip.[6] In fact, she is just one of several women who have played key roles in bison restoration from the establishment of captive herds in the 1870s and 1880s to the activism for free-ranging bison in contemporary society. Additionally, close inspection of Native bison restoration reveals noneconomic, culturally substantive reasons for bringing back the bison, rather than the rationalist economic motivations often seen in mainstream Euro-American society.

The concern with bringing back the bison without a primary focus on economic benefit reveals an ecological side to Native bison recovery. Native Americans always sought a landscape that offered a habitat for bison. Indians fought to protect their home. In many areas, these homelands provided range for bison; hence, they fought to protect the bison homeland. Evidence that Native people entered into treaty negotiations to alter the landscape fails to materialize, especially with respect to the plains. Prior to Euro-American hegemony, Native Americans did not engage in invasive land practices that would deny habitat to bison. In fact, even after full implementation of the reservation system, Indians who became stewards of bison herds ran their bison on ranges as unfettered as possible. Such protection of bison range and offering of sanctuary to bison on reservations to restore the buffalo nation in many ways nullifies revisionist arguments implicating Native Americans in the destruction of the bison.[7] Native Americans sought to maintain free-ranging bison herds as long as possible in the face of a landscape changing because of the Euro-American presence, which significantly differs from the Euro-Americans' idea of saving bison for parks and zoos while transforming the former range of the bison into regions of intensive agriculture. Thus, the historical analyst can conclude that by association with free-ranging bison, Native Americans became champions for a healthy ecosystem, or at least one capable of sustaining large mobile ungulate populations.[8]

Moving toward the present, the contemporary observer witnesses that many Native American bison stewards have entered into alliance with con-servation biologists, proponents of range restoration, or ecosystem scien-tists as they explore options for providing the best oversight for a healthy landscape.[9] Bison restoration in Indian Country greatly accelerated over the past generation, as the growing number of tribes and private Indian owners acquiring bison testifies. The Intertribal Bison Cooperative (ITBC) emerged as a pan-tribal organization that provides a unifying force in In-dian Country for restoring bison's "dignity," meaning as free from human manipulation as possible. At the same time, Native Americans have become more vociferous champions of the bison by rallying against the limitations placed on the bison herd of Yellowstone National Park, which tenuously possesses the status as the only free-ranging bison herd in the continental United States. Still, government personnel shoot the bison when they exceed various politically imposed boundaries. Many Native Americans view these bison as symbols of themselves and take great exception to the high-handed treatment of this icon.

Finally, the Yellowstone Park example touches on another aspect of Native bison recovery in that areas of Canada offer a stark contrast. For example, Canadian First Nations Indians help to manage select public herds at the Mackenzie Bison Sanctuary and Wood Buffalo National Park. These herds can move with far less restriction than those in Yellowstone. Thus, in this respect the Canadian Indian movement to restore the buffalo nation surpasses that found in the United States. However, while this is true in public management, it does not hold true in tribal herd management. Canada does not yet possess a pan-Indian organization like the ITBC to provide cohesion and guidance in bison restoration. The indigenous effort in Canada therefore hinges somewhat more on economic rationale, though the substantive reasons abound there as well. Either way, in both Canada and the United States the history of bison restoration is a story of local people, westerners, bringing back an indigenous resource with indigenous people playing a lead role in restoring "bison as bison" rather than as a breed of woolly cow. Still, future expansion of bison restoration will require consensus building among Native American, government, and private entities in order for it to occur both north and south of the forty-ninth parallel.

A powerful metaphor from buffalo country was provided near the end of the nineteenth- century bison annihilation when a Blackfeet man described the scene as seeing the "tail of the last buffalo."[10] Perhaps he would have been glad to know that the face of the buffalo has returned to its home in increasing numbers, with Native Americans providing stewardship. Still, much of the script for the Native effort toward bison restoration remains unwritten. Yet this effort already possesses a rich history of cultural tenacity and the tightly woven relationship between humans and animals.

1. A Relationship from Time Immemorial

In my body, in my blood runs the spirit of the buffalo.

Arvol Looking Horse (2000)

Bison and Native Americans—in the historical context the two entities seem inseparable. Yet they also merge in contemporary analysis. Native Americans maintain a continuous relationship with the "buffalo nation" that extends back to time immemorial.[1] These indigenous people inculcate the historic relations with ongoing efforts to restore their animal brethren to their position as a landmark species occupying various ecological niches across the North American continent. This restoration—marked by a vision for a healthy landscape, empathy between the animal and human worlds, and cultural perseverance—warrants presentation. For more than 125 years, Native Americans have labored to bring back a healthy, viable bison population imbued with the dignity owed to it by its cultural dependents and stewards. Today, American Indians from more than sixty tribes in the United States and Canada work with more than twenty thousand buffalo. Although the numbers of people and animals acting in concert toward restoration pale in comparison to those who interacted in prehistory and history, the rising numbers define the effort. The bison are making a comeback, and Native Americans in the United States and First Nations peoples of Canada are playing an integral role. Native spiritual elder Arvol Looking Horse makes it clear: "We are the buffalo people."[2]

The story of the restoration must begin with background on the prehistoric and historic relationship between Natives and bison. The hundreds of articles and books already in print on these subjects render any historic endeavor an exercise in bison historiography. That said, room exists for reinterpretation of the material in reconciliation with Native perceptions. Ultimately, descriptions of the buffalo and its evolution alongside the continent's indigens merge with the story of the Euro-American invasion of North America, producing a tragic tale begging for a happier sequel. "Brother Buffalo paid the price, and now we sustain him," states Native American Harry Charger.[3] This comment invites us to first examine the buffalo and then its relationship to Native Americans and the price the species paid.

"If the buffalo were here today, I think they would be different from the buffalo of the old days because all the natural conditions have changed," observed Okute, a Lakota man, in 1911. His intuitive observation possesses a certain timelessness in that change over time defines much of nature, most certainly including the bison and its habitat.[4] The bison Okute observed in his lifetime differed considerably, but recognizably, from their distant ancestors.

Modern-day scientists tell us that prototypes of the bison first appear in the paleontological record perhaps two million years ago. The archeological record, although diffuse owing to its taxonomic complexity, goes back tens of thousands of years. The ubiquitous bison cave art of Paleolithic Europe reveals ancient human portrayals of a recognizable but different-looking bison, the steppe bison (*Bison priscus*). This massive bovid with its impressive sweep of horns possessed nearly twice the mass of today's bison. The creature lived across Eurasia and into North America, thriving into the Pleistocene epoch, which ended approximately ten thousand years ago. The species probably became the parent species for subsequent species of bison in North America, which included another large-horned, large-bodied species known as *Bison latifrons*. As the continent emerged from the Pleistocene with its intermittently recurring glaciation, a gradual diminution of the bison occurred. The prominent bison scientist, Dale Guthrie, speculates that during the course of the glacial periods, *priscus* and *latifrons* lost contact with each other due to intervening ice sheets. The two massive species evolved into somewhat smaller species. North of the ice sheets on the northern plains, a smaller *priscus* form, *Bison occidentalis*, appeared and prospered on the plains. South of the glacial sheets, the *latifrons* line diminished into *Bison antiquus*, which occupied niches from coast to coast and as far south as present central Mexico. About ten to twelve thousand years ago the glaciers retreated, and *occidentalis* and *antiquus* continued their diminution over the course of the next few millennia, eventually merging into the present species, Bison bison.[5]

The archeological record indicates a bison that becomes increasingly recognizable as the contemporary buffalo with the passage from the Pleistocene epoch into the Holocene. Both Bison antiquus and Bison occidentalis appeared much like today's bison, albeit considerably larger. Evidence of the gradual diminution of the bison as the Ice Age relinquished its grip led Canadian archeologist Michael Wilson to assess that "bison standard time," meaning the period when the bison assumed a morphotype quite close to that observed today, occurred approximately ten thousand years ago. He states: "The complications of multiple migrating waves, interbreeding and extinctions concluded about 10,000 years ago." Moreover, the archeological record elucidates itself around that time as well, with discoveries that readily verify that Native Americans interacted with bison in a comprehensive bison culture.[6]

Nonetheless, for Native people, the history of human-bison interaction extends back to time immemorial, to creation itself.[7] In other words, the collective memory of many Natives recalls an existence in which there were always bison. Traditions of tribes historically identified with buffalo and descended from prehistoric bison hunters speak of the presence of the bison, or the buffalo nation, when humans first set foot on earth. For example, the Crow, Cree, and Arapaho nations possess creation stories explaining that the bison's existence predates human life. Humans came to exist based on the premise that animals, specifically the bison, would sustain them. The Lakota and Ute people share a story of humans arising from the blood clot of a buffalo. The Ute tradition explains that an old man and his wife, the predecessors of humanity, received a son born of bison blood in a kettle. The Lakota tradition explains that "Buffalo" adopted "blood clot" as his younger brother and oversaw the sibling's coming to life and rise to prosperity in symbiosis with Pte Oyate, the buffalo nation. Contemporary bison observer C. Wolf Smoke explains, "We evolved from the bison, we used to be bison." He further comments on the reconciliation of formal science and indigenous philosophy: "If you accept Darwin, then you should accept this."[8]

It's worth noting that a significant portion of the oral tradition also accommodates the evolution of the bison from the larger types, such as latifrons, antiquus, and occidentalis, into Bison bison. In many ways linking the paleontological and archeological records with present theories of bison evolution, the legends tell of giant bison that tended to fight with their hunters. Correspondingly, zoologists hypothesize that the early bison, much less of a herd animal than *Bison bison* and often found in environments richer in shrub and wood, probably tended to stand their ground and confront their attackers as opposed to the flight behavior shown by recent bison. This does not negate the fact that *Bison bison* can be a formidable and dangerous prey species. Rather, it suggests that the more heavily bodied, larger-horned creatures favored fight over flight, especially when cornered, which could occur more easily in a wooded environment. This same behavior has been observed with contemporary bison in forested areas, in contrast to those in rangeland. Traditions of the Arikara, Blackfeet, and Cheyenne all share descriptions of the hunting of these massive bison. Their stories, viewed as metaphors by those who seek to reconcile Native historical beliefs and science, describe ancient bison as carnivores who either preyed upon their Native pursuers or competed with them to gain dominance over them.[9] To some modern researchers, this presents an image of aggressive ancient bison willing to stand their ground against hunters, far more than would the bison of recent memory.

Several of the traditions link the bow and arrow, or archery, to the changed relationship with the bison nation in that with the new weapon humans gained both permission and the ability to harvest when deemed necessary. According to Blackfeet, Cheyenne, and Lakota tradition, the bison either agreed to or recognized human prowess once the tribes acquired archery. The bow and arrow established a more even playing field between the bison and humans. Again, this makes sense in reconciling oral traditions with the archeological record in that the bow and arrow minimized the risk to Natives of hunting a large defensive prey species. Native people could more easily harvest the bison, a seemingly beneficent twist of fate in their relationship with the species that was often vital to their very survival and welfare. The archeological record suggests some anachronism, however, in that the implementation of archery, approximately fifteen hundred to two thousand years BP (before present), probably postdated for the most part the diminution of the larger forms of bison, *Bison antiquus* and *Bison occidentalis*, into *Bison bison*.[10] It's worth noting that the use of the bow enabled Native people more successfully to harvest any bison that became defensive, whether on the grasslands or in the woodlands, where bison tend to develop a larger frame and exhibit behavior reminiscent of the great megafauna herbivores. The scientific records and Native traditions merge into a sensible testimony on the evolution of a relationship between the Indian and buffalo nations.

For many scientists, the application of technology, such as archery, in exploiting a resource by America's indigenous people poses the question: did prehistoric Native people overexploit their resources, specifically, the large mammals, including *Bison bison* prototypes such as *latifrons* and its megafauna neighbors in late Pleistocene and early Holocene North America? The overexploitation predates archery on the continent when spears, atlatls, fire, communal hunting, and sheer cunning were the Natives' weapons. The large prehistoric bison often lived in a mosaic landscape similar to the savannah of Africa with a mix of grasses, forbs, shrubs, and trees. University of Alaska professor Dale Guthrie likens the landscape to a plaid pattern of biodiverse microenvirons with rich nutritious flora in a comparatively warm, moist climate. That is, the arid West was not so arid then and much less inclined toward temperature extremes, especially on the cold side. The early bison moved across this landscape, sharing the same rhythms as other megafauna, including the mammoth, mastodon, camel, giant ground sloth; their predators such as the American lion, short-faced bear, dire wolf; and more familiar animals such as the gray wolf, grizzly bear, pronghorn antelope, and moose. Inhabiting this landscape, the Paleo-Americans found their niches, often becoming the hunters of the great mammals. The archeological record, again, makes it clear that such a relationship existed. The most famous landmark archeological finds came in locations near Clovis and Folsom, New Mexico, early in the 1900s. These discoveries, followed by numerous others, led archeologists to designate a Paleo-American "Clovis Culture" largely associated with mammoth hunting some ten thousand years or more before the present and a "Folsom Culture" largely associated with bison dated to a slightly more recent time.[11]

Combining the preponderance of archeological evidence showing that Paleo-Americans hunted the megafauna, such as the mammoth and large bison, with the fact that none of these animals existed when Europeans arrived on the North American continent begs an answer to the question of what happened to the "charismatic megafauna," the large mammals that evoke a sense of near sacred nostalgia in humans.[12] Theorists have lined up in a continuum between two sides known as the "overkill" and "overchill" advocates.

The overkill theorists, led by Paul S. Martin, generally speculate that the beginning of the end for most of the megafauna occurred with the arrival of humans on the continent. This means that when the Paleo-Americans arrived, they began overexploiting the large mammal species. The humans' ability to organize and utilize lithic technology along with their intimate knowledge of animal behavior enabled them to harvest almost at will. The inability to control harvesting when practicing communal hunting drives, for example, often resulted in the killing of more animals than the Natives could utilize at once. Moreover, such hunting techniques did not save the young and the female buffalo from death, which resulted in decreasing bison fertility rates. As well, the overkill theorists maintain that the Native people most likely did not possess a sense of conservation. Rather, their relationship to the animals was less as stewards than hunters who believed that correct behavior and ritual would replenish the herds as opposed to limited and selective take. Environmental historian Dan Flores explains that "in local isolation the Paleolithic shamans either misunderstood or could not grasp the implications; that their way of life, their way of using the plains was over" when they exterminated the animals in their region.[13]

Specific to bison, Jerry McDonald emerges as the leading proponent of the overkill theory. McDonald hypothesizes that Native hunters influenced the selective regime of nature. Bison that stood their ground and fought with their pursuers, although doing so was viable against other animals, could not contend with organized, cunning, well-armed humans. Bison that fled their pursuers could easily outdistance humans unless tremendous snowfall prohibited such movement. Thus, the bison giant *latifrons* became a terminal line, and the comparatively large-formed *Bison occidentalis* and *Bison antiquus* became doomed unless they evolved into smaller forms, for example, *Bison bison*, which were less vulnerable to human hunting. More aptly put, Indians killed off a species and doomed others, an argument that has been extended to the fate of the mammoth as well.[14]

The Native tradition rejects this paradigm. As stated earlier, the Native American tradition explains the change in the bison as renegotiation of the relationship between nations, resulting in a changed bison morphology. Other critics of the overkill theory, advocates of the overchill theory led by

Dale Guthrie, argue that although humans probably impacted megafauna populations, they did not kill off the large mammals. Rather, a combination of climatic and flora changes drastically altered the habitat, rendering it unfit for the great beasts and their dependent predator species. More specifically, with the close of the Pleistocene and its merging into the Holocene with its cooling and drying characteristics, the landscape became less hospitable for the megafauna. The rich mosaic of vegetation gave way to much more definitive biomes characterized by less diversity. For example, savannah and shrub land yielded to shortgrass prairie and evergreen forest. Guthrie describes this as a plaid landscape changing to a striped landscape. Much less diversity and less nutritious forage defined any given area. This decline in forage quality becomes important when we consider that the majority of the megafauna possessed a monogastric (single-stomach) digestive system as opposed to a ruminant digestive system. Monogastric animals require comparatively higher quality forage, as their systems have less capacity to garner nutrients from forage than do ruminants. For example, the monogastric horse gets less nutrition from the same low-quality feed as a ruminant cow and therefore needs larger quantities to sustain itself, which often earns the modern-day horse the epithet "hayburner." Thus, the less nutritious forage became problematic for the majority of the megafauna. In addition to the problem of decreasing total digestible nutrients, the increasing severity of winters and droughts put further stress on the animals. Especially important, the long gestation periods of the large mammals (in excess of nine months and approaching a full year) meant that fertility rates declined as mothers and offspring increasingly faced seasons of hardship. A decrease in habitat quality then combined with the comparatively high maintenance demands of the monogastric megafauna to cause a slide into extinction perhaps fueled by, but not caused by, humans.[15]

Bison survived extinction because of their ability to digest and utilize large quantities of low-quality forage, their comparatively high reproductive rates, and their tendency to flee from pursuers. Although they can sustain themselves with browsing, they much prefer to graze, and the "striped landscape" did not hinder them. They inhabited the grasslands, referred to by Guthrie as the "Great Bison Belt." When able, the bison occupied niches anywhere from coast to coast that offered suitable grazing. Invariably, such colonizations ebbed and flowed with climate and habitat quality. Nonetheless, bison survived the extinction of the great North American megafauna. The comparatively diminutive stature of Bison bison and its survivability inspired environmental historian Dan Flores to label it a "dwarf weed species." His description underscores the animal's persevering ability to thrive in a changed environment, better viewed as occupying a vacant niche under ideal conditions. Though the term weed implies something not useful to humans, Natives in fact utilized bison as fully as possible whenever they interacted with their fellow survivor of the Ice Age.[16]

The continuing arguments over the harvesting ethic of Native Americans acknowledge the very thorough interaction between bison and indigenous people. Russel Barsh, Canadian social scientist and pioneer in the field of indigenous science, addresses Paleo-American communal hunting when he states: "What's important in all this discussion is not whether Indians killed more than they could use or how much they killed; rather, what's important here is how they managed to harvest the bison." Utilizing his extensive research on the northern plains with his focus on the area surrounding Parks Canada's Head-Smashed-In Buffalo Jump in southwest Alberta, Barsh theorizes that Native people deeply immersed themselves in their environment in order to commune with their food source. This "becoming of" the bison and their environs "dissolved the borders of the inner and outer worlds" between humans and their surroundings.[17]

To answer the question of how humans could move bison herds predictably for more than fifty miles to a community kill site such as a buffalo jump, Barsh hypothesizes that human hunters inextricably intertwined themselves with wolves, the attendants of any bison herd. Essentially, people "shadowed wolves shadowing bison." Domestication, arguably, and habituation, certainly, of wolves occurred under these auspices as theorists and archeologists believe that wolves sought the "leftovers" of human kills. The relationship of humans, bison, and wolves "verged on pastoralism," with an archeologically documented history spanning eleven thousand years in southern Alberta.[18] One Blackfeet legend that attributes the feeding of a human family by wolves perhaps offers a metaphor of the dependency fostered by early bison hunters and the wolf. The bison drives, involving hundreds of square miles of landscape with entire communities participating, unfolded like an orchestrated dance across a terrestrial map, with rock cairns signifying the gathering basin and drive lanes. Estimates at Head-Smashed-In alone, just one of dozens of such sites, indicate that some 123,000 bison passed over the cliffs during a span of nearly six thousand years. In addition to emulating the wolf, the Paleo-Americans and their progeny utilized fire to enhance forage and sculpt the landscape. This made bison movements more predictable as they self-rotated onto richer forage.[19]

In the boom-and-bust cycle of productivity found on the plains, the bison's ability to convert unusable (to humans) forage into digestible nutrients—that is, bison beef—proved a virtual godsend. This defines the charm of "charismatic megafauna." The intensive interaction between Native Americans, wolves, fire, and, of course, buffalo, inspired Dale Guthrie to label Paleo-American communal drive hunting as a "risky free-range husbandry." Moreover, archeological records indicate that bison eaters became larger than non–bison eaters, suggesting the physical windfall offered by any bounty of bison. The Blackfeet acknowledged this nutritious benefit by calling bison meat *natapi waksin*, which means "real food," and all other food *kistapi waksin*, meaning "nothing food." Such epithets suggest that wherever bison existed, from the east coast to the west coast, Native people utilized them as fully as possible, either from hunting or trade with hunters.[20]

The phenomenal usefulness of bison to humans is well-known. Most novice students of American Indian life can explain that Indians fed themselves with buffalo meat and provided themselves with clothing and shelter using the skins of the shaggy beasts. In fact, Native people utilized more than one hundred parts of the bison, including the guts as containers, the dung for fuel, the bones for tools, and the sinews for adhesive and cordage, to name just a few of the parts and some of their uses. However, what may make bison unique among mainstays of Native Americans food ways and base economies is the complete dependence on bison fostered by the grassland environment. For example, the Great Plains, without the presence of bison, posed a nearly inhospitable environment to human groups of any size beyond that of an extended family.[21] Bison made the plains hospitable. No other animal in North America, perhaps even in the world, proved so critical to its dependents.

When we think of recent pre-Columbian nonagricultural North American aboriginal peoples who are identified with primary prey bases besides bison, images of salmon fishers and caribou hunters come to mind. Both of these groups certainly maintained integral relations with their food sources.

However, both of them typically possessed supplemental food sources. For example, salmon fishers of the Northwest could fall back on marine resources or significant root and berry crops, with some ungulate presence as well. The caribou hunters, in recent memory probably the closest to the bison hunters in dependency on an ungulate species, tended to access marine or riverine resources as well.[22] These aquatic-based nourishment options existed largely outside the realm of plains dwellers. The plains dwellers needed the bison, and other peoples who lived around bison enjoyed the boon offered by this remnant of the megafauna.

The bounty of the bison, aside from its ecological niche, mainly comes from its carcass. The meat transforms the energy of forage into energy for humans. *Bison bison* carcasses yield on average approximately 550 pounds for a bull, 400 pounds for a cow, 110–165 pounds for subadults, and 50 pounds for calves. *Bison occidentalis* yielded an additional 25 percent for each category. Considering the caloric content of bison beef (about 635 calories per pound), and the human requirement for calories (an average of 2,400 calories per day considering varied sizes and ages), then approximately 3.8 pounds of bison beef per person each day would suffice for healthful living. Humans can eat between five and six pounds of fresh meat per day and up to ten pounds during feasts. Drying significantly reduces the mass of the meat down to between 10 and 20 percent of the original mass. Thus, less than one-half pound of dried bison beef could sustain a human each day. Native Americans also pounded the meat, adding fat and fruit such as chokecherries to make a high-calorie fuel known as pemmican. The pemmican powered both the humans and their canine companions, which were critical to humans' existence for both hunting and transportation before the arrival of the horse (reflected in the late renowned plains anthropologist John Ewers designation of this period as the "dog days").[23] This means that bison offered a conversion of seemingly unusable steppe areas into usable nourishment. However, Native Americans needed to process their harvested bison in order to extend the benefits of any successful hunt.

Plains archeologist George Frison estimates that small-group and individual hunting probably harvested more bison than the more spectacular communal kills, even though the latter receive more attention owing to their greater archeological imprint. Small group and individual hunting techniques varied from stalking, with hunters often disguised in wolf skins to appear as the herd's attendant wolves, to pursuits in deep snow, mud, water, or ice. Hunting implements included spears, atlatls, and arrows, once archery arrived on the scene. Some theorists argue that these hunters became quite proficient.[24] Communal hunters, also efficient once the herds approached the kill zone, used the terrain to perform mass harvests. Bison jumps, where runners chased and enticed bison over cliffs, surrounds by groups of armed hunters, and impoundments into land forms such as arroyos, sand dunes, or wetlands in addition to human-made barricades of wood, rock, snow, and/or soil all comprised the communal hunting arsenal. Efficiency emerged as an issue among Native Americans as they sought to kill the entire herd during a given hunting event in order to prevent the bison from becoming savvy about the communal hunt techniques. Owing to the sacred nature of such complete interaction with the environment, shamans typically served as the "poundmasters," or hunt leaders, the custodians of bison knowledge that originated from divine sources.[25] Quality, or even the preservation, of life depended on the hunt's success in taking advantage of the bison's ability to convert browse into the digestible nutrients offered by its flesh.

However, the physical impact of the bison on its human hunters ranged far beyond simple nutrition. Rather, the bison-hunting Paleo-Americans and their pre-Columbian descendants organized themselves in accordance with the availability of buffalo. Typically, at the family level everybody participated in communal drives, and equal distribution of the harvest occurred. At the band and tribal level, greater accessibility and predictability of bison translated into a higher degree of organization and aggregation of hunters. With respect to the plains, this meant that the areas with the greatest forage offered the most potential for human organization. Typically, the farther north and east the traveler goes on the plains, the greater moisture and subsequent forage he finds. Therefore, the northeastern plains theoretically spawned larger, more organized tribes.[26] The Algonkian and Siouian speakers who eventually made their way onto the plains in the proto-historic period offer such evidence. However, even in areas of lesser predictability to the south and west, people cooperated to high degrees when possible to harvest larger groups of bison, which tended to congregate in response to varying conditions such as the rut or the weather. The rut of late summer and early fall, the bison's seeking of shelter in river bottoms in the winter, or even calving in the late spring, all provided enhanced opportunities for communal harvesting. Thus, Native people organized themselves along the same lines as another social species, the buffalo. When the buffalo coalesced into large groups, then, so too did the Native Americans. These assemblies inevitably proved critical to the health and welfare of the people, not to mention their sociopolitical associations. Nonetheless, the large groups invariably dispersed into smaller groups, both human and bison, that were more capable of living within the parameters offered by the environment of the plains. Indeed, the fluctuating characteristic of bison presence and absence across a vast landscape prevented the development of a large human population on the plains. Yet, as the generations passed, peoples on the eastern and southwestern margins of the plains came to practice and spread agriculture onto the plains; thus, the buffalo became an integral part of increasingly complex societies with access to a variety of foodstuffs. In fact, bison drives became more sophisticated with the passage of time. As George Frison explains, "Communal bison procurement reached its peak in the late prehistoric period," just prior to the arrival of Europeans and their influences.[27]

Indeed, the arrival of Europeans spawned what scholars widely acknowledge as the "Columbian Exchange," which drastically altered the fate of Native Americans and bison after several millennia of relative stability in the "discordant harmony" of ebb and flow in range and population. This massive invasion of Old World biota both augmented and transformed the interdependency of Native people and bison. A snapshot of the "day before America"—North America just prior to 1500 AD—reveals the increasing range of the bison beyond its Great Plains hearth.[28] While probably sustaining their populations in the boreal forest-parkland areas of the northern plains, bison spread into the mountains and valleys west of the Rocky Mountains, deeper into the coastal prairie area of present-day Texas, and into the prairies of the Midwest ranging from present Wisconsin across Indiana and into Ohio. However, the "widowed landscape" resulting from the Old World invasion accelerated the bison's expansion. This proved especially true in the East, where the destruction of the indigenous human population by European diseases such as smallpox and measles and an increasing forage area provided by slash-and-burn agriculture facilitated the bison's movement in the 1600s to the Atlantic and Gulf Coasts of the present southeastern United States and west of the Appalachian Mountains north to Lake Ontario. Although numerically inferior to the herds west of the Mississippi River, the eastern herds became significant. Historian Ted Franklin Belue explains that by the dawn of the historic era, the buffalo were a welcome novelty for Indians in the lower Mississippi drainage. In the South, the Cumberland Valley, the Bluegrass region, and the Upper Mississippi basin, wild beef supplemented the Indians' fluctuating food supply. Upon entering this new ecological niche, the buffalo thrived. Herds increased. Range expanded.[29]

The chronicles of the Euro-American visitors to the region reflect the buffalo material culture shared by many of the tribes who experienced the boon of the expanded bison range. As early as 1541, Hernan de Soto's men found the Tula Indians of present Arkansas with piles of hides and stores of bison beef. Later in the sixteenth century, an English scout of Sir Walter Raleigh's found evidence of buffalo material culture in present North Carolina. Nearly a century later, Spanish chroniclers in the Southeast continued to find Natives harvesting bison to the point of describing the Appalachee Indians as hunting "abundant" buffalo.[30]

The French made similar observations in their empire in the Mississippi River drainage during the seventeenth century. French explorers dubbed the Siouian speakers they found in present Minnesota in 1662 the "Nation du Boeuf" because of the tribe's reliance on buffalo (boeuf) hunting. Jesuit missionaries and French explorers found ample evidence in present Illinois and surrounding areas of bison-rich culture, including indications that the Illinois, Iowa, Miami, Ottawa, Kickapoo, and Potawatomi people practiced communal hunt techniques and distribution not unlike those of ancestral Paleo-Americans. During the period 1718 to 1734, Frenchmen observed heavy reliance on the bison by the Sauk and Fox tribes in and around present Illinois and Iowa. They witnessed buffalo rituals and clan names in neighboring tribes, including the Caddo, Shawnee, and Winnebago. Meanwhile, they also documented buffalo hunting by the southeastern Choctaw, Chickasaw, and Creek tribes. One Frenchman even identified buffalo as the primary staple of the Natchez people, who dwelled deep in the South during this period.[31]

English and American colonists made similar observations, particularly during the latter half of the 1700s as the French and Spanish influence diminished in the Trans-Appalachian region. The Anglophone adventurers found buffalo material culture pervading the inland tribes, from the Chippewa,

Wabash, Ottawa, Potawatomi, Winnebago, Illinois, Sauk, Fox, Mascouten, Kaskaskia, Miami, Kickapoo, Delaware, and Shawnee in the north down to the Creek, Chickasaw, Choctaw, Cherokee, and Natchez in the South. Kanta-ke, "land of the great meadows," known presently as Kentucky, provided a bison-rich environment jealously guarded by the Shawnee and perhaps became what historians later referred to as a "buffer zone," that is, an animal refuge on the boundary between hostile peoples. In this case, the Americans, Shawnee, and Delaware people all competed for hunting dominance of Kentucky in the 1770s.[32] In any event, the pressure brought to bear on the buffalo herds east of the Mississippi River overcame their ability to propagate in that landscape. By the 1830s, no record exists of bison running wild east of the great river. Yet, for several generations the historic record makes it clear that Native people and buffalo co-existed without domestication or intentional annihilation. Moreover, tribes, such as the Shawnee, fought invaders to preserve their bison landscapes. As well, some historians argue that the forefathers of the Lakota, Nakota, and Dakota people developed their interdependence with the bison when the buffalo nation came to the Siouian speakers' homeland on the Atlantic seaboard in the wake of the widowed landscape. The human ancestors then followed the retreating animal population back to the plains hearth where together they made a nearly final stand only a little more than a century ago.[33]

However, many more tribes than those nestled in the East developed bison-related culture during the first three centuries of the Columbian Exchange. Far to the west across the Rocky Mountains, greater numbers of Indian nations increasingly came to embrace a culture heavily influenced by bison. The archeological records make it clear that prehistorically any people of the intermountain West and Pacific Northwest harvested bison when available. The historical record more clearly quantifies and qualifies some of the archeological details. For example, we know that Apache peoples came out of their mountain strongholds in the Southwest to hunt and acquire bison products for trade with Puebloan nations. Tribes of the Uto-Aztecan language group moved out of the basins and ranges farther north to become intertwined with the bison culture. From that group, the Comanches left the mountains forever while the Ute, Shoshone, and Bannock foraged in and out of the mountains. Meanwhile, the plateaus and river valleys even farther north and west harbored the bison hunters who were emerging from the Salishan and Sahaptian speakers, such as the Salish, Spokane, Coeur d'Alene, Nez Perce, Walla Walla, and Yakama nations. Other plateau tribes of differing linguistic stocks including the Cayuse and Kutenai became bison hunters as well.[34]

A significant difference exists between the bison cultures of the West and those of the East in the wake of the Columbian Exchange. Those of the West responded far more to the acquisition of the horse from Euro-American sources—for example, the Spanish of the upper Rio Grande drainage—than to the expansion of the buffalo's range. Still, as time passed, the horse also brought other heretofore unmentioned tribes from the forested fringes east out onto the plains to enmesh themselves in bison material culture. Algonquian speakers such as Arapaho, Blackfeet, Gros Ventres, Cheyenne, Plains Ojibwa, and Plains Cree joined Siouian-speaking Mandan, Hidatsa, Ponca, Kansa, and Osage along with Caddoan speakers such as the Pawnee, Arikara, and Wichita to populate the plains to unprecedented levels. Some of these tribes, notably the Mandan, Hidatsa, and Pawnee, maintained horticultural connections while others such as the Blackfeet and Cheyenne eventually abandoned agriculture altogether.[35]

Ultimately, by the nineteenth century, some three dozen different ethnic groups would occupy the Great Plains, which became the last refuge for the bison in numbers capable of sustaining entire culture groups. Although some historians view this equestrian migration to the plains as a cultural "genesis," others view it more as an intensifier of a "cultural whole previously formed" by preceding pedestrian bison hunters. Certainly, Native people throughout the course of prehistory and history demonstrated a desire to harvest bison and maintain a material culture imbued by the animal. The advantage the horse offered in facilitating the interaction of Native people and bison was to increase the "effective density" of the bison resource owing to decreased search, pursuit, and travel time required by equestrian bison hunters. This allowed greater aggregation of bison hunters into bands, which coalesced in direct proportion to bison predictability and availability. The inhospitable plains became quite inviting once the horse arrived. The famous Plains Indian "high culture" peaked during the late eighteenth and first half of the nineteenth centuries, which led plains traveler John Fremont in 1842 to observe that "Indians and buffalo make the poetry and life of the prairie."[36] The popular image of Native America emerges from this time when Indians on horses pursued innumerable buffalo across the sweeping landscape of interior North America.

Like the images of prehistoric America and the Paleo-American role in it, the vision of the historic West and its indigenous inhabitants' role in it also warrant presentation and analysis. This is especially true in light of the present movement by Native people to restore the buffalo nation. Interpreting historical data from the eighteenth- and nineteenth-century bison landscape attracts controversy. This is largely because for many the popular image of Native America poses a romantic standard, a faulty myth, or a threatening throwback to yesteryear. For Native people, the image of the historic West conjures collective memory of cultural autonomy, a time when "the buffalo was everything to us," as the eminent Crow statesman Plenty Coups stated as the buffalo days culminated in the late nineteenth century.[37] The salient arguments revolve around the numbers of bison and the respective historic roles played by Native Americans and Euro-Americans in the demise of the great herds.

Upon seeing a great many buffalo, a group of Lakota informed the post clerk at Fort Pierre on the Missouri River in 1834 that it appeared that "the dead ones have all come to life again." The metaphorical reference seems quite vague, yet it bears similarity to the guesses made by Euro-American observers and later historians in trying to quantify the size of the bison population after the waves of Euro-Americans overran the buffalo range in the eighty years from Lewis and Clark's crossing of the region in 1804 through 1806 to the last crack of the commercial Euro-American hide hunters' buffalo rifle in the mid-1880s. With a comparatively conservative estimate, William Clark marveled in 1804 about "buffalo in such multitudes that we can not exaggerate in saying in a single glance we saw three thousand of them." Twenty-eight years later, George Catlin, the renowned painter and early advocate of a grasslands national park protecting Native people, flora, and fauna alike, observed that "the almost countless herds of these animals [bison] blacken the prairies for miles together." Eminent newspaper editor Horace Greeley seemed similarly astounded in 1854 on his cross-country stagecoach trip when he wrote, "I know a million is a great many, but I am confident we saw that number yesterday." Southern plainsman Charles Goodnight offered astronomical observations when he described his memory of the southern plains during the Civil War prior to the hide-hunting boom: "The whole country was covered with what appeared to be a monstrous moving brown blanket, the length and breadth of which could not be determined. The number of animals it contained was beyond the human mind to estimate."[38]

The guesses of historians, ranging in the low millions to as high as 200 million, reflect the same variation as this small sample of observations. For years, sixty million, a number generated by naturalist Ernest Thompson Seton in 1906, became the standard. The scrutiny of environmental historians over the past thirty years has diminished current estimates. Largely utilizing grazing capacity estimates based on livestock, these historians, such as Tom McHugh, Dan Flores, and Andrew Isenberg, estimate that the West contained some twenty to thirty million bison early in the nineteenth century. However, the scientific community remains skeptical of such estimates. Biologists such as James Shaw, Mary Meagher, and Valerius Geist, giants in the field of bison studies, point out the flaws of comparing livestock grazing and range capacity with that of bison. As well, the tremendous habitat fluctuations make estimates approximate, at best. These scientists offer that "tens of millions" of bison roamed the West early in the nineteenth century, but that could mean as few as ten million depending on numerous variables. Still, these scientists echo the words of Plenty Coups on the significance of bison: "No other large mammal in North America can match the American bison in relation to presettlement numbers, effects on the landscape, and historical importance."[39]

The scientific and history communities reach greater consensus when explaining the probable exaggerations of contemporary chroniclers and the subsequent overestimation by later analysts. Bison tend to wander in small groups ranging from five to fifty animals. Depending on conditions, these groups coalesce into far larger groups. Therefore, at times, large areas of the plains contained what appeared to be huge herds while other areas contained no bison. For example, Lewis and Clark saw bison on just 15 percent of the days they spent in buffalo country. Moreover, refugia, areas of large concentrations of animals, formed in the buffer zones between hostile tribes. When observers traveled into these areas, they saw unrepresentative large numbers of game, western historian Elliot West explains the result: "Comments from early observers are nearly worthless. Suddenly confronted by vast numbers of animals in the unfamiliar openness of the plains, white emigrants fall back on vague, if memorable metaphors."[40] The estimates of many bison historians revolve around the observations of early Euro-American travelers. The most recent scholarship suggests that millions of buffalo existed, but we really do not know just how many. Still, this does not at all affect the significance of the buffalo nation in the lives of the indigenous people. But how did Natives and buffalo interact during this time of profound change created by the intensification of the Columbian Exchange as Euro-Americans increasingly encroached deep into buffalo country?

At the heart of the answer to the question lies the blame for the near demise of the bison from millions to hundreds in the nineteenth-century West. The arguments go as far back as contemporary observations of Native American harvesting of bison and extend to the present, in scholars' debates in professional journals and monographs. Some primary chroniclers carefully documented that Native Americans refused to waste and overharvest buffalo. Others claimed that Indians readily wasted. Two 1874 editions of Forest and Stream symbolize the sides of the argument. A January article stated: "There never was a greater mistake to suppose that the Indian places no restraint on his powers of securing game. He only kills to eat and not for the amusement of slaughter." Three months later, another article argued: "The Indian kills many times the amount that he needs, but this he considers one of his inalienable rights, and I believe it impossible to prevent this useless slaughter so far as the Indian is concerned." The conflicting arguments in the same periodical probably reflect more the individual perspectives of their authors than quantifiable evidence. Writing on the heels of contemporary observers, academicians at the turn of the nineteenth into the twentieth century often viewed the vast destruction merely as a part of a larger historical process resulting in the ascendancy of Euro-American hegemony on the North American continent. Fur trade scholar Merrill Burlingame epitomized this view in 1929 when he wrote: "That the twentieth century America might exist the buffalo and the Indian had to go." Such discussion of historical determinism heralded the arguments made by later generations of twentieth-century historians. Roughly stated, these historians, including general theorists such as Immanuel Wallerstein and Fernand Braudel, proposed that regions and countries around the globe, including their indigenous biota, became sucked into a world system that exploited them. The indigenous populations could not withstand this globalizing pressure and became part of a process typified by overharvesting of resources. These types of assertions find direct application in the question of Native American and bison interaction in that, to many analysts, the fur trade rendered the Native Americans cultural dependents. The Indians felt the need to acquire Euro-American goods and utilized bison robes and beef in the form of pemmican to fulfill their desires. For these dependency theorists, North America's indigenous people simply failed to overcome outside pressures exerted upon them by Euro-American technology, materialism, biotic invasion, and coercion.[41]

Historians, though generally in consensus about the heavy role of Euro-American harvesting in the obliteration of the bison herds, continue to draw sides in the debate over the roles of Natives in the demise of the bison. If, as we have seen, the first academic trial was over the role of the Paleo-Americans in the destruction of the megafauna at the end of the Pleistocene and beginning of the Holocene epochs, then the second trial has focused on possible Native American overharvesting associated with the fur trade and potential explanations for Native American involvement in that trade.[42]

The popular romantic notion that the buffalo-hunting tribes curtailed harvests to preserve the bison, supported at times by bison historians such as Frank Gilbert Roe in The North American Buffalo (1951), has come under increasing scrutiny from revisionist environmental historians. Western historian Richard White's landmark study, The Roots of Dependency (1983), links the romantic notion with more recent academic work by describing Native American efforts (for example, Lakota and Pawnee) to engage in selective takes of the bison, a practice that became moot due to the increasing Euro-American encroachment on the plains.[43] The most recent revisions come out of the field of environmental history and include the work of Dan Flores, Andrew Isenberg, and William Dobak. These scholars focus on the plains in three zones: the southern plains, the central and northern plains of the continental United States, and the Canadian plains, respectively.

Asking the question whether Plains Indians overharvested bison in the nineteenth century, therefore hastening their own cultural destruction, all three authors answer in the affirmative with qualification that changes brought on by the advance of Euro-American influences forced the Native Americans into unsustainable hunting. Flores asserts that wolf predation, climatic variation, increased grazing competition with horses, greater numbers of Native hunters, and introduced diseases made southern bison populations vulnerable. When Native Americans began selectively harvesting young cows for pliable robes sought after in the fur trade, they began to decimate the southern herds. Flores suggests that "Native Americans did not grasp the implications of the market" and that even without the presence of the Euro-American hide hunting culminating in the 1870s "the buffalo would probably have lasted another thirty years."[44]

Isenberg echoes the reasoning of Flores with respect to factors that made the overall bison population vulnerable as well as Flores's assertion that Native hunting broke the proverbial back of the buffalo nation. He writes, "In the mid-nineteenth century, the combination of Indian predation and environmental change decimated the bison." According to Isenberg, prior to the 1840s Plains Indians killed bison at the sustainable rate of approximately five hundred thousand each year. After the 1840s, in order to maximize the robe trade, the Native hunters began killing at the unsustainable rate of more than six hundred thousand each year, with an increasing selection of young cows. His analysis contends that the loose social bonds of the equestrian nomads prohibited the enforcement of mandates against waste.[45]

Discussing the Canadian grasslands, Dobak minimizes the impact of disease and environmental conditions such as drought. Rather, he maintains that sheer hunting pressure destroyed the great herds of Canada. The region's population increased by two-thirds from 1820 to 1880. Mixed-blood hunters known as "Métis," an ethnic group grown largely out of the fur trade from the intermarriage of Euro-Americans and Native Americans, emerged as a distinct commercial bison culture on the Plains and joined First Nations people in seasonal rounds hinged on the presence of bison. These hunters supplied not only buffalo robes like their southern neighbors but also vast quantities of pemmican to fuel the legions of trappers and traders plying the waters and lands of British North America. Dobak asserts that the robe trade alone encouraged these "Native" people to take 30 percent more animals than necessary. Insisting that First Nations groups such as the Cree and Assiniboine believed that bison populations were infinitely renewable, Dobak claims that mere exclusion of competition served as a perceived suitable conservation tool.[46] In essence, he agrees with Flores that the indigenous people did not understand the impact of the market economy on their life ways.

The notion that Native Americans failed to grasp the passing of the buffalo receives historiographic debate as well. Revisionists such as Dobak or Jeffrey Ostler scour the historical records to produce theses that Native people either could not see or could not understand the diminution of the great buffalo nation. Others, led by Richard White and Dan Flores, argue that Indian people perceived bison availability as being linked more to kinship relations between human and buffalo nations than to harvest numbers or conservation. Often, historians point to a Native belief that buffalo came from the ground, thus preserving an infinite supply. When the end of the bison era grew near, tribes believed that the buffalo had returned to their underground hearth.[47]

Yet the historical records also clarify that Native Americans did fully understand as events unfolded toward the near extermination of the bison. As early as 1763, a Creek chief, The Mortar, complained to the governor of Georgia that white settlers and livestock persisted in driving the buffalo off the land. A century later, Satanta of the Kiowa lamented at the Medicine Lodge Treaty Council (1867) that white soldiers constantly cut down wood and killed off bison. At about the same time, the Hunkpapa Lakota Black Moon stated that the Euro-Americans "ruin our country with impunity." Red Cloud echoed his compatriot's sentiments on two occasions just over a decade later, even before the demise of the northern herd. He explained that whites killed the buffalo, divided the land, and brought starvation, and that "where the Indian killed one buffalo, the hide and tongue hunters killed fifty." In 1878, a Blackfeet man told Commissioner John Young, "The time is close when the tail of the last buffalo will be seen disappearing from the prairie." Reflecting on his life during the days of the buffalo's diminution, Chief Plenty Coups of the Crow nation enhanced the Blackfeet man's statement: "Anybody could now see that soon there would be no buffalo on the plains, and everybody was wondering how we could live after they were gone."[48]

Moreover, Native Americans did perceive their own role in the reduction of bison numbers. In 1868, Thunder Bull, a Cuthead Yanktonai, took responsibility for Native American use of guns as a factor in driving game away. Long Mandan of the Two Kettle Lakota complained of Métis pressure on the northern herd. Nez Perce hunter Yellow Wolf recalled his worry over the plight of his grandchildren without the buffalo hunt to sustain them, admitting: "I killed yearlings mostly. It was robes we were after more than meat."[49] Such comments indicate that at least some Native Americans remained cognizant of the end of the buffalo and observed that the causes included Euro-American influences.

Nonetheless, in the "trial" of Native Americans as conservationists during the demise of the bison contemporary Native American scholars criticize the revisionist positions. The late writer and political scientist Vine Deloria Jr. vehemently disagrees with the revisionist position in a recent statement: "It's nonsense. The Indians did not make any appreciable dent in buffalo numbers in the Northern Plains. It's anti-Indian stuff." Fellow Lakota scholar Jim Garrett focuses on the obvious variable of the increased Euro-American human presence on the plains in the nineteenth century as the key to any study of bison destruction. He especially concentrates on the use of alcohol as an inducement in the robe and hide trades. The use of such a drug to extend hegemony by the Euro-Americans allocates responsibility to them regardless of whether the shooter of the bison was Euro-American or Native American. Garrett's argument hearkens back to the words of Plenty Coups: "They told us not to drink whisky, yet they made it themselves and traded it to us for furs and robes until both were nearly gone." In the words of another Lakota scholar, Edward Valandra, Euro-American abdication of responsibility in the destruction of the bison vexes Native Americans: "For the western world, the killing of millions upon millions of buffalo registers nothing more than a blip on an accountability seismograph." The Native American response to revisionist assessments of their relationship with bison is poignant, especially given that the Native reaction receives support from the scientific community. For example, environmental science professor Valerius Geist believes that the revisions of the dominant environmental historians on the subject are faulty. He voices concern that their studies reflect "historian playing ecologist."[50] Thus, the sides remain drawn in the debate over the motives and actions of the Native people during the time of the near loss of the great buffalo nation.

Richard White makes a compelling argument with his statement that "The ubiquity of the Indian as environmentalist unfortunately tends to reduce most research about Indian people and the land to briefs for and against the recent canonization of Indians into environmental sainthood. Such arguments have outlived their usefulness." Still, given the emotional response by the public to issues such as free-ranging bison, Native hunting rights, and environmental protection versus development, one more argument regarding the Native role in the destruction of the bison begs for consideration. After all, Dan Flores makes an equally compelling statement with his assessment that "How a society or group of people with a shared culture makes adjustments to live within the carrying capacity of its habitat is not only a valid historical question, it may be one of the most salient questions to ask about any culture."[51] To date, most of the analyses revolve around motives in bison harvesting, for example, formalist economic or substantive cultural, and around numbers of bison harvested. Yet, even in the field of contemporary wildlife conservation, the paradigm has shifted from more simplistic game animal management to ecosystem stewardship. This understanding provokes a reinterpretation of some reasonably well-known Western historical events in order to uncover Native American motives and intentions at the twilight of the buffalo days. In keeping with the notion of ecosystem stewardship as a key to wildlife conservation, then, perceptions of the landscape become an appropriate lens for viewing the past.

Given any piece of countryside, respective cultures will shape their own mental landscapes of it. Geographer Yi-Fu Tuan tells us that "landscape is a sector of reality, a construct of the mind and feeling." Historian Simon Schama adds that human perception forms the difference between simple natural elements and landscape. He explains: "Landscapes are culture before they are nature; constructs of the imagination projected onto wood and water and rock."[52] Kiowa author and humanist N. Scott Momaday offers a similar Native assessment: "Man invests himself in the landscape, and at the same time incorporates the landscape into his own most fundamental experience."[53] Undoubtedly, the Native American ancestors of Momaday and their brethren from other tribes sought to maintain their landscape and life ways throughout the nineteenth century. They proved less managers of game and more stewards of habitat and environment, heralding recent trends in wildlife conservation.

The Plains Indian wars and treaties receive much attention by historians. The presentations of this material vary, but reading through it from the perspective of landscape history shows that Plains Indians fought and negotiated in a "natural" effort to preserve their landscape and hence provide a suitable habitat for their cultural mainstay, the buffalo nation. Tuan explains the natural drive to preserve landscape: "Yearning for an ideal and humane habitat is perhaps universal. Such a habitat must be able to support a livelihood and yet cater to our moral and aesthetic nature." For example, Native Americans successfully negotiated to maintain the chase of the buffalo as part of their treaty rights in the two biggest treaty events of the plains, Medicine Lodge Creek (1867) for the southern plains and Fort Laramie (1868) for the northern plains. At the same time, they sought exclusion of Euro-Americans to the greatest extent possible. The Red River War of 1874–1875 on the southern plains and the Lakota resistance of 1876–1877 on the northern plains occurred when these treaty rights broke down because hide hunters and soldiers invaded the southern hunting grounds preserved by treaty, and another Euro-American invasion occurred in the northern hunting grounds. Native Americans responded by sacrificing their lives to preserve their landscape. Famed Lakota spokesmen Black Elk and Luther Standing Bear recollected this time of landscape change. Black Elk explained the detrimental effect of the reservation process: "The Wasichus [whites] came, and they made little islands for us and other little islands for the four-leggeds and always these islands are becoming smaller." Standing Bear clarified a Native view that the Euro-Americans failed to understand their adopted landscape: "The white man is still troubled with primitive fears; he still has in his consciousness the perils of this frontier continent. But in the Indian the spirit of the land is still vested."[54]

Comments such as those of Black Elk and Standing Bear note the conquering, fearful mentality of Euro-Americans as they spread onto the plains. Confinement of the Natives followed by transformation of the landscape was the death knell for the buffalo culture pursued by the Plains peoples. The Indians had desired to maintain a landscape capable of sustaining the great buffalo herds, in essence, the stewardship of an intact ecosystem. Given the latitude to police their own Native American ranks with respect to harvesting, the great buffalo nation potentially could have persisted. If the intertribal warfare had continued, then buffer zones would have remained as refugia for bison.[55] If intertribal peace had been permitted to prevail, then self-regulation might have occurred as Native Americans began to realize that the buffalo nation was in dire circumstances. Either way, the Native people of the Great Plains did not receive an opportunity to prove their stewardship of their environment, the last bastion of the immense bison herds.

The army confined the Indians to reservations and applauded the demise of the bison; Euro-American hide hunters blasted the herds into oblivion; the American government failed to lift a finger to prevent such injustice; and Euro-American agriculturalists carved up the land while changing the biota, which ultimately prohibited any possible resurgence of free-ranging bison herds reminiscent of those in the preceding millennia.

For its part, the American government proved all too glad to see the passage of the bison. On the front lines, army commanders indiscriminately slaughtered buffalo, supplied ammunition to and protected the Euro-American hide hunters including scofflaws who were inconsiderate of Native hunting rights, and lobbied for prohibiting protection of the herd. Exemplifying this, George Armstrong Custer was the most ardent and wasteful buffalo hunter in the Seventh Cavalry. Meanwhile, Custer's colleague, Col. Richard Irving Dodge, applauded Euro-American hunters with the directive: "Kill every buffalo you can. Every buffalo dead is an Indian gone." Around the same time, Custer's boss, Gen. Philip Sheridan, made comments around the country lauding the destruction of the bison. Back in Washington DC, attempts by Congress in 1874 to pass a bill protecting bison received a pocket veto from President Ulysses S. Grant. One congressman epitomized the prevailing attitude of policymakers bent on transforming the western landscape forever: "The best thing which could happen for the betterment of our Indian question would be that the last remaining buffalo should perish."[56]

For their part, the hide hunters, Euro-Americans who shot bison merely for their unprocessed hides destined for tanneries to the east and occasionally for some of the meat such as the humps and tongues, readily complied with the wishes of the army and eastern politicians. These market hunters hit the plains en masse following the invention of processes to convert bison hides into leather in Germany and in the United States in 1871. Bison hides became industrially processed robes, blankets, overshoes, machine belts, cushions, furniture, wall coverings, and military uniform accouterments. The "buffalo runners" (hide hunters) used large-caliber guns to shoot as many bison as possible. They killed millions and their efforts reduced the last of the herds to remnants of small groups or individuals. They hastened the end of the buffalo nation on the southern plains by 1877 and on the northern plains by 1885.[57]

Meanwhile, cattle supplanted bison on the plains during the 1870s and 1880s. Some historians believe that diseases, including anthrax, brucellosis, and tuberculosis, carried by cattle provided yet another death sentence for the once prolific bison herds. In the 1880s, farmers began to dominate the region, and the open range essentially ended. The agriculturalists busted the sod and planted Eurasian crops such as wheat in a quest for a dominant monoculture. These agriculturalists also partitioned the land with fences and fields. Their concept of a habitable landscape did not include the restoration of the buffalo nation. It's worth noting that the decision to exclude the bison clearly comes from a Euro-American cultural construct. After all, farming Indian tribes of the plains, including the Mandans, Hidatsas, and Pawnees, among others, never sought to drive the bison out of their food ways. Rather, they sought a comprehensive food culture mixing agricultural produce and bison beef. Nonetheless, while the hide hunters completed the destruction of the bison, the Euro-American farmers transformed the landscape and completely ended the potential for any quick return to the buffalo days.[58]

Regardless of the causes of the destruction of the bison, the effect on the Native Americans proved nearly cataclysmic. Bison historian Martin Garretson summarizes the impact: "It was a decimation of race as well as species." Examining just one tribe reveals the consequences of the loss of the bison. In 1877, the Blackfoot of Canada enjoyed more than adequate nourishment, which was largely derived from bison beef. When between six and ten thousand Indian refugees from the United States invaded the Blackfoot hunting territory in 1877 and 1878, the death knell sounded, and the Blackfoot were starving in Canada by the winter of 1879. South of the forty-ninth parallel, the Blackfeet tenuously clung to their bison culture until 1883 when the hide hunters wiped out the herds depended upon by the tribe. In 1884, more than one-fourth of the twenty-three hundred Blackfeet in the United States starved to death.[59] During the 1940s, John Ewers, resident anthropologist of the Blackfeet nation, observed lingering effects of this end of an era. He wrote: "Poverty that still exists on many reservations of the northern plains is stark proof of the persistence of Indian inability to adjust the changed conditions which followed the sudden death of the fur trade [buffalo days] in this region . . . and the horrible example of the effect on human lives of the extermination of the buffalo must continue to haunt those who are concerned about the future of man's relationship to his environment in North America." Two Native American statesmen of other tribes, Plenty Coups and Sitting Bull, eloquently articulated similar effects on their respective nations. Plenty Coups stated: "When the buffalo went away we became a changed people. Idleness that was never with us in buffalo days has stolen much from both our minds and bodies." He added: "When the buffalo went away the hearts of my people fell to the ground, and they could not lift them up again." Sitting Bull made a similar statement: "A cold wind blew across the prairie when the last buffalo fell—a death wind for my people."[60]

As the virtual apocalypse caused by the demise of the buffalo nation neared, spiritual ceremonies multiplied across Indian country in an effort to restore a landscape that would again be home to the bison. Archeologist Michael Wilson characterizes the impact of the near extermination of the buffalo nation as a virtual end of the world from a philosophical perspective: "[It] removed far more than a food source: it knocked out the underpinnings of an entire cultural pattern, from subsistence to ceremonialism. Their prime link with the Creator disappeared as much a memory as the unfenced open plains." The spiritual movement that resulted culminated with the ceremony known as the Ghost Dance. For Plains tribes, for example, the Lakota, the ceremony possessed four key elements reflective of the Native desire for land stewardship. First, the earth would regenerate. Second, the buffalo would return. Third, the Euro-Americans would go away. Fourth, the Indian population would multiply. The movement ended tragically and symbolically at Wounded Knee Creek in South Dakota on December 29, 1890, when Seventh Cavalry soldiers massacred 350 men, women, and children of the Lakota tribe led by Chief Big Foot of the Minniconjou band.[61] In many ways, this tragedy marked the nadir of Native American existence. Their near demographic collapse would hit bottom within a dozen years, casting them into the depths of marginalization.

The buffalo also hit its nadir at this time. In 1886, William Templeton Hornaday left his eastern headquarters as chief taxidermist for the Smithsonian to go to Montana to gather specimens for the museum while buffalo still existed. Ironically, he managed to track down and shoot nearly thirty animals for his collection. This event spawned Hornaday's study of the extermination of the bison in the late 1880s. He estimated that across the West outside of Yellowstone National Park approximately 85 bison still ran wild. Another 200 roamed in Yellowstone. Perhaps as many as 550 were scattered about in the parklands and forested areas of present northern Alberta and the Northwest Territories. He guessed that another 256 existed in captivity, for a total of 1,091 in 1887. Euro-American hunters and poachers continued destroying the remnants of the wild population, so that by turn of the century only a couple of dozen bison survived in Yellowstone, and other wild bison south of the Canadian border ceased to exist, with the exception of one small herd in the Texas panhandle. The herd in Canada continued to diminish as well.[62] The buffalo nation had been brought to its knees.

Poachers in the snows of Yellowstone slaying some of the last of the buffalo; soldiers in the snows of South Dakota slaying some of the last of the Indians—the parallels are ominous. A relationship generated by ancestors over thousands of years teetered on the edge of extinction. Ultimately, Native Americans perished as they struggled to preserve a way of life based on the buffalo nation and its unfettered landscape, which both partners deemed home. As they lay dying on the frozen ground, Chief Big Foot and his followers probably did not realize that in some small way their prayers were beginning to get a positive answer. They would not live to see the fulfillment of their desires and the intentions of the Ghost Dance ceremony, but Native people, honoring an ancient implied covenant, were working to save brother buffalo and hence the land and its indigenous people. By 1890, Native Americans had caught bison calves and had successfully established protected bison herds that would guarantee survival of the species and spread its progeny across North America for generations to come.

BORDERS.

BORDERS #434
4314 Milan Road
Sandusky OH 44870
419 626-1173

STORE: 0434   REG: 02/65   TRAN#: 6957
SALE   04/11/2008   EMP: 00168

UFFALO NATION

                  ST T   19.95
rder#:40908

              Subtotal   19.95
              OHIO 6.25%   1.25
1 Item   Total   21.20
              CASH   21.20

        04/11/2008 11:37AM

For returns accompanied by a Borders Store Receipt, the purchase price will be refunded in the medium purchase (cash, credit card or gift card). Items purchased by check may be returned for cash after 10 business days. For returns within 30 days of purchase accompanied by a Borders Gift Receipt, the purchase price (after applicable discounts) will be refunded via a gift card.

Merchandise unaccompanied by the original Borders store receipt, Borders Gift Receipt, or presented for return beyond 30 days from date of purchase, must be carried by Borders at the time of the return. The lowest price offered for the item during the 6 month period prior to the return will be refunded via a gift card.

Opened videos, music discs, cassettes, electronics, and audio books may only be exchanged for a replacement of the original item.

Periodicals, newspapers, out-of-print, collectible, pre-owned items, and gift cards may not be returned.

Returned merchandise must be in saleable condition.

BORDERS.

Returns to Borders Stores

Merchandise presented for return, including sale or marked-down items, must be accompanied by the original Borders store receipt or a Borders Gift Receipt. Returns must be completed within 30 days of purchase. For returns accompanied by a Borders Store Receipt, the purchase price will be refunded in the medium of purchase (cash, credit card or gift card). Items purchased by check may be returned for cash after 10 business days. For returns within 30 days of purchase accompanied by a Borders Gift Receipt, the purchase price (after applicable discounts) will be refunded via a gift card.

Merchandise unaccompanied by the original Borders

Map 1: Bison Maximum Range, Remnant Herds, and Captive Founding Herds.
Sources: Roe, *North American Buffalo*, appendix map, and Hornaday, "Discovery, Life, History, and Extermination of the American Bison," 525.

Fig. 1. Forage conversion: the benevolence of the bison. © William Campbell, Homefire Productions, Inc.

Fig. 2. A remnant of the once prolific charismatic megafauna. Photo by author (1999).

Fig. 3: Bison hoof and human hand:
a relationship set in stone. Snake Butte, Fort
Belknap, Montana. Photo by author (1999).

Fig. 4: A First Nation's buffalo hunting oracle, used for a
millennium. Writing-On-Stone Provincial Park, Alberta,
Canada ["Hoodoo Interpretive Trail" brochure and signs,
2004]. Photo by author (2004).

Fig. 5: A staggering transformation of the landscape for Native people, reduced to collecting buffalo bones. 1886, Dakota Territory. Photo by F. J. Haynes. Courtesy Haynes Foundation Collection, Montana Historical Society, Helena.

2. Saving the Buffalo Nation

Through some ministration of the Great Spirit a few buffalo were given to an Indian warrior. These buffalo have multiplied and they are now the most valuable herd in the world.

Duncan McDonald, Salish Elder (1904)

Despite the tragedy defining the end of the buffalo days, some remarkable and uplifting developments were taking place simultaneous to it. During the decade and a half from 1875 to 1890 the wild bison population tee-tered on the brink of extinction, particularly south of the parklands and boreal forest of present northern Alberta and the Northwest Territories. In this same period, five groups established captive breeding programs that guaranteed survival of the species. During the 1870s, James McKay and Charles Alloway of Manitoba, the Goodnights of Texas, and Samuel Walk-ing Coyote and Sabine of Montana established and increased captive herds. In the 1880s, they were joined by the Dupuises of the Dakota Territory and Charles Jesse (Buffalo) Jones of Kansas. In three of these households (those of McKay, Walking Coyote and Dupuis) ran the blood of Native Americans who primarily sought the preservation of the buffalo nation for cultural purposes. Jones and Goodnight sought restoration for nostalgic purposes as well but expended considerable effort in attempting to turn a profit by developing a cattle-bison hybrid. Regardless of the motives, the efforts of these households buffered the beleaguered bison while the legal slaughter of the 1870s and 1880s and subsequent poaching into the 1890s persisted.[1] The hindsight of history reveals that these households did not stand alone in capturing and raising bison and also that the bison might have survived without their efforts. However, if they were not the first to capture and raise buffalo calves, they were the only groups who maintained a captive bison operation from start to finish, allowing the calves to grow to adulthood and successfully procreate with the progeny remaining in the protected herd. As well, historical analysis tells us that disease and poaching loomed as significant threats to the buffalo. The fact that these saviors of the bison augmented not only the buffalo's numbers but also its genetic diversity owing to the disparate geographic origins of their herds cannot be emphasized enough. In fact, experts agree that the genes of these five seed herds exist in most of the bison living today.[2]

Before describing and analyzing the stories of these bison saviors, with emphasis on the Native Americans, we must set them in context. Today, most students of the American West can provide a rough synopsis of the bison's plight: The Indians and the buffalo coexisted in relative harmony. Then, Euro-Americans arrived on the Plains and brought firearms, livestock that spread disease and competed for resources, horses that enhanced Native American hunting, and trade goods including alcohol that encouraged Indians and buffalo hunters to harvest unnecessary numbers of buffalo. These factors nearly combined to wipe out the buffalo. Near the end of the slaughter, lawmakers saved some bison by setting aside habitat on federal land with the protection of government forces, namely Yellowstone National Park under the protection of the U.S. Army in the United States and crown lands over-watched by the Royal North-West Mounted Police in northern Canada. Bison eventually prospered and their progeny exist across the United States and Canada in parks, zoos, refuges, and on private ranches.[3]

This brief version of the buffalo's predicament satisfies general knowledge, but it fails to detail the precise nadir of the bison population. Also, it does not convey the numerous attempts to raise bison prior to their near extinction, nor does it give credit to those front-line conservationists who were successful. Filling in these gaps must begin with some details about the wild bison's demise.

During his 1886 expedition to Montana, William T. Hornaday, the renowned hunter-naturalist, found it difficult to locate any buffalo for his Smithsonian Collection. Subsequently, he began an arduous study of the demise of the bison and created a map showing the numbers and locations of wild bison. As noted in chapter 1, Hornaday believed that 835 bison still ran wild in North America. The largest herd numbered 550 and roamed the

Peace River country of Canada. The second largest herd, of 200, foraged in Yellowstone National Park. Smaller herds included 25 in the panhandles of Texas and Oklahoma, 26 in south-central Wyoming, 20 in eastern Colorado, 10 in east-central Montana, and 4 in the western Dakotas.[4] Hornaday's figures potentially underestimated bison numbers and locations slightly, as some of the documented killing noted in this chapter will suggest. Nonetheless, he did illustrate the extraordinarily tenuous position of the once prolific bison, now reduced to a few wandering bands and with its possible extinction looming large.

Threats to the very survival of the species, particularly from hunters but also from disease, still lurked. People continued to kill bison even after the end of the great herds. For example, when hunters found a "hidden" herd of 165 animals near Jackson Hole, Wyoming, during the winter of 1884-1885, they annihilated it. Two years later, Texas cowboys killed fifty-two bison they had discovered and sold off the heads and hides for taxidermy. In 1897 hunters found and eliminated four isolated bison in Lost Park, Colorado. Worse yet, poaching plagued the herd in Yellowstone National Park through the 1890s and into the first decade of the twentieth century. In a 1902 survey Yellowstone Park officials located fewer than thirty animals, and the superintendent deemed it necessary to supplement the herd with captive bison. Following the herd's plight for two more decades reveals that even as the herd increased it remained in danger, losing forty members in 1925, for example, when they wandered out of the park and into Montana's Gallatin Valley and were quickly slaughtered by hunters. Reminiscent of the events south of the forty-ninth parallel, the apparently isolated bison ranging Canada's Peace River country had dwindled to fewer than three hundred near the turn of the century. Given such low numbers of animals, disease also posed a threat; for example, twenty-two Yellowstone bison perished in 1912 because of hemorrhagic septicemia.[5] Given the limited bison population, disease and hunters unconcerned with preservation of the species undoubtedly threatened the very existence of the bison at its nadir. The captive breeding programs provided a major bulwark against extinction due to the protection they afforded the animals within their herds.

Although such successful programs failed to materialize until the near complete demise of the bison, the history of attempted captive breeding of bison, particularly by Euro-Americans, extends back all the way to the

initial occupation of buffalo country by Europeans. In the late sixteenth
century, the first Spanish governor of New Mexico, Don Juan de Oñate, ordered a capture of bison for domestication. This unsuccessful effort spanned
thirty-one years. In 1701, Huguenot settlers in Virginia tried to raise buffalo. Later in the same century, Virginians in western counties attempted
to raise bison. Alexander Henry caught bison calves in the Red River Valley
in 1800 by leading them behind his horse once their mothers could no longer be found. Robert Wickliffe raised buffalo for thirty years in Kentucky
beginning in 1815. He attempted cross-breeding with cattle to produce an
enhanced hybrid. The bison captives' ferocity ended his experiment. Artist
George Catlin raised several calves during his time on the northern plains.
Fur trapper and trader Dick Wootton took care of buffalo calves from 1840
to 1843 in southeastern Colorado. Eventually he tired of the enterprise and
drove the buffalo across the plains to market in Independence, Missouri.
Famed newspaper editor Horace Greeley, while "going west," saw captured
calves in Kansas in 1859. In fact, calf-napping was nearly ubiquitous as stage
station managers, soldiers, fur traders, and even buffalo hunters kept bison
calves as pets. A particularly compelling story is Montana plainsman Vic
Smith's recollection of catching fifty calves in 1879 and penning them on
the breaks of the Yellowstone River forty miles north of the stream. Gros
Ventres tribal members set the calves free by breaking down the fence.[6]

Ultimately, none of these ventures led to bison increases and dissemination through captive breeding. The reasons for this lack of success become
clear in the testimony of British sportsman John Mortimer Murphy, written
in the same year that Smith caught his calves. As Murphy explained:

> Lassoing calves is most interesting sport, as the creatures run well. Hunters
> who wish to obtain calves for menageries or private persons often resort
> to the method of capture [leading bewildered calves behind horses], as the
> animals are more likely to live than if they were driven hard for several
> miles before being lassoed. Thousands of them are captured alive annu-
> ally by being run down with horses, but the greater number die, owing to
> the severe manner in which they were chased, or else to their grief at being
> separated from their kindred and the nutritious grasses and freedom of
> the plains. I have seen a troop of cavalry lasso one hundred of them in two
> days, and bring them to the barracks, and although they had plenty of
> room in a corral to run about, and an abundance of hay and grass, few of

them lived more than a week. The same mortality was noticeable among those captured by expert lassoers and regular hunters, so it is evident that they cannot stand much hardship.[7]

Indeed, to keep bison alive, protect them, and meet their needs required an inordinate amount of perseverance. Buffalo Jones, an eventual savior of the bison who captured more calves than any other of the original founders of successful programs, even said of the nearly sixty bison he caught and used to start his herd, "this number does not include the scores I captured when shooting buffalo on the plains for 50 cents a piece; the calves that I captured I generally sold for $5 each, and were probably used for beef purposes." Even as the saving efforts for the sake of posterity got underway, few individuals persevered with their bison captives to ensure success. One such reasonably well-documented case typifies that lack of follow-through and comes from the McKoy brothers who caught two calves, a male and female, near Beaver, Oklahoma in 1883. They sent the two to Rand Park in Keokuk, Iowa, in 1885. The park then sold two offspring to Page Woven Wire Fence Company of Michigan. The company continued raising the bison, with some finding themselves at the New York Zoological Park in 1904. From that herd, in 1907, fifteen buffalo went to one of the first restored public herds in the Wichita Mountains of Oklahoma in 1907.[8] This example combined with the numerous examples of calf-napping underscores the historical importance of the successful captive breeding programs initiated by people who hunted, caught, raised, and increased bison to guarantee the survival of the species.

The two most famous bison-savers, Charles Goodnight and C. J. "Buffalo" Jones, seem to pop right out of the Old West with their legendary biographies.[9] From their stories, some of the themes threaded through the successful bison-saving efforts appear. First, front-line conservationists emerged from the ranks of Western bison hunters, Native American and Euro-American, to ensure the survival of the species they had extraordinary familiarity with. Second, women played a key role. Third, the respective efforts of the Euro-Americans and Native Americans reflected important cultural differences even though both groups possessed a keen sense of nostalgia for the animal. Individualist capitalism characterized the enterprises of Goodnight and Jones. Communalism better describes the work of the Dupuis and Walking Coyote families along with the purchasers of their herds. James McKay, a Métis, falls somewhere in between these characteristics.

By the time his biographers caught up with him, Charles Goodnight was a Texas frontier legend. He had served as a scout for the Texas Rangers and was renowned for pushing cattle across and establishing ranches on the south plains. He was also quite cantankerous. His biographer, J. Evetts Haley, once recollected, "I hesitatingly crossed his ranch-house yard to face the flow of tobacco juice and profanity." Laura Hamner, another biographer, chose to soften Goodnight's demeanor by accompanying him on rides and visiting with him in his den.[10] In the end, both Haley and Hamner broke through the tough veneer and conveyed the story of Charles Goodnight.

On the plains of Texas in 1866, Goodnight decided to capture some bison calves. He used an old stockman's trick of chasing a herd until the calves tired and could be separated from their mothers and led along. When one unwilling mother charged Goodnight, he defended himself and his horse by shooting her. Sixty-two years later, he explained, "The older I get the worse I feel about having to kill that cow." Goodnight's first capture of bison calves ended like those of so many others. He agreed to let a friend raise them on half shares, but the friend tired of the enterprise and sold the captives. At that point, they vanished from record.[11]

It took the intervention of Mary ("Mollie") Goodnight to guarantee the successful establishment of a Goodnight captive breeding program for the besieged bison. In 1878, during the horrendous slaughter by the hide hunters, Mrs. Goodnight took charge. At this critical point, she explained to her husband "the advisability of preserving to Texas and the nation a few of the buffalo." She abhorred the suffering and hated to think of the "certain extermination of this race of animals." Acting on her suggestion, Charles and Mary's brother roped four calves. The calves were each given a milk cow to suck. They adopted their new mothers and new range and went on to become the beginning of the Goodnights' permanent herd. Their progeny spread all over the country, including Yellowstone, to enhance the existence of their once near-extinct species.[12] Mary Goodnight ensured that the calf captures of 1878 did not end like those of 1866. The Goodnight story blends front-line conservation and women's activism. The Goodnights emerge as the consummate Western ranchers, living and working on the southern plains. Their conservation effort took place at their home. Mary inspired the enterprise and persevered until it succeeded. Perhaps her goodwill is what makes the Goodnight story synonymous with the theme of hunter-conservationist or developer-conservationist.

Charles Goodnight, like other plainsmen, was a product of his time and environment. He hunted and killed buffalo. When he established his ranch in the Palo Duro region of the Texas panhandle, he stationed camps of cowboys to drive the bison away from available grass and water so his cattle could feed at will. Goodnight claimed that civilization necessitated the buffalo slaughter and that the buffalo hunters were a "fearless body of men . . . who by killing out the buffalo stopped forever the terror of the settlers, the depredatory tribes of the plains Indians."[13] Clearly, he did not exhibit the characteristics of an environmentalist concerned that nature reign supreme and unchecked.

Still, Charles Goodnight studied nature. According to J. Evetts Haley, Goodnight always laced their conversations with "observations upon the growth of the land with particular attention to varying forms for latitude and altitude, humidity and aridity." Haley said that Goodnight believed that "Everything in nature is useful." According to Laura Hamner, Goodnight's "books were woods and streams . . . by day and stars by night." Goodnight told Hamner that as a ten-year-old boy new to Texas he had seen his first buffalo. He "felt a pull that something in the beasts had for a responsive element in him . . . his spirit was roaming the prairie with that animal, powerful, alone, free."[14] Maybe Goodnight's spiritual empathy with the nomads prompted his efforts. Although he helped destroy the buffalo, his wife's influence and his love for nature combined to mitigate the destruction.

The Goodnights reaped both intangible and tangible rewards from conservation. Visitors frequented their ranch to see the living symbol of the western frontier. They invited a band of Kiowa to stage a buffalo hunt, for whom eating buffalo meat held special significance. Bison had played an elemental part in Goodnight's past, and one of his last meals was a Thanksgiving buffalo roast in 1929. More tangibly, buffalo did bring considerable income, and the Goodnights battled to earn a decent living. Perhaps they anticipated the future value of buffalo when they began their captive breeding program. Bison hide value increased from $2.50 in the 1870s to more than $100.00 a few years later. Mounted heads and horn products also commanded top dollar. Buffalo meat became a relatively high-priced luxury food. Ever the capitalist, Charles also developed buffalo wool, tallow, and soap products for sale. His rugged individualism showed when he established new ranches in west Texas, when he forged the Goodnight-Loving Cattle Trail, and when he developed catalo, a hybrid cross between cattle and buffalo, whose meat brought comparatively higher prices than regular beef.[15]

The idea of developing catalo did not originate with Goodnight any more than did the idea of calf-napping to start a captive breeding herd. In fact, both Oñate and Wickliffe had envisioned such a hybrid, and apparently others had sought such an animal as well.[16] This proved true enough to spawn the following critical observation from an observer in 1872:

> The idea of their [bison's] domestication at once entered their heads [western developers], and, from that time to the present, many attempts have been made to domesticate them, or, by crossing with domesticated cattle, to impart to the latter some additional valuable quality; but I believe that hitherto all such attempts have proven abortive. Now and then, upon the western frontier, you may see the dun color, high shoulders, and somewhat restless disposition, that indicate a cross between the domestic cow and buffalo bull, but, like the red-blood of the Indian, the mighty throng that is pressing on, soon absorbs it, and obliterates effectually its marks, if not wholly its effects.[17]

Still, Goodnight expended considerable effort to establish a mixed-blood animal and received some notoriety as one of the few successful breeders of the catalo.[18]

Goodnight pursued this manipulation of the bison for decades and foresaw "great possibilities in this cross-breeding." He even became quite defensive about his operation when questioned whether it was he or Buffalo Jones who first developed a successful hybrid breeding program. Lively correspondence about this debate reflects that both men sought credit for such an enterprise. Ultimately, the hybrid program failed due to infertility problems, but the failure does not indicate a lack of concerted effort by Goodnight, who experimented with a variety of crosses and cattle breeds to pull off the enterprise.[19] In the end, the western plainsman and his wife helped resurrect the bison from the brink of disaster, but Charles's effort at hybridization went beyond simply saving the species for its own sake. Notions of Euro-American development played a heavy role in his work with the bison.

Economic development also characterizes the motives of the other famous bison-saver, Charles Jesse Jones, colorfully known by his more common name of Buffalo Jones. A resident, like the Goodnights, of the southern Great Plains, his adventures took him from his home in Kansas to the frozen Canadian north and the steaming jungles of Africa. His exploits varied from farming, buffalo hunting, and serving as game warden of Yellowstone National Park to lecturing on his experiences in Africa. Actually, these enterprises comprise only a small portion of his accomplishments. Still, preserving the buffalo was his greatest contribution to posterity.

Jones claimed that he conceived his rescue idea in 1872. He still hunted buffalo for a living, but he sought to atone for his slaughter. To this end, between 1886 and 1889 he and his staff embarked on four rescue missions ranging from Garden City, Kansas, down into the Texas panhandle and catching an estimated fifty-six buffalo calves. These provided the start for a domestic herd that served as the foundation for other private and public herds throughout the United States, including one herd used by journalist Ernest Harold Baynes to promote the American Bison Society.[20]

Jones's entertaining tales of his expeditions detail roping calves, grabbing their tails, and hand-throwing them. He explained to his biographer, Henry Inman, that on his first calf-catching expedition he protected his charges from wolves that closed in on the thrown and tied calves. Jones could not stop while he labored to catch as many calves as possible, so he left an article of clothing with each calf to deter the hungry wolves. Half-naked and burdened by a calf under each arm, Jones rode back to aid his captives. Finally, his support wagon, furnished with pails of milk, arrived and saved the day.[21]

Correspondent Emerson Hough, accompanying Jones's second expedition, provided a near magical description of one Jones capture: "Up came his hand, circling the wide coil of the rope. We could almost hear it whistle through the air . . . in a flash the dust was gone, and there was Colonel Jones kneeling on top of a struggling tawny object." Later on in the expedition, Jones, like Goodnight, was "compelled to kill [an attacking mother buffalo] with his revolver." Hough related that this as "an unwished result, and was much deplored, for we came, not to slay, but to rescue." Nonetheless, Jones successfully captured his calves and nurtured them on milk cows, which usually entailed an initial brawl until the calf and cow became accustomed to each other on the long drive from Texas back to Kansas.[22]

Buffalo Jones's last two calf-napping expeditions in 1888 and 1889 proved noteworthy for two reasons. First, Jones tried but failed to catch and drive adult bison. Jones explained that the adults "took fits, stiffened themselves, then dropped dead, apparently preferring death to captivity." Second, it was on this expedition that the last wild buffalo calf of the southern range was caught. Jones described the moment: "I whirled the lasso in the air. I laid the golden wreath around the neck of the last buffalo calf ever captured."[23]

Like other savers of the bison, Jones, a westerner, saved buffalo where he worked and lived. Guilt motivated his hunter-conservationism. In the 1870s he had been one of the foremost buffalo hunters; he, himself, claimed killing "thousands" of the creatures, even though many times he tried to break his rifle over a wagon wheel and quit the slaying business. Then, hearing the boom of other hunters' rifles, he rationalized that with or without his presence, the bison were doomed. He would shoulder his rifle and head off for another day's shooting. Later he said, "I am positive it was the wickedness committed in killing so many that impelled me to take measures for perpetuating the race which I had helped almost destroy."[24]

Similar to Goodnight, love for nature and a drive to control it motivated Jones. He often longed to "be by himself in the timber or fields where he could indulge his love of nature untrammeled by any uncongenial companions." Jones saw nature as something beautiful, but something created to serve humankind. As a child he would catch little animals and "tame them in his own peculiar way." In fact, he made his first money by capturing and selling a squirrel, a "transaction," Jones said, that "fixed upon me the ruling passion that has adhered so closely through life." He compared the nearly extinct buffalo to the biblical reference to the "stone which the builders rejected," insisting that the domesticated buffalo would become the chief of all ruminants, as the rejected stone became the cornerstone. Jones claimed he would "chain" and "dominate" the buffalo. He spoke of "dominion" over the creature.

Jones's comments suggest that he hoped for economic benefit while exercising his "dominion" over the bison. Like other buffalo savers, Jones battled most of his life to make a respectable living. He prospered and suffered as a farmer, buffalo hunter, town developer, and rancher. Jones believed that one day buffalo would supplant cattle as the lords of the domestic range.[25] He spent a great deal of money on his expeditions and undoubtedly hoped for a return on his investment. His capitalist motivation appeared in his bid to develop the catalo, vying with Charles Goodnight to earn recognition as the champion breeder of the cattle-bison cross.[26] Jones bought and sold buffalo for several years, dealing in tens of thousands of dollars. During the 1890s, he lobbied the federal government both for a bison preserve and assistance for his hybridization program.[27] Jones's conservation, motivated by guilt, Euro-American ideals about dominance over nature, and capitalist fervor, combined with the efforts of the Goodnights to help save the bison of the southern plains.

Meanwhile, the northern plains bison had their advocates as well, with Native people dominating the efforts. James McKay, a mixed-blood giant of a man with a Scottish father and Métis mother, conceived of preserving the bison as early as 1872. An annual participant in the Red River hunts where Métis families went out on the prairie en masse for coordinated harvesting by their hunting brigades, McKay became alarmed at the lack of bison after their hunt took them much farther west than usual. His business partner and assistant in the bison-saving effort, Charles Alloway, described their thoughts on saving the bison: "We talked it over, and through that winter concluded that the buffalo could not last much longer." Thus, in the spring of 1873, with the assistance of French Métis hunters, McKay managed to acquire two heifer calves and one bull calf from the Battleford area on the Battle River. Alloway recollected that they lassoed the calves or ran them down after hunting as the pitiful calves approached the hunting camp. Like others before and after them who successfully maintained healthy calves, McKay put the new young charges with milk cows and kept them at his ranch at Deer Lodge (near Headingly on the Assiniboine River, twenty-eight miles west of Fort Garry, present Winnipeg, Manitoba). Alloway explained: "We fed them hay and tended them in shelters much the same as domestic cattle." In April 1874, McKay again went out with the Métis hunting brigades of between eighty and one hundred hunters, supported by nearly two thousand women and children clambering along in the distinctive Red River carts or on horseback. Alloway described the hunting party as "migratory tribes of Indians or half-breeds." In May, the group encountered bison to the west along the Milk River breaks, near the forty-ninth parallel southward between present Moose Jaw and Regina, Saskatchewan. They caught three more calves (one bull and two heifers). The young male subsequently died, and McKay's small captive herd back at Deer Lodge contained five members after the 1874 hunting expedition.[28]

The small protected herd grew, and in 1877 Samuel Bedson, the warden of the penitentiary at Stony Mountain, Manitoba, bought four young bulls and one heifer from McKay. McKay lived just two more years, but his herd increased to thirteen pure-bred bison and three cross-bred catalo. The subsequent developments involving his herd connected with those of the bison restoration efforts south of the forty-ninth parallel. At McKay's estate sale in 1880, Bedson purchased another eight bison and acquired another three from other sources. The warden grew his herd to eighty-three bison in 1888, but he left the bison business, marked both by increase and attempted cross-breeding, when he sold his herd, totaling fifty-eight pure bison and twenty-eight cross-breeds, to Buffalo Jones. At the same time, McKay's neighbor, Lord Strathcona, Sir Donald Smith, began a herd, presumably from McKay's bison, on behalf of the Canadian government. Smith kept his herd until 1898, when he donated his thirteen animals to Rocky Mountain Park at Banff. They became the last Canadian breeding population outside of those animals left in the parklands and woods to the north.[29]

McKay's motives are not reflected in the historical record as readily as those of Goodnight and Jones. Still, the evidence from his partner Alloway's recollections indicates a simple desire to preserve an animal that was very important to the northern plains and prairies. McKay, a speaker of Cree and several other First Nations dialects (along with both English and French), eventually became the provincial secretary of Manitoba.[30] Both a businessman and politician, he appears not to have used the bison to advance either business goals (he owned a freighting enterprise that moved goods between St. Paul, Minnesota, and Edmonton) or political ambitions as a dominator of nature. As well, he did not engage in widespread breeding programs aimed at developing the catalo. Like others who maintained bison alongside cattle for the latter's calming effect, he did get mixed-breed animals in his herd. The numbers do not, however, indicate an extraordinary attempt to create a "super cow" like that desired by Buffalo Jones. Nonetheless, McKay lasted in the business just a few years, long enough to preserve the bison, but not long enough to develop a full-blown program from which one could determine his full intentions beyond simply saving the species. The Red River hunting brigades retain some measure of fame for their intensive bison harvesting, which combined both sustenance of the herd and commercial robe and pemmican industries. Indeed, these hunts provided a blend of both communalism and individualistic capitalism. McKay's effort to save the bison reflects influences of both his First Nations and Euro-Canadian heritages.

While McKay's bison work represents a cultural middle ground, the efforts of the two Native American households, Salish and Lakota, that saved bison on American soil more firmly symbolize Native American communalism, which was driven by something other than capitalist economic instinct. The first of these two stories emerges from northwestern Montana, where a Salish family engaged in a near epic effort to bring bison back to the Flathead Valley from the northern plains across the Rocky Mountains. The somewhat controversial story first appeared in the public record in 1902 when editor George Bird Grinnell, western adventure writer and Boone and Crockett Club founding member, published it in a July issue of *Forest and Stream*.[31] Interested in the origins of domestic bison herds, Grinnell asked a hunting guide friend, Jack Monroe, to investigate the origins of the Flathead Valley herd. Monroe met with the owners at the time, mixed-bloods Michel Pablo and Charles Allard, and acquired a testimonial correspondence from Montana entrepreneur Charles Aubrey. A former fur trader, buffalo hunter, and rancher, Aubrey, who like others had tried and failed to establish a captive bison program, articulated the details of the herd prior to its purchase by Pablo and Allard.[32] His richly detailed account illustrates an effort far different in its inception than that of Goodnight, Jones, or McKay.

Aubrey explained that in the winter of 1877–1878, he occupied his trading post on the Marias River just south of present Shelby, Montana.[33] The popular Native wintering ground, though firmly within the home territory of the Blackfeet, claimed residents from many other Indian nations as well, including Sarcee and Stony from the north; Klamath, Kootenai, Nez Perce, and Salish from the west; Assiniboine and Gros Ventres from the east; and even a family of Crow from the south. Aubrey maintained that the wake of the Nez Perce conflict created a feeling of sympathy among the tribes so traditional animosities abated.

Meanwhile, a drama unfolded within the trading encampment when a Pend d'Oreille man named Samuel Walking Coyote, married to a Salish woman named Sabine, became involved with a Blackfeet woman. The affair caused a domestic dispute, which Aubrey attempted to mediate by asking the Blackfeet to restrain their young lady while he attempted to settle matters between Walking Coyote and Sabine. Tempers flared through the winter, but the Blackfeet woman left in the spring following a quarrel in which Walking Coyote injured Sabine. Aubrey explained to the Salish man that the circumstances had become grave and that neither the Salish community back home in the Flathead Valley nor the Jesuit priests there would treat Walking Coyote kindly in light of the incident. Aubrey stated that he and the fearful Walking Coyote then devised a plan to make amends for the transgression. Because bison did not range in the Flathead Valley, Walking Coyote could capture and take bison calves back to the community and the priests. The gentlemen agreed.

The next day, Walking Coyote and Sabine prepared to leave with plans to rope calves and bring them back to Aubrey's post to habituate them with milk cows. The plan worked and within a couple days, the husband and wife team returned with a heifer and bull to pen with the cows. Walking Coyote told Aubrey that the Salish family, which probably included their teenage son Joseph Attahe, would return to the hunting grounds to catch more calves and that the herd already was moving north toward its summer range near the Saskatchewan River.[34] Thus, Walking Coyote feared that the family would run into enemy hunters and would not return for more than a week either way. Eight days after departing, they successfully returned with three more heifers and two bulls. Walking Coyote related to Aubrey some of the details, including the loss of one heifer to a broken neck during a roping accident. Sabine took this as an omen to end the effort, and they then hobbled the calves and led them back to Aubrey's post. The fur trader remembered that they left within a few days in a pack train, with Sabine leading the family with pack horses and the calves following, with Walking Coyote trailing.

Aubrey did not see them again, although he did ascertain knowledge of their return trip. They crossed the Teton and Sun Rivers, went up the Dearborn River to cross the continental divide at Cadotte Pass, and descended along the Blackfoot River. They then passed through Hell Gate, skirted alongside the Bitterroot Valley, and climbed through the Koragen defile, where U.S. Highway 93 now runs to drop into the Flathead Valley. They lost one bull after an injury. Whether Walking Coyote experienced vindication for his actions remains unclear. In any event, they made it back home and began raising their small herd.[35]

During Monroe's interview of the prominent valley residents Michel Pablo and his wife, the couple verified much of the story and remembered the arrival of bison calves back into the valley. Similarly, Charles Allard, another locally well-known rancher, explained in an 1889 letter to George Bird Grinnell that his and Pablo's bison came from calves "bought from the Indians." Others remembered the early story of the calves as well. Longtime Flathead Valley resident Duncan McDonald recalled in an interview late in life "that Whista Sinchilape or Walking Coyote found three little heifer and three little bull calves wandering" and that "Mary Sabine" and "Joe Attahe" helped drive the calves back to the St. Ignatius area of the Flathead Valley. Duncan's brother, Joseph McDonald, also remembered "Samuel" and the calves. Noting that the community became excited each year during the calving season for the bison, he added that the Salish family confined them to a small pasture. However, eventually they often wandered freely in the vicinity of Fort Connah, a former Hudson's Bay Company post located just a few miles across the valley from St. Ignatius. Flathead Valley resident Antoine Morigeau added details about the commitment of the Native community to the small herd's survival. Samuel, Morigeau said, kept a close guard over his young buffalo. Every Indian in the valley, believing these to be the last ones, aided in their protection. They were permitted to roam wherever fancy led them, but always there was an Indian rider in their vicinity.[36]

Another Salish man named Que-que-sah also recalled the calves, commenting: "I remember Samuel Welles whom the white people called Indian Sam and Indian Samuel. . . . I was in the village of St. Ignatius that day in 1873, when Welles rode in with his pack string." Que-que-sah remembered the initial pasturing and later free-ranging of the small herd. Community members often gathered after church on Sundays to watch the bison for a moment of reflection. He also acknowledged that Pablo and Allard bought these bison to start their herd. Que-que-sah went on to say that he believed that they acquired a few calves later from Blackfeet to augment their captive breeding herd. Father Lawrence Palladino, a priest at St. Ignatius during this period later wrote about the Pablo-Allard herd, claiming that it "all sprung from two calves captured and brought to St. Ignatius in our first days on the place by Indian Samuel."[37]

Pablo and Allard bought the bison from Walking Coyote's family in 1883 or 1884. Sources usually fix the number purchased at between eight and fourteen. The numbers and dates regarding the exact origins of the Salish bison are frustratingly imprecise. As well, the allusions to bison brought by other Native Americans besides Walking Coyote and Sabine must figure into the analysis of the herd's beginning. When weighed against the overwhelming support provided by existing documentation none of this complicating data disproves the couple's effort or its establishment a breeding program. Still, given the various testimonies that do exist, we may well conclude that by the mid-1880s, if not earlier, small additions to the herd living in the Flathead Valley were made by other Native American sources, most likely Salish or Blackfeet hunters during the late 1870s or early 1880s. Still, by the time Allard wrote to Grinnell in 1889, the partners owned thirty-four head in a vibrant herd that would eventually increase into the hundreds.[38]

Comparing the efforts of Walking Coyote and Sabine to deliver bison to their homelands and thereby perpetuate the species to the efforts of other bison saviors points out important similarities and differences. First, these people lived and worked in the West on the front lines of both buffalo harvesting and conservation. Their culture depended on the bison. Second, as Native people, they did not concern themselves with cross-breeding experiments or genetic manipulation. Rather, they raised bison as bison and not farm cows even to the point of allowing their buffalo open range. Most importantly, the Salish nation members of the Flathead Valley clearly offered their approval to bringing back the bison since they allowed the herd free run of the reservation and even took it upon themselves to provide guardians. Third, Sabine played a key role in perpetuating the species, right down to hunting and herding the calves. The generations of Native women intimately involved in the bison-human relationship continued on through her involvement. Moreover, this primary participation by Native women also characterized the effort of the fifth and final household that saved the bison, the Dupuises of the Lakota nation.

The Dupuises, also known as the Dupres, Duprees, or Dupris, received far less renown than the Goodnights or Buffalo Jones. Nonetheless, their life stories are comparable. Frederick Dupuis, a French Canadian, arrived at Fort Pierre in present South Dakota in 1838. A fur trader, he first worked for Pierre Chouteau's American Fur Company then traded independently. Documentation from his trading days in 1860 and 1861 reveals that he largely concerned himself with Indian activity, trade goods, and the whereabouts of the buffalo. Eventually, Dupuis left the fur trade and became a rancher until his death in 1898.[39]

Dupuis lived in South Dakota for sixty years, witnessing the Plains Indian horse culture at its prime; the steady resource exploitation by fur trappers and traders; the Black Hills gold rush; the domination by the blue-coated federal soldiers; the destruction of the buffalo; the establishment of towns, farms, and ranches; and the massacre of his Lakota neighbors at Wounded Knee. Dupuis married a Minniconjou Lakota named Good Elk Woman who took the name Mary Ann Dupuis. They had nine children. The Dupuises established a large ranch on the Cheyenne River that served as a camp and hub for Indian activity, with at least fifty people served supper daily.[40] Serving as a bridge between two cultures, the Dupuis household also linked the old wild herds of bison and the captive herds that ensured survival after the slaughter.

A Dupuis expedition to save the buffalo occurred sometime between 1881 and 1882 somewhere on the hunting grounds along either the Grand, Moreau, or Yellowstone Rivers in the present western Dakotas or in eastern Montana (different reports give different dates and locations). An account of a Dupuis hunting expedition at this time lends insight into the family's life in buffalo country. At the invitation of a Dupuis son-in-law, Clarence Ward, the Reverend Thomas Lawrence Riggs accompanied the Dupuis family on what he labeled the last winter buffalo hunt of the Dakotas. After seeking permission from the family for Riggs to accompany the hunt, Ward announced to the clergyman that the Dupuis boys and Mary were excited about his presence and wished him to share their tent. Frederick did not go along on the hunt. Riggs described a communal Indian hunt with horses, travois, and dogs. The Dupuis family took a buckboard and tents. About half of the hunting party consisted of women. The hunters were successful, and the Dupuis family took care of Riggs during the hardships of the hunt. He concluded that the industrious, good-natured Native Americans possessed great expertise at buffalo hunting.[41] Riggs never mentioned that the Dupuis boys captured live calves on this hunt, although it seems certain his detailed account would have recorded such an event.

Curiously, George Philip, a close relative of Scotty Philip who eventually purchased the Dupuis bison herd, insisted that it was during an 1880–1881 hunt that Pete Dupuis, Frederick and Mary's son, caught the live calves. Apparently, the hunt Philip referred to was not the same as that described by Riggs. Philip specified that Dupuis caught the calves after an exhaustive chase in the breaks of the Grand River, then loaded the youngsters onto a wagon for a ride back to the Dupuis ranch on the Cheyenne River. He put the calves in with the Dupuis cattle where they ranged on the Cheyenne River Reservation without incident.[42]

Another account, possibly primary, exists concerning the capture of the calves. Basil Clement, a companion of Frederick Dupuis, related his version of the story to Circuit Judge John F. Hughes of Fort Pierre, who years later told Clement's story to Charles Deland. Clement maintained that he, Frederick Dupuis, and one of Dupuis's sons headed west toward Montana to capture buffalo calves. When they found a herd, they stayed downwind and watched the animals graze until the calves bedded down and the mothers wandered off feeding. Then the hunters stole the little creatures, which instinctively remained motionless. The hunters loaded the orphans on the buckboard and took them back to the Dupuis ranch. Charles Deland, the recorder of Hughes's story, noted that contemporary eyewitnesses confirmed that four young bison lived on Dupuis land in the fall of 1883. Apparently, the Dupuises had acquired these animals during the previous spring or summer.[43]

Regardless of the exact details surrounding the capture of the bison calves, the Dupuis family helped save buffalo. By 1888, the successfully growing herd numbered five cows, four bulls, and seven mixed-blood catalo. The hybrids resulted from ranging the bison with domestic cattle to keep them from wandering away rather than from an attempt by the Dupuises to create a mixed-blood breed. The Dupuis story shares the themes found in the other bison-saving endeavors. These front-line conservationists lived and worked on the northern plains. Their sense of communalism becomes evident when examining their hospitality and hunting. Mary, a full-blood Minniconjou experienced in the buffalo culture, proved instrumental in the effort. Riggs's account of the 1880–1881 buffalo hunt suggests that she administered the Dupuis hunting party, and she clearly helped guide the family. Frederick Dupuis told the *Pierre Free Press* in 1890, "Many years ago, I married a good Indian woman." When asked about taking land in severalty, he demurred: "My old woman can take land if she wants to." Frederick honored his wife's wishes. One observer of the French-Canadian fur trappers and traders noted that the "only authority [they] acknowledged was that of [their] Indian spouses." Indeed, Mary, Good Elk Woman, influenced Frederick and her sons to save a few of the remaining buffalo. The oral tradition among descendants of Frederick Dupuis and Good Elk Woman fully celebrates the leading role she played in bringing back the bison. Given the tribe's traditional characterization of White Buffalo Calf Woman as the architect of a covenant between human and buffalo nations, the role for a Lakota woman of reconciling the two entities appears quite familiar.[44]

Thus, as disaster struck Indian country in 1890, symbolized by Wounded Knee, a small promise of hope existed in the consolidation of protected bison herds. Walking Coyote and Sabine's herd descendants numbered in the thirties and represented the largest herd under the aegis of Native people, namely, Michel Pablo of the Salish-Kootenai Reservation. The Dupuis herd possessed at least nine full-blood bison grazing on the Cheyenne River Reservation. Meanwhile, McKay's Métis-gathered herd did not find its way to a First Nations reserve, but did become a small seed herd for Rocky Mountain Park along with a large addition to Buffalo Jones's herd on the southern Plains. At the dawn of the 1890s, the southern plains did come to contain the largest number of privately protected bison, with Jones and Goodnight maintaining several dozen bison each.

Yet even as the bison in Indian country maintained some degree of autonomy on an open range, those days would end as increasing pressure toward a Euro-American restructured landscape dominated even the apparent safe havens of Native American reservations. Much as North America's indigenous people faced their greatest challenge in the demographic and cultural collapse that followed the conclusion of military hostilities, so, too did the bison, which had come to range in protected Indian country. At the turn of the century and for several succeeding decades, both the Native people and the buffalo would suffer the loss of their autonomy and the benefits of their covenant relationship. The bison and the American Indians would soon follow the way of their Canadian brethren, who no longer maintained bison herds following the sale of the McKay herd.

Fig. 6. Northern plains Métis hunting brigade contemporary to that of James McKay. Undated. Courtesy Montana Historical Society, Helena.

Fig. 7. The Dupuis (Dupree) family. Frederick, son Peter, and Mary Ann (Good Elk Woman). Undated. Box P148. Photo courtesy of the South Dakota State Historical Society—State Archives.

3. Indians and Buffalo, 1890–1990s

It is a singular fact, and contrary to general belief, that we owe much to the Indians for saving the buffalo from extinction.

Martin Garretson, Secretary, American Bison Society (1938)

In 1997, as he watched several bison leave a corral and emerge onto the prairie, much to the delight of several Native American onlookers including students from a local school, Lakota environmental scholar Jim Garrett commented: "The resurgence of the buffalo. That's happening. But it's happening a hundred years later."[1] His observation hearkened back to the Ghost Dance ceremony and the lamentations of Indian people across the West during the late 1880s and early 1890s to restore the earth and bring back the buffalo. However, Garrett's statement also came with the hindsight of someone viewing the history of the past one hundred years. Ethnohistorian David Rich Lewis summarizes the origins and marginalization of Native American life in the twentieth century:

> The pace of change in Native American cultures and environments increased dramatically with Euro-American contact. Old World pathogens and epidemic diseases, domesticated plants and livestock, the disappearance of native flora and fauna, and changing patterns of Native resource use altered the physical and cultural landscape. Nineteenth-century removal and reservation policies reduced the continental scope of Indian lands to islands in the stream of American settlement. Reservation lands were largely unwanted or remote environments of little economic value. The Dawes General Allotment Act of 1887 provided for the division of some reservations into individual holdings as part of an effort to transform Indians into idealized agrarians—yeomen farmers and farm families.

> In subsequent acts Congress opened Indian Territory, withdrew forests,
> reservoir sites, mineral and grazing lands, regulated Indian access to
> those areas, and even circumvented the trust period to speed the transfer of
> lands into non-Indian hands. These policies contributed to the alienation
> of more than 85 percent of Indian reservation lands—a diminishment of
> land, resources, and biotic diversity that relegated Indians to the political
> and economic periphery of American society.[2]

Yet, all the while, Indians tenaciously kept the bison integral to their
culture.

Even as Native Americans including Sabine, Walking Coyote, the Dupuises, Michel Pablo, and Charles Allard labored to save the bison and preserve its integrity on the range, the continuity of the physical Indian-buffalo
relationship remained in question as Euro-American forces continued to
reshape the landscape and its Native inhabitants. These bison-savers helped
determine the biological survival of the bison from past annihilation. They
could not, however, determine the political survival. The American government would do that. The century, from the time of the establishment of safe
captive breeding herds under Native American aegis in the late nineteenth
century until the proliferation in bison numbers in Indian country—largely
due to pan-Indian organization through the Intertribal Bison Cooperative
in the late twentieth century—marked a period in which the whims of the
American government bore heavily on the ability of Native American people
to persevere as the "buffalo people."[3]

Students of Indian-white relations often can recite the salient points of the
past century and a quarter, such as the boarding school movement, Dawes
Act (1887), Indian Reorganization Act (1934), Termination Policy of the 1950s
and early 1960s, and Indian Self-Determination Act (1974). The ability of
Native Americans in the United States to maintain adequate influence over
the plight of bison in their ongoing struggle for cultural autonomy often
parallels these policies and legislative acts. Under the detrimental impact
of the "Americanization" programs, which concentrated on Native youth
in boarding schools and alienated Natives from communal Indian lands,
Indians and their allies lost a protracted battle to keep bison ranging in Indian country.[4] With the improved treatment offered by the New Deal, which
reinstated respect for Native American culture and communal landholding,
bison began to return to Indian country, with the blessing of a sufficient

number of federal policymakers and warm encouragement from Native Americans. The arrogance of the termination period temporarily checked Native American autonomy, just as revised livestock policies impacted the range of the buffalo. Yet the activism and advocacy of the 1960s and 1970s, often led by Native Americans, improved the position of Native people before the law and also helped to intensify bison stocking programs on reservations. Thus, by the 1990s, Indians and buffalo could finally become the subject of a modern success story after a century of riding a virtual bucking bison bull of interference. The prayers of a century past were getting a favorable answer, but the self-reliant initiative of a few determined Indians at the outset was instrumental in earning that long-delayed victory.

Far and away the more prolific of the two Native American bison programs in the early 1890s lay in the Flathead Valley of northwest Montana. There mixed-blood ranchers Michel Pablo and Charles Allard grew their herd from around a dozen head in the early 1880s to several hundred by the end of the 1890s. Their story confirms several of the themes inherent in Native American efforts to save the bison, including conservation by front-line Westerners often with women involved, a strong sense of communal responsibility to Native America, and the desire to maintain bison herds with as little human interference as possible in virtually a free-range environment.

Both Pablo and Allard possessed Native American mothers. For his part, Pablo, also known by his Indian name Chilth-mit-chin-noo, was born in 1844 or 1845 in Fort Benton, Montana, in the home range of his Blackfeet or Piegan mother. His father, a Mexican or New Mexican, worked there as a wrangler. Pablo's ties to the Flathead Valley came through his 1864 marriage to a Salish woman named Agathe Finley, who worked as a cook at the Flathead Agency, and whom presumably he met through his work as a wrangler and interpreter. Agathe reputedly held considerable influence in household decisions with respect to the bison. The couple established a ranch on the south end of Flathead Lake in 1881, and it was there that the Pablos ran their bison with Michel's partner, Charles Allard, following the purchase from Samuel Walking Coyote.[5]

Allard was born in Salem, Oregon, in 1853 to a Native American mother and Euro-American father. He moved to Montana in 1865, where his father participated in western Montana's gold rush. Young Charles eventually grew to become a successful stockman. He also made the Flathead Valley his home, where he began a ranching partnership with fellow mixed-blood Pablo. As for Pablo, the purchase of the Walking Coyote bison initiated Allard's effort to bring back the buffalo.[6]

Tony Barnaby, a son-in-law of Michel Pablo, elucidated the reasons behind the purchase from Walking Coyote in an interview several years after the inconspicuous business deal that forever impacted the restoration of bison in the United States:

> Many people today, while appreciating the fact that Indian Samuel, Michel Pablo, Chas. Allard, Sr., and Andrew Stinger [a bison wrangler associated with Pablo] were the ones who saved the buffalo from extermination, question their motive. Some say that the plan was to build up a vast herd, that later, could be sold at a great profit. Perhaps that is a very natural view; but we, who were associates of these four men, know it is erroneous. The acquisition of money meant little to men of their type. But the preservation of the bison, well, this latter reason was their duty, privilege and pleasure. Pablo, for instance, did not consider a buffalo as just a great shaggy beast of the plains; but rather symbolical of the real soul of the Indians' past—something grand, that with the culture of his own race, had somehow managed to survive the undesirable features in the white man's system.[7]

With this sense of purpose, Pablo and Allard sought to grow their small herd, which for the most part wandered freely in the Round Butte area of the Flathead Valley. Through natural increase, assorted purchases, and the acquisition of a few calves from Piegan hunters and perhaps other regional sources, the herd contained twenty-seven head by 1888 and thirty-five head just one year later. In 1893, the partners made a significant purchase of twenty-six pure-blood bison and eighteen hybrid cattalo from Buffalo Jones. Displaying his keen abilities as a bison steward, Pablo drove a few of his herd to Butte, Montana, where he met the new herd recently arrived by railroad and in the safekeeping of his partner. The two and some hired hands then drove the combined and more habituated herd back to the Flathead Valley. Never happy with the hybrid catalo, Pablo and Allard quarantined them on Wild Horse Island in Flathead Lake. The two ranchers did not want the cattle blood in the veins of their bison herd, which now possessed both southern herd blood and a bolster of northern herd blood because Jones had infused his herd with bison and their progeny that James McKay and Charles Alloway had initially acquired on the prairie near the United States–Canadian border. Pablo and Allard did not keep the catalo for long and re-sold them to Buffalo Jones, who possessed a keen interest in mixed breeding that contrasted with Pablo and Allard's less manipulative bison philosophy. Nonetheless, by the time of Allard's untimely death from complications following an accidental injury in 1896, the herd possessed a full 300 animals.[8]

Allard's death, though a heartfelt loss, did not disrupt the progress of building of the herd. Pablo split the herd of 300 into two groups of 150. He kept one group and Allard's heirs split the remainder. Three individuals quickly acquired these animals and spread them across the West, becoming important seed stock for later herds. Charles Conrad of the Kalispell area received several animals. He, too, passed away prematurely, but his widow Alicia Conrad provided the main body, which totaled thirty-four animals of the original herd established on the National Bison Range in 1908. Howard Eaton took several of the animals he received from Allard's heirs and dealt them to the federal government, fifteen of these becoming part of the Yellowstone National Park herd. Meanwhile, the third recipient of the herd from Allard's heirs, Judge Woodrow of Missoula, sold his to the Miller Brother's 101 Ranch in Oklahoma.[9]

Pablo used his 150 head to continue building the largest herd in private hands in the world. In 1900, his herd of 259 totaled twice that of Charles Goodnight and Buffalo Jones combined. After the turn of the century, as much as 80 percent of the nation's bison possessed some blood from the Pablo-Allard herd. Meanwhile, the beneficence of Pablo's bison effort was not lost on his neighbors. For example, Salish spokesman Que-que-sah recalled that the owners would occasionally butcher an animal to share with neighbors. In particular, he said of Pablo: "[He] was very generous to his friends. Often he would tell our Indians to butcher a fat buffalo. We all liked and respected Mr. Pablo and no Indian would steal any of his herd." Pablo's son-in-law, Tony Barnaby, described him as "lavishly generous to friend and foe; lover of both races; fond of all animals." About Pablo's bison savvy, Barnaby added: "With a keen eye to his animals' welfare, he knew at all times, just about where his buffaloes were grazing. He soon realized that they were increasing at a rapid rate: and after he returned from each daily ride on the range, he remarked: 'it is well'."[10] Shortly after the turn of the century, however, Pablo could no longer say, "It is well." Forces beyond his control would end his bison restoration effort and nearly complete the alienation of the physical relationship between Native Americans and bison.

In 1904, President Theodore Roosevelt signed a bill into law that ordered the execution by 1909 of the 1887 General Allotment (Dawes) Act on the Flathead Reservation. This translated into the alienation of the tribes from reservation lands, which were divided into individual landholdings with the unallotted lands opened up to settlers. Thus, the protected communal lands that served as the Pablos's bison range would no longer exist. Realizing in 1905 and 1906 that time was running short, Pablo reportedly petitioned for a grazing allotment for his herd, which by then was approaching six hundred animals. When the government denied his petition, he responded with an overture to Congress that the federal government buy his herd for $250 a head. The congressmen rebuffed his offer. Pablo then struck a deal with the Canadian government.[11] Tony Barnaby described Pablo's reaction to the rejection by the United States government and subsequent deal with Canada:

> Only upon one occasion, was Pablo really discouraged. When he was positively assured that the reservation was to be opened to white settlers, he knew that free, open range was ending and that his beloved herd must go. He vainly sought to sell them to our own Government in hopes they would find a haven in some refuge set aside for that purpose. We know that when Pablo heard that our Congress could not be induced to appropriate a purchasing fund, he was moved to manly tears. Only as a last resort, did he sell them to the Canadian officials.[12]

Canada's point man for the business negotiations, the Métis Canadian emigration agent Alex Ayotte, hailed from Great Falls, Montana. He knew of Pablo's dilemma, and after some quick checks with his superiors in Canada, Ayotte brokered the deal with Pablo so his fellow Native's bison herd could be preserved in Canada. Pablo signed the final agreement with Howard Douglas, the commissioner of Dominion Parks, which indicated that the Canadian acquisition relied on the Canadian national government's sponsorship of a bison recovery program in its parks. They closed the deal in March 1907, promising to pay $245 per animal, including the shipping that would take them to their new home near Wainwright, Alberta. Pablo received a down payment of $10,000 and began planning the roundup and shipment of the herd to begin in the late spring of 1907 and conclude in 1908.[13]

Although the sale proceeded smoothly, neither the roundup nor the shipment transpired easily. The plan included a roundup along the Pend d'Oreille River, trailing the herd twenty-seven miles to the rail station at Ravalli, then a multiple-stage railroad journey utilizing five separate railroad companies and culminating with the herd's arrival at Elk Island Park in Alberta, where the bison would remain until crews finished the fence at Wainwright. Pablo supervised the construction of the loading facilities at Ravalli, including strengthening rail cars, installing troughs, and building wings for the chutes. Pablo's cowboys, full-blooded and mixed-blood Native Americans led by Charles Allard's sons, Charles Jr. and Joe, hoped to separate bulls and young animals from the main herd for the initial shipment.[14]

The cowboys met their match in trying to round up and load the herd. Bison gored horses, men sustained injuries, and occasionally cowboys shot bison in self-defense. In the first roundup, spanning two weeks, they managed to commandeer fewer than 250 head. Pablo accompanied this first group all the way to their destination to ensure their safe arrival. In fact, however, this would be the most success they saw in the entire process. By spring 1908 the stockmen had managed to gather and ship only about 400 of the more than 600 Pablo bison. The planned two-year roundup and shipment failed. Meanwhile, the remaining herd continued to reproduce. For all of 1909, Pablo's men shipped just over 200 animals. In that year, they switched from trailing the herd to Ravalli to transporting them in crated wagons from the roundup site. The roundups continued but tapered off over the next three years, with 68 bison shipping in 1910 and 7 in both 1911 and 1912. Estimates vary, but approximately 700 bison eventually made the trip. The cowboys never did succeed in rounding up the entire herd, and stragglers remained.[15]

The event, which spanned several weeks each year from 1907 through 1912, became a bit of a media spectacle. Even today, customers can find postcards commemorating the event in curio shops in Montana. Although photojournalists covered the event, some of the most colorful and insightful descriptions came from the pen and paint of famed Montana artist and author Charles Marion Russell. Russell participated in the roundups in both spring 1908 and fall 1909 and reflected on his attendance in three letters from 1909 and 1910.[16]

His correspondence and supplementary sketches and watercolors yield a plethora of information about the landscape and the cowboys as well as the difficulties executing the roundup. First, Russell commented on the open range preserved for the bison on the reservation: "It was shure good to bee in a country without fences" [sic]. About the buffalo wranglers, he added that "the riders were all breeds [mixed-blood] an[d] fool boods [full bloods] a wild looking bunch that looked good to me." He augmented these comments with a watercolor of nine riders galloping across the prairie. The riders sport long dark hair, many in braids, cowboy hats, feathers, vests, long-sleeve shirts, bandanas, riding quirts, and western rigs on an assortment of horses. Another watercolor, entitled "one of Pablo's riders," provides more detail: a single rider who appears much like the nine just described but with jacket instead of a vest and with a colorful blanket under the saddle.[17]

Russell elucidated the arduousness of this monumental effort by Native Americans to save the bison. He sketched a diagram of the bison-holding facility, which utilized an oxbow, and the cliffs along the Pend d'Oreille River and also painted bison hurtling into the river. The cowboy artist explained:

> The first day they got 300 in the whings but they broke back an[d] all the riders on Earth couldn't hold them. They only got in with about 120. We all went to bed that night sadisfide with 120 in the trap but woke up with one cow the rest had climed the cliff an[d] got away. The next day they onely got 6 an[d] a snow storm struck us an[d] the roundup was called off till next summer.[18]

Russell elaborated on this description in another letter:

> These bluffs were nearly straight up an[d] made a natural fence that would have held any cow on Earth an[d] from looks I'd bet nothing with out wings could have made the git away but since I seen where they got out I wouldn't bet what buffalo cant do they had 300 in the wings the first run but when they sighted the fence they split running in all directions an[d] there aint no such thing as lieding a buffalo hel [he'll] go through under or over you an[d] a rider that runs in front of a buffalo is a green hand.[19]

Given such challenges, the determination of these people to get the buffalo off the increasingly unprotected reservation and under the aegis of the

Canadian government was remarkable. After all, the few bison that Pablo's wranglers did not catch quickly met the fate of millions of their predecessors at the hands of buffalo hunters.

The remaining bison, a cagey group of survivors termed "outlaws" by *Forest and Stream*, eluded capture "without fear or respect for horse, man, rope or fence," and "if overtaken and roped, they threw the horse and his rider and went off with the rope." Pablo hoped to conduct hunts for local residents to harvest this remainder of his once prolific herd. He began staging hunts, but Montana's attorney general declared that the allotment of the reservation placed the leftover bison under the jurisdiction of Montana law. Without the Native American community's protection, poachers quickly obliterated the last of Pablo's bison.[20]

A noteworthy side story to the end of the Native American bison herd of northwestern Montana is the establishment of the National Bison Range on alienated lands once grazed by Pablo's buffalo on the Flathead Reservation. Largely in response to the failure of the United States government to protect the bison through the purchase of the Pablo herd, several eastern conservationists gathered in New York in December 1905 to form an organization aimed at establishing a national bison range. The participants formed the American Bison Society, headed by William Templeton Hornaday and with President Theodore Roosevelt as the honorary president. The organization and its supporters, which included a fundraising women's group, acted quickly to get bison into the public domain in addition to the Yellowstone herd. The Roosevelt administration oversaw the 1907 stocking of the Wichita Mountains Wildlife Reserve in Oklahoma (formerly part of the Kiowa-Comanche Reservation prior to allotment) with fifteen bison from the New York Zoological Park. The American Bison Society subsequently proposed to Congress in March 1908 that it would provide a herd to run on a fenced range of approximately twenty square miles adjacent to the Flathead River near St. Ignatius. In return, the federal government would purchase and fence the land. The government responded favorably, and the American Bison Society purchased the Conrad herd of thirty-four buffalo to stock the new preserve. They hit the ground on October 17, 1909.[21]

Though many of the American Bison Society members and supporting congressmen advocated saving the bison on these ranges for reasons similar to those of Native Americans— nostalgic more than economic—the circumstances reveal some important differences. First, the government deprived the Native Americans of their land, then took that land, and reestablished bison there, much as Native Americans had initially preferred. Moreover, the American Bison Society developed unfulfilled plans to repeat this process on both alienated Lakota and Crow lands, but these tribes eventually established their own herds. Second, the Eastern conservationists did not envision a bison open-range landscape at the expense of Euro-American farmers and developers. Environmental historian Andrew Isenberg explains: "The bison preservationists acceded to the economic exploitation of the grasslands by the ranchers and the farmers who had displaced the bison and the Indians in the nineteenth century. They sought only relatively small parcels of land for parks and game preserves, and were rather more concerned that the ranges be accessible to tourists." Third, Hornaday developed resentment for Pablo as a result of the Canadian deal for his herd. In a letter to the American Bison Society's northwest Montana range consultant, Morton Elrod, Hornaday explained that he refused "to ask favors of a half-breed Mexican-F'head" just to get a few Pablo bison to stock the future National Bison Range.[22] Thus, while both Native Americans and Euro-Americans worked to preserve the bison of the United States at the turn of the century, their effort reflected the federal government's hegemony in executing policy and eastern conservationists' ethnocentrism.

Meanwhile, Canada's bison program received a numerical boon with the arrival of the Pablo bison. The herd quickly outgrew its temporary pasture at Elk Island Park, where a few remained after the transfer of the bulk of the herd to the larger facility at Wainwright. Still, by 1923, the herd threatened to overgraze its range. The Canadian government responded with a reduction program in which surplus animals were slaughtered. By 1933, the Canadian government was slaughtering fifteen hundred to two thousand bison annually to keep the herd in line with the park's grazing capacity. As well, policymakers decided to make a controversial transfer of several hundred buffalo to Wood Buffalo National Park in northern Alberta and the Northwest Territories. The controversy arose because of positive tuberculosis tests in the Wainwright herd and concern over the mixing of the transferred bison with the bison already indigenous to Wood Buffalo National Park.[23] Certainly, "prolific" describes the Pablo bison and their progeny both while on American and Canadian soil.

Although less prolific, the Dupuis herd also holds a place of paramount importance in the history of the Native American effort to retain a continuous physical relationship with the bison. Its story contains many of the same themes found in the story of the Sabine and Samuel Walking Coyote-cum-Pablo herd: a transfer of ownership, a sense of community and loyalty to the bison-Indian relationship, the influence of Native American women, and the hope of raising the bison in an open-range environment as much as possible.

During the 1890s, Pete Dupuis, Frederick and Mary's son, took control of the family's herd and increased its number. He passed away in 1898, and the executor of the family's estate decided to sell the herd to family friend Scotty Philip. Philip continued grazing the herd on the Cheyenne River Reservation for three more years. In 1901, he and five other men moved the animals nearly one hundred miles to his more than 10,000-acre "Buffalo Pasture" on his Fort Pierre ranch, near present-day Pierre, South Dakota. The herd contained fifty-seven pure-blood bison and approximately two dozen hybrid cattalo. Uninterested in establishing a catalo enterprise, Philip declared that the hybrids "weren't worth a damn" and promptly slaughtered them. Philip thus quickly displayed his intention to replicate bison herds as he had known them while growing up on the northern plains.[24]

James "Scotty" Philip's western experience began when he left Scotland in 1874 as a fifteen-year-old adventurer seeking gold in the Black Hills. By 1877, his work experience consisted of jobs as a guide, scout, freighter, rancher, and dispatch rider out of Fort Robinson, Nebraska. Two years later, he met and married his lifetime mate, Sarah Laribee (Larvie). Soon thereafter, the couple moved onto the Great Sioux Reservation in Dakota Territory and began ranching near Bad River by present-day Philip, South Dakota, in the "west-river" country. About that time, Philip met and became friends with the Dupuis family. Enjoying, like the Dupuises, the communal landholding and subsequent open-range opportunities, the Philips became very successful ranchers, eventually running tens of thousands of cattle on the Dakota rangelands. In the early 1890s, they shifted their base of operations off the reservation to Fort Pierre. Philip rode his ranching success to positions as a real estate broker, banker, and even state senator. His ability to succeed spilled over to his bison-saving effort as well, which lasted as long as he lived, until 1911. Yet, as was true with his friend Frederick Dupuis, Scotty's drive to raise bison was influenced by his wife.[25]

For her part, Sarah Laribee, often called "Selly" in her husband's brogue, was the daughter of Joseph Laribee, a French fur trader once employed with the Hudson's Bay Company and later a cattle rancher, and his Cheyenne wife. In fact, Joseph served as Scotty's initial partner in ranching. One of four daughters and a sister-in-law of Crazy Horse, the multilingual Sarah moved easily between the Native American and Euro-American worlds. Her Native American blood allowed the Philips to live on the reservation and placed them in circles of friends who had mixed-blood marriages and mixed-race children. Sarah's nephew, George Philip, described her as a "splendid woman" and "self-sacrificing helpmate . . . always willing to do her part." Her influence on Scotty paralleled that of Mary Dupuis on her husband, both instances of Dakota fur trader Basil Clement's observation that the "only authority acknowledged was that of Indian spouses." She was similar to Mary Goodnight in that both their husbands had failed to start bison herds before the involvement of their spouses. Prior to his marriage to Sarah, Scotty attempted to corral a large herd on the Grand River, only to watch them escape his grasp. Moreover, sources indicate that Sarah's advice to Scotty resulted in his purchase of the Dupuis herd in 1898.[26]

However, more than just Sarah's advice provided impetus for the Philips to help preserve the bison from extinction. The Philips possessed a keen sense of responsibility for their Native American neighbors. James Robinson, one of the Philips's ranch hands and later biographer of Scotty Philip, explained: "Among his great ideas were the lessening of misery among his friends, the Indians; [by] saving the buffalo from extinction." Nephew George Philip, who helped herd the bison from the Dupuis ranch to the Buffalo Pasture, added this about his uncle: "He was one man who always believed that the Government policy of tutelage and dependence was against the best interests of the Indian." The nephew further assessed that Philip "always remained to the end a staunch and stern champion of their rights."[27] Such comments reveal that as an already successful cattle rancher, Philip entered the world of bison raising to help his adopted people, the Lakota and Cheyenne nations.

His actions as a bison steward indicate Philips's desire to restore bison on an open range rather than as shaggy, penned-in cattle undergoing constant genetic manipulation to create a hybrid super-cow. With natural increase and sundry acquisitions from neighbors, the Philip herd grew to eighty pure-blood animals by 1904. Philip continued butchering or selling hybrid animals. Within two years, Scotty managed to wrangle from Congress a 3,500-acre land grant along the Missouri River with the expressed purpose of enlarging his bison's range. The "Buffalo Pasture" then became 16,000 acres enclosed by fence on three sides and the Missouri River on the fourth. The herd prospered on the expanded pasture and eventually grew to more than nine hundred animals, thereby exceeding the grazing capacity. The herd easily migrated out of its designated range when the Missouri River froze during the winter. Like Pablo, the Philips envisioned that the federal government should purchase and take responsibility for the herd. Scotty Philip hoped that the government would create a great open range for bison in the unused portions of western South Dakota. His dream never transpired. Scotty died in 1911.[28]

The closest development to Philips's vision of a "buffalo commons" was the establishment of South Dakota's Custer State Park in 1914. Though much smaller than anything envisioned by Philip, Custer State Park quickly became a very prolific bison-producing area, originally stocked with thirty-six animals sold to the park by Sarah Philip. Owing to an active reduction program, the park since its inception has furnished thousands of buffalo to bison handlers across the country.[29]

After Scotty's death, the Philip family's bison effort began to diminish. Sarah, affectionately called "Mother Philip" or "Grandma' Philip" by ranch staff, continued to visit the bison as late as 1920. That same year, her son-in-law, Andy Leonard, initiated the first of several sell-offs. Staged hunts and sales led to the diminution of the herd, and by 1926 it no longer existed.[30] Thus, 1926 marked the date when the physical relationship between Indians and buffalo broke. True, the National Bison Range persisted as a federal enclave within the confines of the Flathead Reservation, but no longer did Native Americans or their advocates serve as primary stewards for the buffalo nation. North America's aboriginal people hit another level of dependency. The disruption would prove temporary, however, because buffalo would return to Indian country in the next decade.

The period from the Ghost Dance until the New Deal in many ways represented the nadir for Native Americans. Their population dipped to an unprecedented low at the turn of the century, approaching a scant two hundred thousand individuals from a population that once numbered in the millions. They lost the majority of their communal landholdings, and boarding schools stripped their youth of their indigenous culture. Although mainstream American culture often focuses more on the damage caused to Native Americans by disease and military conquest culminating in the late nineteenth century, Native Americans themselves often state that the greatest injuries they sustained were the result of the subjugation efforts that stemmed from the Dawes Act (1887) and boarding school movement.[31] It is little wonder then that the greatest blow to the Indian-bison relationship came at this same time.

Native Americans persevered through this period, never forgetting either their culture or the importance of maintaining a solid physical relationship with the buffalo. It becomes obvious to any observer that treatment of bison and Native Americans paralleled each other. Euro-Americans subjected both of them to slaughter, disease, a marginalized landscape, deprivation of community, and alienation from their ways of living by concentrating them away from preferred habitat. Indian spokesman John Lame Deer reflected on this parallel treatment: "There are places set aside for a few surviving buffalo herds in the Dakotas, Wyoming and Montana. There they are watched over by Government rangers and stared at by tourists. If brother buffalo could talk he would say, 'They put me on a reservation like the Indians.' In life and death we and the buffalo have always shared the same fate." A further analogy between the Indians' and buffalos' fate during this period of reservations and boarding schools lies in the confinement of Native Americans in close quarters where disease spreads, much as it had among bison exposed to disease and restricted in movement in confined spaces. In some cases, the very same lethal disease, tuberculosis, victimized the Native people and the animal.[32]

Yet although Native Americans and bison continue to face problems, since the 1930s their situation in Indian country has steadily improved, albeit with some interruptions. Indeed, most buffalo on reservations today came from the public sector. The Meriam Report of 1928 admitted that government policy toward America's Native people stood in great need of correction. Subsequently, the 1934 Indian Reorganization Act ended the allotment process, made provisions to restore unallotted lands back to the tribes, and established a precedent for honoring Native culture and customs. Thus, the

Indian desire to return bison to Indian country received acknowledgement and some degree of redress by the federal government.[33] The Crow Reservation offers a good example of this process.

At the ongoing request of Robert Yellowtail, superintendent of the Crow Agency, Yellowstone National Park and the National Bison Range made several donations of live bison to the Crow Reservation in southeast Montana in the mid-1930s. Some slight variations exist in the available statistics, but during the two winters of 1934–1935 and 1935–1936, Yellowstone National Park shipped approximately 177 bison to the Crow. The National Bison Range furnished an additional 26 animals. Superintendent Yellowtail made additional overtures for more animals in 1937. His request received a relatively cool reception from Yellowstone superintendent Edmund B. Rogers due to concerns over the supervision of the bison on the reservation. With natural increase and some supplemental purchases from private bison ranchers, the Crow herd numbered more than 350 head in 1937. Roaming as they do, many of the bison made their way south into Wyoming. This infuriated stockmen and state officials in the Cowboy State who worried about disease and grazing damage. Nonetheless, the National Park Service furnished the Crow Reservation with an additional 12 bulls in 1942.[34]

Although opinions will vary over virtually any program tied to the government and some Crow cattle ranchers expressed concern over the reintroduction of the bison, many Crow appreciated the return of bison to their stewardship. Jeanne Eder, a Dakota Native studies professor and author, recalled her adopted Crow mother's explanations of the restored pride and feelings of goodwill elicited by the reintroduction of the bison in the 1930s. The Crow woman, Georgianne Bad Bear, reminisced about the sense of security and stability the presence of the herd gave her as she grew up on the reservation. Attempting to create as much grazing range as possible, by 1942 the Crow had utilized twenty-four thousand acres, with the original pasture encompassing fourteen acres on a high plateau in the Bighorn drainage. The topography minimized fencing requirements by cutting off buffalos' access routes through draws and ravines, but still the bison managed to find their way to roaming the landscape without regard for political boundaries. Part of the bison's desire to expand their range came from the population increase the herd experienced. The number reached near 1,000 head in 1942, with a subsequent reduction program harvesting 100 to 200 each year. In the spirit of community, the harvested bison went to ceremonies, school lunch programs, and family consumption. The herd's population dropped to 746 in 1946 and decreased even further to just above 500 in the mid-1950s. Nonetheless, it burgeoned again to nearly 1,100 in the early 1960s.[35]

However, the 1950s saw a lurch toward federal and state government interference in dealings with Native Americans. First, during that decade the federal government pursued the termination policy, which persisted into the 1960s.[36] This policy sought to solve the perceived "Indian problem" by encouraging Native Americans to leave their reservations and enter mainstream American society's increasingly urban and suburban environments. Termination never affected a large number of tribes, but its imposition proved that government manipulation of Native Americans did not vanish with the New Deal. The parallel between Native Americans and buffalo extends to termination as well: the government's concern over brucellosis-infected bison resulted in the complete eradication, or "termination," of the Crow herd.

In 1950, the director of the National Park Service declared that live bison shipments from National Park sites were now under the jurisdiction of the Fish and Wildlife Service. About the same time, the acting director of the Fish and Wildlife Service, Hillory Tolson, announced the decision to end further shipments of live animals because studies revealed the presence of brucellosis, a disease that causes abortions in pregnant cattle. Tolson explained: "Because the park herds roam over extensive areas and cannot be handled and treated as can cattle, it is impossible to fulfill the sanitary requirements that have been set up by Federal and State agencies to govern the interstate shipments of livestock."[37] These standards and the government's restricted landscape vision for open-range grazing definitively ended shipments from both Yellowstone and Wind Cave National Parks.

By this time, however, the Crow herd needed no more supplementation. However, the increasingly stringent regulations and enforcement brought federal pressure on the Crow Agency, culminating in the initiation of an eradication program in 1962. Additionally, area ranchers wanted a slaughter because bison-cattle contact had been confirmed in the winter range off the flanks of the Bighorn Mountains. It's worthy noting that the Crow bison stewards never observed the effects of brucellosis, for example, early births, in their herd. In any event, the shipments in the 1930s were never tested while the 1942 shipment of twelve bulls tested negative, meaning that the bulls did not carry brucellosis. The eradication slaughter took two years, with poachers finishing off stragglers in 1965.[38] Thus, termination was complete. The Crow lost their bison herd to outside interests.

The Crow survived this second break in their physical relationship with the bison, however. The early 1970s brought a restoration of their bison project, much as the Indian Self-Determination Act (1974), achieved through Native American activism and advocacy in the late 1960s and early 1970s, brought greater autonomy for Native Americans nationwide. After the Crow began constructing enhanced fencing and handling facilities for vaccinations and brucellosis testing, the Secretary of Interior authorized the importation of disease-free bison from Theodore Roosevelt National Park. The second reintroduction commenced with fifty animals in the late summer of 1972, with the stipulation that the tribe round the herd up and test it annually for brucellosis until the county acquired a "certified brucellosis free" status.[39]

From this point in the 1970s on, the Crow's physical relationship with the bison and subsequent cultural strength solidified. The tribe increased its peninsular bison paddock to thirty thousand acres on the Bighorn Plateau. Annual roundups became more than just working events, but also an annual cultural tradition. By 1990, nine hundred bison moved across the reservation landscape, and they increased to more than twelve hundred by 1995. As an original member of the Intertribal Bison Cooperative in 1992 and provider of seed stock to other tribes the tribe became a leader in the Native American bison comeback. The bison return led one tribal member to state in 1995: "The buffalo mean everything to the Crow. Not only do we now have meat for our celebrations, but we eat the meat and it makes us feel good. We tan the hides. We keep the skulls. It just makes us feel Indian again. We lost a part of our way of life, our culture. Now it makes even little kids happy to know we have buffalo running up there."[40]

Certainly, the Crow's relationship with the bison and government policy did not evolve in a vacuum. After all, by 1992 approximately twenty-six tribes ran nearly thirty-six hundred bison in Indian country. Although the Crow possessed the largest herd, their twentieth-century history with the bison most closely mirrored the Lakota of the Pine Ridge Reservation. Also recipients of federal bison from more than one site, in this case both Yellowstone and Wind Cave National Parks in the 1930s and 1940s, the Pine

Ridge Lakota grew a rather large herd. They also suffered herd eradication and then reintroduced bison in the 1970s.[41]

Others joined the Crow and Lakota in getting seed stock and beginning modern herds in the late 1960s and 1970s. Moreover, the broad geographic range of the few tribes portrayed here reveals the widespread desire by Native Americans to enhance their association with the bison. For example, the Shoshone-Bannock of southeastern Idaho brought twenty-one bison from Theodore Roosevelt National Park in 1966 to begin their reservation's contemporary herd. The Assiniboine and Gros Ventres nations of the Fort Belknap Reservation in northern Montana started their now very successful herd with just twenty-seven animals, originating from both the National Bison Range and Theodore Roosevelt National Park in 1974. The tribes put their new charges next to the tribal headquarters for a short time before moving them to a 2,000-acre pasture in the visually striking Snake Butte area. Also in 1974, twelve other bison from Theodore Roosevelt National Park went to the Kalispel Reservation in eastern Washington. A donation from the National Bison Range in 1979 added ten more animals to the Kalispel herd. Bison returned to the Cheyenne River Reservation as well in the 1970s, near where the Dupuises once watched over their captive seed bison.[42]

In some ways, these developments constituted a full circle in that the Dupuis, a Lakota family, saved bison off the range, lost the small herd in an estate sale with the passing of son Pete, only to have descendants of the Dupuises witness the return of bison to their homeland after an absence of some eighty years. This circle of association with the buffalo produces family and tribal pride.[43] After all, it was Jim Garrett, descended from the Dupuis family, who uttered the thought that opened this chapter: that the reintroduction of bison answers prayers uttered a century ago. This source of pride and comfort also reveals the very personal aspect of the presence of bison in Indian country. Often suffering the whims of government policies and cultural breakdowns caused by subjugation and dependency, Native Americans persevered through the twentieth century in maintaining a relationship with the buffalo. At times, the physical relationship broke, but the cultural affinity remained strong and set the stage for the burgeoning witnessed in the 1990s.

Fig. 8. Michel Pablo and buffalo in the Flathead Valley, Montana, ca. 1907. Photo by N. A. Forsyth. Courtesy Montana Historical Society, Helena.

Fig. 9. Charles Allard Sr., 1896. Photo by the *Missoulian Souvenir National Irrigation Congress*. Courtesy Montana Historical Society, Helena.

Fig. 10. Agathe (Finley) Pablo, ca. 1908. Photo by Norman K. Luxton. Courtesy Montana Historical Society, Helena.

Fig. 11. Charles Allard Jr. and his buffalo wranglers on the Flathead Reservation roundup, 1908. Photo by Norman K. Luxton. Courtesy Montana Historical Society, Helena.

Fig. 12. Michel Pablo leading the bison crates, ca. 1908. Photo by N. A. Forsyth. Courtesy Montana Historical Society, Helena.

Fig. 13. Indian woman reaping some of the last rewards of the Flathead bison in 1908 after this buffalo broke its neck charging a corral fence. Photo by Norman K. Luxton. Courtesy Montana Historical Society, Helena.

Fig. 14. Scotty (seated, back) and Sarah (Laribee) Philip (seated, far left) with family and friends at the Philip Ranch. Courtesy South Dakota State Historical Society—State Archives (undated).

Fig. 15. The Crow Agency's tribal sign. Photo by author (1999).

Fig. 16. The progenitors of these Fort Belknap bison grazing near Snake Butte arrived in 1974. Photo by author (1999).

4. The Intertribal Bison Cooperative

You people are doing the most important thing of any group, Indian or non-Indian, that's going on today . . . by bringing this animal back, this animal that has tremendous power, you're going to change everything in the Great Plains.

Vine Deloria Jr., ITBC conference, 1998

A pan-Indian buffalo restoration movement became a reality in the winter of 1991 when representatives of more than a dozen tribes from across the western United States gathered in South Dakota to create an umbrella organization aimed at bringing back the buffalo nation. The Intertribal Bison Cooperative, more often referred to as the ITBC, formally came into existence when the tribal members reconvened the following year in Albuquerque. As a result, bison and bison range proliferated in Indian country in the 1990s. During the decade, herds under the care of Native Americans rose from fifteen hundred animals to more than nine thousand head in 1999. At the same time, reservation bison range increased by one hundred thousand acres.[1]

Although Native American bison restoration had made headway in the two or three decades prior to the establishment of the ITBC, the effort lacked both synergy and a philosophical bond. For example, on the Native effort to restore bison Yellowstone National Park biologist Mary Meagher concluded in 1973 that "there seems to be a confusion of opposing motives, opinions, self interest and fact." Heavily involved in the ITBC and in his own Lakota people's effort to restore the bison on the Cheyenne River Reservation, Jim Garrett articulated reasons for the apparent confusion some two decades after Meagher's observation: "Until this cooperative movement was established, tribal efforts at restoring the buffalo to their lands was a singular experience for them. Many did not have sufficient experience in raising buffalo and needed guidance. Prior to the ITBC, while restoring buffalo populations was making some inroads, there was little to no effort to reintroduce the cultural, economic, and ecological significance of the buffalo to the tribal community." In 1995, ITBC member Mike Fox echoed this assessment of the importance of the ITBC's coordinating role: "With ITBC, we've done more in the last three years than they did in the last fifteen." Fox was referring to the fact that between 1992 and 1995, the ITBC established seven new tribal herds, tripled the number of buffalo in Indian country, and restored twenty-five thousand acres to buffalo range.[2]

Indeed, by the end of the decade, the list of the ITBC's accomplishments was remarkably long. Besides a growth in the number of bison and size of their range, highlights included an increase in member tribes from nineteen to fifty, provision of technical expertise to initiate herd introductions for twenty-five tribes, the creation of more than five hundred tribal jobs, development of two projects entitled the Native American Bison Refuge and the Yellowstone Rescue Facility Initiative, establishment of policies to ensure the acquisition of seed stock from national parks and wildlife refuges (with, for example, 160 bison going to member tribes in 1998), the Best Industrial Video Award from the American Indian Film Institute for its promotional video Return of the Native, a Renew America Award for environmental excellence, entrance into a memorandum of understanding with the National Wildlife Federation to prevent the Yellowstone bison slaughter, the acquisition of more than fifteen thousand signatures for the Yellowstone Bison Draft Environmental Impact Statement, and the acquisition of millions of dollars in grant money from government and private sources.[3]

In terms of its institutional precedent, the ITBC developed out of an interest group within the Native American Fish and Wildlife Society. Nurtured in this structured environment, the founders of the ITBC quickly developed some organizational frameworks for its function and form. With an understanding that "reintroduction of the buffalo to tribal lands will help heal the spirit of both the Indian people and the buffalo," the group generated the following mission statement[4]:

> The Intertribal Bison Cooperative is a non-profit Native American organization dedicated to the mission of restoring buffalo to Indian lands in

a manner which promotes cultural enhancement, spiritual revitalization, ecological restoration and economic development compatible with tribal beliefs and practices.[5]

The cooperative defined its purpose in the following terms:

The role of the itbc, as established by its membership, is to act as a facilitator in coordinating education and training programs, developing marketing strategies, coordinating the transfer of surplus buffalo from national parks to tribal lands, and providing technical assistance to its membership in developing sound management plans that will help each tribal herd become a successful and self-sufficient operation.[6]

The ITBC's membership has consisted of a board of directors comprised of each member tribe's chosen representative, sometimes but not always the tribe's bison wrangler. The head of the organization consisted of an executive council, with a president, vice president, executive director, secretary, and treasurer. The ITBC also maintains a donating member list, but these individuals do not participate in the decision-making.[7]

To implement its purpose during its first decade of existence, the ITBC typically operated with four departments who utilized money received from government and private grants and from private donations. The organization's four departments were Development, Tribal Business Management, Publications/Cultural Education, and Technical Services. The Development department raised funds; employees lobbied the government, foundations, and corporations. Publicity campaigns supplemented direct mail-outs, recruitment of individual donors, creation of planned-gift options, and the formation of partnerships with businesses that capitalized on the bison products market.

The Tribal Business Management department furnished business plans to member tribes if requested. The department also offered business training through workshops addressing budgeting and cash management in a bison operation. At the same time, business consultants also conducted feasibility studies for land, herd, and capital expansion.

Meanwhile, the Publications/Cultural Education department produced the quarterly newsletter and created a coloring book entitled *Gifts of the Buffalo Nation*. The award-winning *Return of the Native* video production stands as one of the proud accomplishments of this department. As well, the development of an educational CD-ROM and traveling buffalo box for school use and the performance of presentations marked the ITBC's educational efforts.

Finally, Technical Services performed the most direct work with the tribes. Members of this department gave technical assistance on features of bison restoration such as fencing, range restoration, transport, and medicine. The department also coordinated congressional funding and the distribution of bison from the federal parks and wildlife refuges system as well as funding from other donors. In keeping with the ITBC's concerns over the bison of Yellowstone National Park, the Technical Services department continued research into disease and transportation issues surrounding the controversies over the Yellowstone herd. Moreover, the Technical Services department often joined with other departments for field visits to member tribes in order to facilitate business plans, help with technical aspects of bison operations, and even supervise bison delivery.[8]

With respect to the organization's member tribes, a composite typical tribe was usually from the West and possessed a bison hunting tradition. The tribe probably joined the ITBC in the 1990s and established its herd in the same decade with surplus bison from a national park or wildlife refuge. Wind Cave National Park, for example, quite possibly provided the original animals, which the ITBC helped move to the receiving reservation. The typical foundation herd increased on its own and through the arrival of supplementary animals from another tribe, private ranches, or more surplus from the government. The typical tribe's bison program, though not perhaps self-sufficient financially, often enjoyed a very high level of ideological support from the tribal government and reasonably strong support from the tribal community. Community members regularly served as the tribal stewards of the bison that were nurtured by the reservation's ranchers or wildlife biologists. The typical herd consisted of approximately seventy-five animals ranging over nearly five hundred acres.[9]

These bison stewards, or caretakers, most often utilized a hands-off approach in developing their herds. In other words, they handled their bison as little as possible. Still, they needed to provide for their charges as challenges appeared. These challenges included maintaining genetic diversity, matching animal numbers to range capacity, maintaining positive public relations, and the general concerns faced by anyone working with wildlife or livestock, such as the potential negative consequences of human-animal interaction. As the Yakama herd program supervisor, Tracy Hames, put it: "Buffalo are real good at being wherever they want to be, which may not be where some people want them." The stewards usually augmented their herds to prevent inbreeding. Most tribes put their animals to pasture, and provided limited feed supplementation during drought or winter. The harvest or reduction of animals usually entailed an element of the sacred, and accompanied by a ceremony or personal prayer. At the request of tribal members or the tribal council, harvested bison were often distributed to the tribe for ceremonial purposes, community service (such as care for the elderly or less affluent), and/or a health program in which bison meat was made available to help prevent diabetes or heart disease. Ultimately, the typical program succeeded in its short-term goals, and stewards remained optimistic that the restoration of the buffalo would continue with further acquisition of rangeland.[10]

The fact that so many member tribes complied with the ITBC's mission statement and purpose validated the cooperative as an influential organization and indicated the existence of effective leadership. This proved true to be the case from its inception, as the ITBC realized in many ways the dreams of its leading founder, Fred DuBray. Years ago, DuBray, a Lakota rancher from the Cheyenne River Reservation, dedicated his life to restoring Pte Oyate, the buffalo nation. In 1995, he reflected on the impetus for his leadership: "I've always felt there was something missing here. My ancestors are buried here. The buffalo's ancestors are buried here. All the grasses, everything's native here. That's the context that I always thought in. All these things need to be here. That comes from cultural understanding." As he formulated his plans for bringing back the buffalo, a Lakota elder posed an important idea to DuBray: he should first ask the buffalo if it wanted to come back. Several Lakota held a ceremony for guidance and emerged with an answer in the affirmative. They would work to restore the bison, but with "dignity." The proposition apparently influenced DuBray, as he made it quite clear that "in a feedlot, it's not realistic to think that they would want to come back."[11]

Such rhetoric was typical of the ITBC's articulate leader, and over the course of the organization's life, into 2004, he intermittently served as the cooperative's president. Whether DuBray led the organization or someone else was serving as the president or executive director, several lines of rationale emerged from the organization's leaders: the need for pan-Indian collaboration and commitment, the parallel fates of Native Americans and the bison, and the desire to treat bison not as livestock but as wildlife, that is, with minimal manipulation, in order to take care of the land.[12]

When the tribal representatives first met in Albuquerque in 1992, delegates acknowledged the diverse situations of the respective tribes. Ernie Robinson, Northern Cheyenne, declared: "Individually our goals may be different, but as a whole our goal is to get the buffalo back to the Indians again." DuBray responded that "there are going to be obstacles on the way and we're going to need each other's strength to draw on." DuBray gave a very real example of this collective capability by noting that if one tribe approached Congress about getting money for a bison program, "they'd probably just close the door in our face. But if we got thirty-four or thirty-eight tribes saying the same thing, they still may close the door in our face, but at least they're going to hear us." Seven years later, then president Louis LaRose of the Winnebago tribe commented, "We are all growing in our understanding of the restoration of the bison." Ben Yates, Nambe O-Ween-Ge of New Mexico's Pueblo tribes, echoed the initial commitment of the ITBC founders and its continuing mission through the 1990s when he was asked in 2003 about the future of his tribe's herd: "As long as my kids are around, then we'll have buffalo."[13]

The leadership of the ITBC saw their fate as being inextricably intertwined with that of the bison. Comments by DuBray throughout the 1990s affirmed this association. At the founding meeting, the organization's future president explained, "As we bring our buffalo herd back to health, we also bring our own people back to health, and that's what it's all about." He brushed away any doubt about the meaning of his words when he noted that "buffalo are the very heart of our culture . . . if they can't be saved, then we can't either." The next year, an Associated Press news release quoted ITBC President DuBray as follows: "Before it was military strategy to eliminate the buffalo and eliminate our culture. Common sense would tell you that bringing buffalo back would bring people back into a healthy situation." Four years later, a similar DuBray quotation appeared in the New York Times: "When they destroyed the buffalo herds, they were destroying our culture. They severed the physical relationship, but the spiritual relationship remains." DuBray's linking of bison and Native Americans continued right into the next decade when he spoke at the bison conference hosted by the University of Nebraska in 2000. Just days ahead of his scheduled appearance before the United Nations on behalf of indigenous people, he explained: "Buffalo are our relatives. We are obligated to take care of them."[14]

The course of bison interaction and land management for member tribes emerged fairly concretely from the initial meeting establishing the ITBC. Regarding the restoration of bison onto reservations, DuBray clarified: "The only way that we can justify doing this is to allow them to be what they are." The delegates came out against tinkering to develop "super buffalo" or bison with large meaty hindquarters. The ITBC emphasized soon after its inception that it wanted to preserve the "wild integrity" of bison using a "traditional philosophy" and remained stalwart against practices of intensive management, including feed lots, dehorning, chronic medication, breakup of natural social units, premature slaughter, genetic engineering, and artificial insemination. In short, the ITBC came out in strong opposition to the treatment of bison as cattle. DuBray stated, "We're trying to take a holistic approach."[15]

Thus, most tribes attempted to make their herds as free ranging as political geographic limitations would allow, and the ITBC leadership charged the board of directors to treat their bison with as much of a hands-off approach as possible. Vice President Carl Tsosie of Picuris Pueblo echoed DuBray's heralding remarks when he proclaimed at the 1999 ITBC Annual Conference: "We are stewards of nature." He told the buffalo handlers in the audience that "buffalo handling is like a marriage, it's not a hobby," adding: "You're the one, the base to all this, the answers to the prayers. You're the warriors. It may take years, it may take lifetimes, but we will never give up."[16] His strong rhetoric reflected the resolve of the ITBC's leadership.

However, the work of the ITBC went beyond organization, effective rhetoric, and the commitment of its bison stewards. For its first ten years, a myriad of concerns confronted both the cooperative's central administration, located in Rapid City, South Dakota, and its member tribes. Facilitation of funding and the distribution of surplus bison from parks and refuges dominated the agenda of the ITBC. Other important matters included collaboration with tribal colleges for bison management education and validation of existing programs while creating a prospectus for new herds. Tribes and tribal programs, in cooperation with the parent organization, possessed agendas of day-to-day functions such as feeding, breeding, and troubleshooting any problems along with the omnipresent need to reconcile economics and holistic management, the development of health programs, and the implementation of new policies.

With an estimated potential twelve million acres on reservation lands capable of sustaining 120,000 bison, the ITBC largely concerned itself with the acquisition of funding in its first decade. Since large chunks of land in Indian country fell out of tribal hands following the passage of the Dawes Act (1887), tribes have struggled to get back their originally sanctioned domains. This requires money, and the peak amount the ITBC received in any year during the period 1993 through 1996 amounted to $660,000, equivalent to about 10 percent of the financial requirement to implement full expansion into potential bison range. Receiving its usual distribution from the Department of Interior, in 1999 ITBC leaders lobbied Congress and Secretary of Interior Bruce Babbitt in 1999 for additional funding. The following year, the cooperative did succeed in obtaining money from the Department of Labor for application toward the ITBC's education outreach. By 2000, the Technical Services department fully implemented a funding system whereby tribes would write grants through the ITBC for congressional money. Funding priorities went to tribes that demonstrated a program for fencing and range improvement. Meanwhile, the solicitation of private donations and grants continued unabated. The funding efforts in the first decade failed to achieve the ITBC's ultimate goal of financial security, but succeeded in maintaining an operating budget capable of providing for expanded services and departments.[17]

Hoping to increase bison numbers along with bison range, the ITBC assumed a primary function as the conduit by which member tribes receive surplus bison from the federal government. Typically, the tribes submitted proposals to the ITBC, which ranked the proposals. Technical Services director Tony Willman reported in 2000 that the ITBC normally received requests for about 300 bison but usually could furnish only about 150. The following year proved especially bountiful as tribes received 450 animals. Government parks donated the animals, but the handling and transportation costs fell to either the ITBC or member tribes. Some of the leading federal donors included Wind Cave National Park, Badlands National Park, Theodore Roosevelt National Park, the National Bison Range, and Wichita Mountains National Wildlife Refuge. Custer State Park also donated considerable numbers of bison to neighboring Lakota reservations. Nonetheless, these surplus bison, although a boon to the tribes, did necessitate careful consideration since they were cull animals, often selected according to what the existing park or refuge herd did not need.[18] The enhancement of tribal herds with these surplus bison served as a major catalyst for the close association of the ITBC and the tribal colleges.

Judi Hebbring Wood, a private bison rancher, former secretary of the National Bison Association, the bison project coordinator for Lower Brule Community College in South Dakota, and administrator for the Northern Plains Bison Education Project, explained in a 2000 professional journal article how the culling process for public herds worked. The respective agencies kept the best animals, sold the next best through public auction, and then donated the leftovers. This, of course, worked contrary to the genetic strength benefit to tribes since they did not receive the fittest animals, the ones that historically would have survived. Wood cautioned tribes to watch the sources and backgrounds of their bison while looking for the expected qualities of healthy range bison. She explained the process simply at the Bison Conference 2000 in Lincoln: "Beware the ugly and abnormal looking ones, if a buffalo looks good, then it's probably OK genetically speaking."[19]

Reminiscent of the key roles played by earlier women in bringing back the buffalo, Hebbring Wood also contributed to the organization of the first three Tatanka Oyate Summer Institutes in 1999, 2000, and 2001. The ITBC combined with the Northern Plains Bison Education Network (NPBEN) to present this annual event in the summer. Each year participants received classes and hands-on instruction in all facets of bison restoration, ranging from historical study and stress-free bison handling to Native food preservation and range dynamics. NPBEN consisted of ten tribal colleges funded in part by the W.K. Kellogg Foundation. Some of these colleges initiated programs to offer associate of science degrees in bison production and marketing. The colleges hoped to blend the science of western culture with indigenous philosophy, to promote study of "wildculture" alongside agriculture.[20] The summer institutes provided an opportunity for the ITBC and tribal colleges to link up and coordinate efforts to restore the bison.

The tie between the tribal colleges and the ITBC became obvious when the ITBC's president Louis LaRose stated in 2000: "Land grant colleges are a key step to restoration. We need bison research for bison." It's worth noting that in 2002, LaRose, former ITBC president, served as the board chairman for Little Priest Tribal College in Nebraska, a member of NPBEN. As well, the mission of the ITBC for a dignified return of the bison dovetailed rather nicely with the "science with soul, or spirit-based science" offered by the tribal colleges. Much like the ITBC, the college programs aimed to restore bison through an "intricate inter-weaving of culture, ecology, workforce development, and spiritual revitalization."[21]

While establishing liaisons with tribal colleges remained important to the ITBC in its first ten years toward the end of that time period site visits provided the ITBC with an opportunity to oversee tribal programs as well as offer the aegis of the cooperative. Although such visits continued regularly, one such trip received documentation in *Buffalo Tracks*, the ITBC's quarterly newsletter, in 2000. The article described a visit by a three-person technical team to the Northern Ute Tribe at the Uintah and Ouray Agencies. The team presented the ITBC and its philosophy to the tribal council and the tribe's fish and wildlife department. Meanwhile, the team collaborated with tribal members to develop economic need, business, and herd management plans. Finally, the team toured the existing Ute herd and its range and evaluated the range and plans for herd expansion with the ITBC's assistance. The visit concluded with a report by the team, which concluded that good potential existed for range and herd expansion if the tribe could acquire the appropriate grazing permits from cattlemen.[22]

Such visits assist tribal bison programs by validating them. At some point, most tribal bison programs have required assistance from the tribal government. It took time and volume for most programs to become self-sufficient. ITBC visits have therefore demonstrated a pan-Indian support structure that has tended to allay tribal leaders' fears about a losing proposition in the form of a resource-draining bison program. As a result, most tribal governments have provided a high level of support even though tribal politics often make the allocation of scarce resources a divisive issue. ITBC board member and Spokane tribal bison steward, Monty Ford, remarked after an ITBC visit to the Spokane Reservation: "Having ITBC here gave our community a good sense of why the bison are such an important commodity to the Indian people . . . that it's OK to be Indian, that it's OK to be cultural."

Comments such as Ford's show that bison stewards must work within their own tribes and with the ITBC to navigate toward the future. As tribes established their programs through the 1990s they received support, but many still encountered obstacles to running a successful bison program over and above the acquisition of a few animals along with a land base and later supplementation with further additions of animals. For example, some tribes experienced enough success with natural increase of their herds that excess animals became a concern. In any interviews with the Northwestern tribes of Washington who have limited bison range, chase stories quickly emerged. Typically, bulls started to seek new range regardless of fences, roads, lawns, or gardens. Stewards found themselves either organizing roundups or sometimes shooting the wanderer.[23] Offering hunts for excess animals also posed a solution to appease tribal councils or members who are concerned with the economic feasibility of their bison programs. In 2000 and 2001, for example, the Assiniboine and Gros Ventres of Fort Belknap responded to drought conditions with a reduction in which surplus bison from Fort Belknap were used to establish the Fort Peck Reservation's herd. Other ITBC tribes still lacking herds, including the Eastern Shawnee, Miami, Nez Perce, Salish-Kootenai, Sault Ste. Marie Tribe of Chippewa, and the Tesuque, sought ways to acquire bison. Meanwhile, the Comanche Tribe, like other tribes in Oklahoma that had little land base left in tribal trust, sought to enhance its bison restoration effort by encouraging tribal ranchers to go into raising bison. Five of them did so by 2003.[24]

Clever solutions to difficult problems defined much of the tribes' work during the first decade of the ITBC. Nowhere did this prove truer than in the synthesis of economics and the altruistic spirit of bison restoration. Unequivocally, virtually all ITBC tribes established their herds for spiritual and cultural revitalization. Nonetheless, a peripheral hope of economic revitalization also often presented itself. Lakota bison consultant Jim Garrett posed the question: "Where does one draw the line between spiritual use and utilitarian use of the buffalo? It is an ethical question that each tribe must ask itself and answer."[25]

Some tribes enlarged their herds to carrying capacity and answered the question of their program's utility by selling live animals for seed herds. However, even this fairly anodyne solution ran into difficulty in the first three years of the new millennium as drought gripped much of the West, and live bison prices plummeted. Tribes, although philosophically prepared to expand their bison restoration, found themselves needing to reduce herd sizes in order to maintain the principle of keeping bison on the range and avoiding heavy supplementation. This explains why after the exponential increase in Native American bison holdings during the 1990s, growth slowed after the turn of the century. Early in 2003, for example, the ITBC reported no more than ten thousand animals held by its member tribes. During the same time, however, the meat market maintained more consistent pricing levels.[26]

Harvesting and butchering buffalo, though certainly not novel concepts in Indian country, always posed a delicate issue for most ITBC tribes. Hence, most tribes performed these tasks with religious overtones. To reconcile the utilization of meat with the organization's mission statement and rhetoric of bringing back the buffalo with dignity, the ITBC lauded free-range and grass-fed bison beef over penned and grain-fed bison beef. Although a miniscule minority of tribes possessed penned herds with heavy feed supplementation, tribes attempted to practice the range-fed philosophy espoused by the ITBC. The harvesting operations of the tribes thus did not resemble the feedlot and slaughterhouse system pervasive in the cattle industry. In fact, the bison stewards typically shot their animals in the field, accompanied by a religious ceremony. It was not uncommon at all for bison stewards to contend that a bison from the herd would actually present itself for the kill.[27]

The butchering process retained a great deal of significance as well. Traditional field butchering dominated for the harvesting of small numbers of bison. However, some tribes wanted to process a greater volume of meat and bison products, such as hides, skulls, and taxidermy heads. They began working to develop a more efficient butchering system. Leading other tribes, the Lakota of the Cheyenne River Reservation looked to another indigenous people, the Sami reindeer herders of Scandinavia, for a processing model.[28]

The Cheyenne River Lakota researched the mobile slaughter unit of the Sami and deemed it culturally compatible. With such a unit the harvest occurs in the field with minimal stress to the animals in contrast to a roundup and shipment to a slaughterhouse. The tribe commissioned the manufacturing firm in Sweden that built the Sami unit to construct a similar model upgraded for the larger-sized bison. The Lakota started using their customized mobile slaughterhouse in 1998. The resulting capabilities enabled the herd stewards to harvest as necessary and furnish at least one ceremonial bison each year to the reservation's seventeen communities and sell stew meat and ground meat in the tribal-owned supermarket. This also supplemented existing bison meat programs for the impoverished and elderly. Moreover, an additional benefit was that the Cheyenne River Lakota could more aptly reach a niche market of more affluent consumers who prefer organically grown and respectfully processed meat.[29]

In-depth analysis by the Lakota tribe's researchers also revealed that historically the Lakota found more than one hundred uses for the bison. Using modern butchering techniques, the tribe had only found eleven different uses for the harvested bison. The mobile slaughter unit increased these uses to more than thirty. Jim Garrett explained the increase:

> Our people have always used the sinew along the backbone for sewing thread. In the modern butchering style, the backbone is cut across to make steaks and this eliminates the long sinew. Our more traditional style cuts the meat lengthwise so that the sinew can be separated from the meat, washed, dried and made into thread. The women can then use this thread in the making of authentic Lakota clothes and shoes that have a higher value on the market. Another example is that specific bones of the animal were used in the past and now we do not have to saw-cut the bones. We save these for our artists to use in their artistic expressions.[30]

In many ways, a standard-bearing tribe for the ITBC, the Cheyenne River Lakota found a culturally sensitive way to blend spiritual respect for the bison with the desire to enhance production for the benefit of Indian people. Ultimately, tribal bison stewards hoped to increase their harvesting to continually grow their herd while providing at least one meal with bison beef each day for each member of the tribe. Ironically, by 2004 the growth of the tribe's bison meat industry combined with state government regulations forced the tribe to immobilize the slaughter facility, although traditional ceremonies continued to mark the butchering process.[31]

Fred DuBray proposed a way to provide bison beef for tribal members while bringing in profits for bison programs. Since federal policies deprived Native Americans of their bison food base in the nineteenth century, they could help restore it in the twenty-first century. The United States Department of Agriculture (USDA) food program could buy grass-fed bison from tribal programs and then distribute the meat on reservations to program recipients. Thus, the USDA could help enhance the health of Indian people with lean bison beef, make some amends for ending a bison-based lifestyle, and help restore buffalo to tribal lands.[32]

The idea of health benefits for Native Americans derived from bison meat obviously did not occur solely to the Lakota. In fact, the ITBC selected "Sacred Buffalo: Restoring Healthy Native Nations" as its third annual conference theme. Although the concept of health at the conference embraced cultural, emotional, and environmental health, dietary health provided a main focus. With diabetes afflicting as many as one out of three people on some reservations, the need to address dietary concerns became part of the agenda of the ITBC. Winnebago bison caretaker and ITBC official Louis LaRose often served as point man at the conference with a model program on his reservation in Nebraska. As LaRose explained at the University of Nebraska bison conference in 2000, "We're only two or three generations removed from picking berries, we were not designed to do all our hunting in aisles A, B, and C."[33]

LaRose and the model Winnebago Bison Project approached the bison meat augmentation effort with a three-pronged approach in the late 1990s. First, the tribe initiated a Kids Café Diabetes Program as a type of dietary triage for the tribe's youth and to get bison into their diet. Second, LaRose and other representatives began lobbying the federal government to put bison into reservation food distribution programs. Third, bison project managers linked the health of their bison range to the health of the bison meat and hence to the health of the consumers of that meat. LaRose elucidated this approach: "In order for us to consider buffalo as a healthy food for us as human beings, we must also look at a healthy diet for the buffalo. The healthy diet for the buffalo was native grasses and native prairie. We have to provide a healthy ecosystem for the buffalo, but it also creates a healthy ecosystem for all the animals that are here."[34] The twenty-first century will become the scene for assessing the success of the Winnebago program and others like it ventured by other ITBC tribes. Yet, a holistic viewpoint and sweeping vision already pervade many tribes' bison restoration efforts.

Examples of such vision have included the plans of Fred DuBray and the Cheyenne River Lakota, Pat Cornelius and the Oneida tribe of Wisconsin, Phil Follis of the Modoc tribe, and Richard Archuleta from Taos, New Mexico, who has worked in concert with other Pueblo bison stewards to enhance Southwest bison restoration. DuBray and many of the Lakota on the Cheyenne River Reservation announced their plans in the late 1990s to eventually restore a natural parkland without fences for their herd. Through 2002, the tribe possessed a recent history of bison range acquisition and herd growth, making it the largest operation in the ITBC, with more than two thousand animals on better than thirty thousand acres. Cornelius, the bison steward of the Oneida herd and a former private rancher, lobbied in 1998 to make fallow agricultural land in the Conservation Resource Program (CRP) available for bison grazing. Laws prohibit agricultural use of the land, but since bison can be classified as wildlife, Cornelius reasoned that the Oneida herd qualified for sustenance on the CRP lands. Government officials disagreed, but she did succeed in getting the seeding of native grasses and herbs on some of these lands so as to enhance prairie restoration. Follis, a Modoc living in Oklahoma—where the federal government concentrated members of his tribe following the Modoc War a century and a quarter ago—initiated a program to bring bison to his people's northern California homeland. He hoped to piece together national forest, Bureau of Land Management (BLM) lands, and Modoc holdings to produce a 3 million–acre bison range. His efforts took him to Washington, D.C., to lobby beltway bureaucrats, who began to mull his proposal early in 2003.[35]

Meanwhile, Richard Archuleta, who rotated in and out of ITBC officer status (namely, as the organization's treasurer) in the late 1990s and early 2000s, envisioned the expansion of his tribe's longstanding and quite successful bison program into the Rio Grande Valley on the highlands above the Rio Grande Gorge near Taos. The Taoseños believe the area once flourished as grassland and became the present sagebrush range only after overgrazing by sheep introduced by the Spanish. Archuleta expressed his desire to reseed the area with native grasses and medicinal plants to support bison and pass on the health benefit to the people.[36]

Meanwhile, in late 1996 and early 1997 members of the Taos Pueblo, including Archuleta, combined with several other Pueblo representatives to directly avert a perceived bison disaster. At an emotional time for the Pueblo people following the reintroduction of bison and the sacrosanct Buffalo Dance across the northern Pueblo tribes in the first half of the decade, a herd of bison managed by the State of New Mexico created an issue. Known as the Fort Wingate herd, the group of as many as two hundred bison roamed western New Mexico near the Zuni Mountains, overlapping the Fort Wingate Military Reservation. With the expiration of the state's land lease, state officials decided to stage a hunt to eradicate the herd. The Native American outcry led by Taos, San Juan, Sandia, Pojoaque, Nambe, and Picuris Pueblos resulted in what equated to a "stay of execution" the day before the hunt's opening. By February 1997, policymakers had decided to donate a significant part of the herd to some of the Pueblos. For example, Sandia started its herd with this donation. Meanwhile, Pueblos, even those not in the ITBC, followed up on this momentous occasion by initiating their own herds. These tribes, maintaining small bands for spiritual revival, included the Cochiti, Isleta, Laguna, and Acoma.[37]

Despite the apparent cohesion of the pan-Indian bison restoration effort of the 1990s, reflected in the leadership and strength of the ITBC, total consensus has not existed in Indian country over the restoration of the bison. Of course, bison restoration ironically represents change, and given human nature change always attracts its detractors. Inherent resistance to bison restoration has always existed to some degree, although the vast majority of bison stewards have detected a high level of support from their communities. Nonetheless, one segment of Indian society, let alone its counterpart in Euro-American society, has shown pockets of the greatest resistance: cattle ranchers.[38]

Certainly not all cattle ranchers have resisted the homecoming of the bison. After all, a significant number of Native American bison stewards emerged from the ranks of cattle ranchers. Cattle ranchers frequently feared the transmission of brucellosis, which causes cattle to abort, even though no record exists of bison-to-cattle transmission of brucellosis on the range. They sometimes became concerned about bison busting fences and harassing their cattle. At least one cattleman in Indian country expressed dismay that the tribe's bison steward did not care for the bison with anywhere near the standards associated with care for healthy livestock and that the caretaker expressed a certain arrogance about the entire undertaking. Yet, these issues usually could be allayed through range monitoring and personal diplomacy. More often the crux of the issue lay in the allocation of resources, which was often perceived as bison versus cattle.[39]

The important resources in question were land and capital. Some ranchers have insisted that tribal bison projects enjoy a "pet" status and draw away funds otherwise destined for agricultural subsidization. Spokane bison caretaker Monty Ford addressed this in a 2000 interview when he explained that on the Spokane Reservation in the previous fiscal year, the range cattle budget received $80,000 from tribal, Bureau of Indian Affairs (BIA), and other federal budgetary sources. In the same time period, the buffalo program received a paltry $1,500. Meanwhile, area ranchers struggled with the concept of communal ownership with a spiritual basis as opposed to individual capitalism with a material base. Some also feared the impact of bison beef on the market.[40]

As the leader of the ITBC, occasional tribal manager of a herd, private bison rancher, and cattleman, Fred DuBray offered insight in a 2004 interview into divisive issues concerning bison programs on reservations, including friction between bison stewards and cattle ranchers. DuBray emphasized that each tribal community would need to resolve the issues arising over its own bison programs. For example, tribal councils and bison herd stewards could best minimize perceived threats by not proposing bison herd introductions or expansions in a threatening manner. For example, with DuBray's input, the Cheyenne River Lakota expanded their range by acquiring previously alienated reservation lands bought from non-Native ranchers. Cheyenne River cattle ranchers thus did not find themselves in competition with bison herd and range increase. DuBray asserted that the arguments over ways of restoring bison back to Indian country were themselves evidence of success. The question had moved from "Should or can Native people bring back the buffalo?" to "How can Indian communities best restore the buffalo nation?"[41]

For their part, members of the ITBC possessed three understandings with respect to the issue of cattle ranching versus bison restoration. First, they viewed the bison as a superior animal for the range health of the American West. Second, they disapproved of the market-driven cattle industry's treatment of its subjects. Third, their vision of the landscape, much in keeping with that of their ancestors, was for a form of nonintensive pastoralism, in sharp contrast to modern monoculture. These understandings have not received widespread acceptance by the western cowboy culture.

Former executive director of the ITBC Mark Heckert made his assessment of the superiority of bison clear: "We've line-bred cattle for a thousand years, which are essentially a wetland, lowland species and we've tried to move them out here into an upland arid area. So they spend endless time in riparian areas, and you've got to keep unfrozen water open for them in the wintertime. You've got to pull the calves because they can't reproduce naturally." Lower Brule Lakota bison steward Shaun Grassel explained that "cattle have a tendency to eat everything down and trample everything down" and added that "buffalo don't tend to overgraze as cattle do." His colleague from Fort Belknap, Mike Fox, supported this contention: "Unlike cattle, they [buffalo] do not bunch around watering holes and destroy riparian areas and valuable prairie wetlands." Fred DuBray agreed in explaining that bison can face storms with their woolly forequarters, get water from snow in the winter, eat a plethora of grasses and forbs, and do not stand around feeding selectively.[42] In short, bison reign in western range adaptation.

Because of the bison's natural adaptation to the American landscape, the ITBC membership never has advocated any kind of manipulation of its mammalian charges. Heckert addressed this issue early in ITBC's history when he stated in a 1996 interview: "The tribes are very concerned that the buffalo will simply become a shaggy-cow money machine for people who don't care about native culture." Technical Services director Tony Willman clarified the ITBC's position with an article in the ITBC's quarterly newsletter in 1999. In it, Willman acknowledged that the "bison industry continue[d] to explode" as ex–cattle ranchers entered the enterprise. Unfortunately, this propelled "the latest rage in physically altering bison directly linked to what certain 'ex–cattle ranchers/now bison experts' feel a bison should look like." He admonished that people should give their bison food, space, and water or not go into raising buffalo. Judi Hebbring Wood described a similar observation antithetical to ITBC's vision: "We are now beginning to see animals that hardly resemble real buffalo. They look more like furry cattle with their thick legs and blocky butts—the most prized on the show circuit."[43] She noted that given such trends in the buffalo industry, Native America remained the bison's best hope for maintaining the wild character of the buffalo.

For ITBC members, certain resolutions emerged from the first ten years of the organization's existence. Bison should look like bison, roaming as unfettered as possible on native landscape. Native Americans restoring their culture with the bison should be central to the buffalo's rejuvenation. Enhanced health for generations to come in both the plant and animal kingdoms should be restoration's goal. This outcome would offer hope for the ITBC and vindicate many of the tribal sacrifices more than a century past.

A more detailed examination of one ITBC tribe's experience sheds light on the bison restoration movement at the close of the previous century and the dawning of our own. The example provided by the Assiniboine and Gros Ventres from Fort Belknap is emblematic because of its concerted public outreach effort. Likewise, the reservation epitomizes many of the trials and tribulations experienced by ITBC member tribes.

When the tribal council originally decided to bring the buffalo back to the reservation lands in 1974, it met resistance. Predictably, some cattle ranchers frowned upon the venture. Other residents feared the loss of funding to other programs focused on jobs, housing, or health care. Reflecting on this friction, Mike Fox, the head of the bison program through much of the 1990s, recalled: "Especially the ranching families. It seems like the ranching community are the ones that have the biggest mistrust of the buffalo; that they're going to take over." [44]

After an initial period in which the bison were penned near the tribal office, a management plan that heralded much of what the ITBC would implement came to guide the Fort Belknap bison program. The herd caretakers opened a large pasture and let the bison roam. They tested new arrivals to their herds and all slaughtered animals to see if brucellosis or other afflictions haunted their herds. Any roundups took place only once a year. By 1990, approximately sixty animals enjoyed a 2,000-acre pasture. The following year the program started to pay for itself with the sale of live calves. The "goal to bring the buffalo back into the daily lives of the tribal people" started emerging as a reality. By 2000, four hundred bison grazed in a pasture of 22,000 acres, with another 20,000 to 30,000 acres ready to come into the program with the transfer of grazing leases. The tribe traded bison and brought new blood in from various locations, including Lakota reservations, the National Bison Range, and Wind Cave National Park. Supplemental feeding became infrequent and occurred only during urgent times of natural stress. The Assiniboine and Gros Ventres herd became a seed herd for other tribes, including the Blackfeet of Montana and members of the Blackfoot Confederacy in Canada, who visited the reservation to observe the success-ful model bison operation.[45]

Like most other tribes, the Assiniboine and Gros Ventres harvested bison for ceremonies and impoverished families. They implemented a somewhat innovative nuance to part of their game management plan by substituting bison meat for a reservation deer tag. Harvests occurred in the pasture, with field butchering, which sometimes included guided hunts for non-tribal members that earned the tribe as much as $2,000 for each permit. The tribe also ran a pilot project on the impact of bison beef on diabetics.[46] However, the Fort Belknap bison program distinguished itself more by the events surrounding its live bison than by bison that nourished the people through harvesting.

The tribe offered its bison pasture as a recovery site for the nearly extinct black-footed ferret. This selection by a multiagency team demonstrated the confidence placed in the holistic range management practiced by Fort Belknap as a model of grassland restoration. Although not an average tour-ist visiting the site because of an advertising campaign, former Secretary of the Interior Bruce Babbitt remarked on his 1999 tour of Fort Belknap, "American Indians are the only people who know how to live in harmony and to relate to the spiritual harmony of the land."[47]

When Babbitt paid his compliment, he was perhaps unaware of one impor-tant piece joining the Native spirit and the land: a program implemented at Fort Belknap that directly linked the people and the bison. In the mid-1990s, the tribal council initiated a Buffalo Watch Program for alcoholics who were having family difficulties and troubled social relations on the reservation. Although the tribe later dropped the program and its effects are difficult to measure, at least one participant told a reporter that after initially resenting it, she eventually learned a considerable amount from the bison, particu-larly from the mothers and their offspring, and believed it would help her become a better parent. Wayne Azure, a former bison steward, intimated a similar success story during a 1999 interview. A woman who had a record of child abuse was sentenced to watch the bison during her lunch hour for several months or forfeit the return of her children from her to the social services office. During her sentence, she eventually developed a different perspective, reunited with her children, and went on to become a "good mother," as Azure described her.[48]

Azure's story itself provides insight into the world of a modern bison steward in Indian country. In his Nakota language, that of the Assiniboine, Azure's name is Tatanka Ska Wuhamní, which translates as White Buffalo Dreamer. He worked in the late 1990s for the tribal fish and wildlife department as a field hand, tourist guide, and bison caretaker. He also served on the tribal health board. Emanating a sense of the sacred in his assessment of the bison program, Azure linked himself, the bison, and public health all in one brief description: "Most people don't realize the buffalo are here to heal the people. I see it coming. I saw the white buffalo in a dream. This herd will have one."[49]

Making obvious reference to the aura Native people associate with the white buffalo, Azure personalized his role in the process. As one of the care-takers, he participated in slaughters. Each time, the shooters began with a pipe ceremony. Next, they approached the herd, and one of the bison would emerge from the herd. The hunters would shoot the loner. Then, each of the nearby bison would circle the downed beast and sniff it before they moved away and the butchering began. The herd would then sniff the stomach contents after the butchering. Azure explained that these behaviors struck a deep chord within him: "I cry when they do that. It's part of my healing process."[50] Obviously, bison stewardship assumes a dimension a majority of people do not perceive in their day-to-day work.

Thus, the acceleration of bison restoration in the 1990s and into the first three years of the new millennium touched an increasing number of people in Indian country. Both tribes and individual Native Americans engaging in bison acquisition augmented the bison restoration movement.[51] The importance of these developments, however, clearly goes beyond objective numbers of bison and acres of land. The cultural connection and spiritual revival hold a much greater importance to both the tribes and individual Indians.

Azure's story extended beyond Fort Belknap. He felt compelled when de-scribing the healing process to offer his sentiments on the bison of Yellow-stone National Park, an offering not without precedent for Native Americans concerned with the buffalo and their culture. Referring to the unprecedented modern slaughter of Yellowstone bison during the winter 1996–1997, Azure lamented: "Why they would slaughter a whole herd when they didn't know how many carried brucellosis? It took me back to the time of my ancestors when they [Euro-Americans] slaughtered the buffalo. I was very, very angry for a long time about what was done. They asked us to go back in 1998 and 1999. I talked to my teacher [spiritual mentor] about it. I wanted to see it—feel it. But the senselessness angered me. I get bitter. Old Ones don't react so emotionally. They take time to find stories—parables."[52] His concerns notwithstanding, the ITBC and bison supporters across Native America took to heart the issue of the Yellowstone bison. In many ways, they found in the fate of these animals the ultimate parallel to their own.

Map 2: Intertribal Bison Cooperative (ITBC) Membership: 53 tribes in 2004. Sources: ITBC website and Roe, *North American Buffalo* appendix map.

Fig. 17: Richard Archuleta and Taos herd. Photo by author (1999).

Fig. 18: Wayne Azure and Fort Belknap bison. Photo by author (1999).

5. The Yellowstone Crisis

We will continue to pray for an end, and will fight the genocide of these sacred animals. We will continue with this struggle until this unethical slaughter ends.

Carle Rae Brings Plenty (1999)

Despite a century of steadily increasing bison population since the Yellowstone buffalo population's nadir in 1902, the winter crisis of 1997 marked both the worst slaughter of "free-roaming" bison in the twentieth century and the worst slaughter of Yellowstone bison since the park's establishment in 1872.[1] By early February 1997, over 800 of Yellowstone National Park's approximately 3,500 buffalo perished just outside the park's boundary at the hands of government officials representing the State of Montana and the National Park Service. Yellowstone bison biologist Mary Meagher predicted that by the end of the winter "a major population crash" would befall the woolly beasts, with at least 2,000 bison ultimately perishing. Her prediction rang largely true as government agents killed 1,084, and another 200 to 300 died from the exceptionally adverse winter conditions by the time the crisis ended. The herd emerged from the winter with fewer than two-thirds of its former members. Environment-sensitive citizens bemoaned the "national tragedy." The Greater Yellowstone Coalition of Bozeman, Montana, led five other plaintiffs in a suit against the National Park Service (NPS) for violation of its own Organic Act and other laws. The coalition also charged that Montana ignored fifty-year-old laws that required the state to establish bison habitat outside the park. Montana's governor, Mark Racicot, one of the most popular political figures in Montana history, shot back that the National Park Service had proved "remiss" in its bison oversight by not reducing the herd. Montana senator Conrad Burns introduced legislation calling for tighter control over and herd reductions of Yellowstone bison. The Montana legislature moved bison from its Department of Fish, Wildlife and Parks to its Department of Livestock so fewer obstacles could be placed in the way of implementing the slaughter policy.[2] In the winter of 1997 the fate of free-roaming bison on the American landscape appeared to hang in the balance across the boundary of Yellowstone National Park. Why?

Part of the answer comes from the National Park Service's controversial "natural regulation" policy for Yellowstone National Park. Established in the 1960s, the policy departed from much of the heavy-handed management of the existing policy, especially with respect to persistent herd reductions by humans and limitations on predation of ungulate populations. For example, when the NPS implemented the policy of natural regulation in 1967, the frequently reduced Yellowstone bison herd numbered approximately four hundred animals.[3] As the herd's population skyrocketed over the next three decades, various groups interested in the herd's plight envisioned differing futures for the buffalo of Yellowstone. Scientists and officials within the National Park Service foresaw an "experiment" whereby they could examine "natural" processes. Cattlemen saw a threat looming on the horizon, which was eventually articulated by Montana's senator Conrad Burns when he stated: "The problem with Yellowstone National Park has always been they had too many buffalo. What we're saying is get the numbers down where the range will support them. It's just good old common sense on how you run livestock." Environmentalists saw nature running its course and hoped that with some subtle tweaking, for example, the introduction of the wolf, the park's ungulates could reach some type of equilibrium. For their part, Native Americans hoped to witness the return of an age-old icon to an existence not unlike the one it had once enjoyed.[4]

Thus, as the herd increased, public officials, ranchers, environmental visionaries, and Native Americans held diverse ideas on the proper relationship of the buffalo to the American landscape. Most specific to the Yellowstone controversy, however, the livestock lobby drew the line of no return for bison outside the park's boundaries. Montana possessed 2.75 million cattle in 1996, of which some 2,000 grazed near the park on six public allotments interspersed with private land. The Montana herd enjoyed a "brucellosis-free" status, which meant that Montana cattle did not require inspection when crossing state lines, and their beef merited acceptance by European

Union standards. Brucellosis, a disease for which about half the Yellowstone bison possess antibodies and only some 20 to 25 percent could possibly transmit, induces abortion in cattle and undulant fever in humans. Ironically, Yellowstone bison probably first acquired brucellosis from mingling with domestic cattle inside Yellowstone National Park sometime between 1915 and 1917. Nonetheless, the native bovid species suffers little from brucellosis but may spread the ailment through reproductive fluids. Scientists believe that cattle can catch it only by ingesting birthing fluids while grazing in infected calving areas. Heat, sun, and aridity readily kill the bacteria. Proof of the rarity of buffalos spreading brucellosis emerged in the winter of 1989-1990 when 900 Yellowstone bison mingled on twenty separate cattle herd range areas and not a single cow tested positive for brucellosis. These observations have led some scientists and onlookers to label brucellosis a "political disease" because its control varies with the political strength of the infected animal's advocates.[5]

Additionally, elk carry brucellosis that cattle can acquire. In Jackson Hole, Wyoming, 40 percent of the elk possessed brucellosis in 1994. Hunters took 4,300 of these animals during that hunting season without one complaint of undulant fever. Moreover, the valley possessed 300 bison. Yet, cattle grazed "nose-to-nose with brucellosis-infected bison and elk for more than 75 years" through 1994 without major brucellosis problems because of timely cattle vaccinations, distancing bison from domestic cattle, and keeping cattle off the range during wild ungulate calving and migration periods. These facts led concerned observers to conclude that a powerful lobby of outdoorsmen and -women, hunters, and outfitters protected elk from the strong livestock lobby while bison lacked protection. The 2,000 cattle grazing around Yellowstone National Park, a range they often shared with elk, commanded an inordinate amount of protection considering that they comprised but .07 percent of Montana's cattle. Reacting to these observations, a Wyoming Fish and Game official who requested anonymity stated: "If the public gets used to the idea that bison, like elk and deer, should be free to roam on federal lands managed by the Forest Service and Bureau of Land Management, then it may lead to a reduction in the amount of public lands forage allotted to livestock. That's what the ranchers really fear."[6]

Such a comment ignores the facts of open range and politics. Open-range cattle have a champion in the form of the enduring cowboy culture, which is protected by conservative politicians. The maintenance of grazing permits, often viewed as subsidization, offers proof of this protection. Elk and deer have received their champions from the ranks of the guide and outfitter industries combined with recreational hunters, both of which maintain powerful lobbies, as can be seen in the vigor of the hunting community in many western states. By contrast, the bison emerged from the winter of 1997 desperately needing a champion. With existing law, neither the National Park Service nor the State of Montana would or could protect the wild bison. A few mainstream environmentalists and their organizations sought to help, but Native Americans, drawing on their age-old relationship with the buffalo nation, became the ones to champion the cause of their animal brethren. Winnebago Bison Project director Louis LaRose epitomized this aegis when he declared on January 22, 1997: "The bison once took care of us. Now we're in the position where we must take care of the bison."[7]

For Native people, who had sought for at least five years to get a different policy for the Yellowstone bison, the need for a change in the treatment of the park's buffalo quickly became dire in the winter of 1996-1997. The Native Americans' typical stand on the issue was to advocate no slaughter of bison. Carle Rae Brings Plenty, education and cultural coordinator for the ITBC, clarified this stance in 1998: "We don't want to see any killed, but if they are, we would like to see them go to Indian people."[8] However, prevailing politics made this unfeasible.

Capitalizing on a tradition tacitly agreed to by the governing entities of the National Park Service and the State of Montana, Native Americans from several tribes went to butcher bison killed near the park's boundary in accordance with existing policies. The voluminous rain, snow, and subsequent ice along with cold temperatures combined that year to force bison to wander in nearly unprecedented numbers to find better grazing. In fact, that year, the bison began eating emergency food, such as evergreen needles and bark, as early as December. Thus, when the Native Americans, already disgruntled over the slaughters of the previous year, arrived they found a vigorous slaughter in process. Since officials could not haze many bison back into the park, the Montana Department of Livestock hauled away numerous bison to death far from the killing fields in accordance with a catch-and-slaughter policy implemented in response to a lawsuit filed in Montana.[9]

These circumstances had two effects on the Native Americans. First, the killing and slaughter of the bison violated the traditions and respect proffered the animal by Native Americans, who normally performed sacred rituals during the butchering of buffalo. Too fast and too institutionalized, the state's slaughter alienated the indigenous people. Second, the number of bison dying at the hands of Montana agents caused a collective shudder among local Indians. Speaking of his tribe's butchers, Lakota Fred Dubray recalled: "What they saw, what they felt, made them so sad they didn't want to go back. It was complete disrespect for the buffalo." ITBC executive director Mark Heckert later remarked: "I don't know how else to say it. It's tremendously bad karma to kill these buffalo."[10]

In January 1997, the Intertribal Bison Cooperative made a bold stroke to preserve the bison. Lakota leader of the ITBC, Fred DuBray, signed an agreement with National Wildlife Federation (NWF) president Mark Van Putten to work toward protecting emigrating Yellowstone bison from slaughter. The ITBC committed itself through the agreement to enlist the widespread support of the federation. DuBray made this clear in his official statement: "To the tribes represented here today, buffalo represent the very essence of our culture and who we are. While the world around us has changed, our spiritual and cultural link to bison is eternal. By working together with National Wildlife Federation's millions of members, we will reestablish healthy bison populations on Indian lands, and reestablish hope for the Indian peoples."[11]

The agreement provided a memorandum of understanding aimed at immediately stopping the slaughter, offering an alternative to the methods of the NPS and Montana, and laying the groundwork for more comprehensive future activism and plans. The partnership offered a quarantine operation as the alternative. The Choctaw tribe of Oklahoma stepped forward to propose harboring a 3,000-acre refuge for animals certified healthy after inspections. The refuge would become a distribution point for healthy excess bison. It's worth noting that Yellowstone bison retain special genetic value in that they are one of the few public herds whose genetic structure remains untainted by cattle genes, a tainting which occurred fairly often during the initial captivities of the late 1800s. Thus, they hold special attraction to those individuals concerned with the purity of their bison and the reestablishment of the buffalo nation.

Yellowstone National Park Superintendent Mike Finley offered the joint proposal to Montana Governor Racicot as a compromise to mitigate the slaughter.[12] Eventually, Secretary of the Interior Bruce Babbitt also asked the state to stop the killing. Meanwhile, offers continued to arrive asking that the bison receive live shipment to the Choctaw reservation for future distribution. Yet Montana's state government did not budge. Racicot refused the overtures, and the executive officer of the State Department of Livestock explained why: "We don't want any diseased animals anywhere in the State."[13]

Still, on February 12, 1997, Tribal Chairman Caleb Shields of the Assiniboine and Lakota tribes of the Fort Peck Reservation delivered a heartfelt oration to a joint session of the Montana legislature. Shields opened his articulation of the significance of the slaughter to Native Americans with:

> The Yellowstone Park bison herd has once again placed Montana in the national spotlight. Montana Indian Nations share a common bond with this herd. Like us, they are the last survivors. Those of our ancestors who survived the 19th century found sanctuary on reservations. In 1894, the last wild buffalo herd—about 20 head—found sanctuary in Yellowstone Park.

> I speak for all Montana Indian nations when I say that the slaughter of this herd must stop. The killing is out of hand. Hundreds of buffalo have been slaughtered without even attempting to test them for brucellosis.

> Our cultures are different on this issue. Under our religion, buffalo are respected. They are good medicine. Their skulls and hides still adorn our most sacred lodges. We will dance, sing and pray to them. What is occurring outside Yellowstone Park is disrespectful.

> Viable alternatives exist.[14]

Shields's address brought up key historical points and heralded others. First, Native Americans possess a long history of interaction with the bison of Yellowstone. Second, for many Indian people, the Yellowstone herd embodies Native America. Third, spirituality and feeling play a huge role in the Native mindset in general and quite specific to the Yellowstone herd. Fourth, the Yellowstone herd merits treatment better than that received.

These facets offer a window into the relationship of Native Americans and Yellowstone bison before, during, and after the 1996–1997 crisis.

The archeological record reveals Native American and bison interaction around the Yellowstone Plateau dating back nearly ten thousand years. The mountain valleys served as a grazing resource regularly sought by bison. Their early human harvesters followed the same ebb and flow through the present-day park area as they hunted and foraged. Archeologists note that varied findings show Native Americans utilized a wide range of flora and fauna including, of course, the buffalo. The obsidian deposits found within the park beckoned the Native masters of lithic technology. Yellowstone obsidian emerges from archeological findings across the country in the form of both atlatl points and arrowheads. Some of those points still retain the blood of bison and, unsurprisingly, suggest the harvesting of the bison resource by Yellowstone Native Americans. Buffalo jumps at Emigrant, Montana, just north of the park indicate that harvesting at times took on a reasonably voluminous dimension.[15]

As the prehistoric record yields to the historic record, analysts have been able to reconstruct some of the tribal affiliations with the park. The Kiowa maintained ties to the park area prior to their departure from the inter-mountain region as did their Uto-Aztecan linguistic cousins, the Shoshone. The Shoshone and the Shoshone-Bannock combination of Shoshone and Paiute speakers probably ranged the park most fully during the period when Euro-Americans began to penetrate into the interior of the continent. Some of the Shoshone, known as "the Sheepeaters," became virtually full-time residents, subsisting quite often on bighorn sheep as implied by their name. Eventually, the equestrian Blackfeet and Crow ventured onto the plateau as part-time users. Tribes to the west and north such as the Salish and Nez Perce and their allies came to know the Yellowstone region during their horseback migrations through the area in pursuit of bison usually found on but not restricted to the plains. During its investigation of tribes to receive the designation "Affiliated American Indian Tribes of Yellowstone National Park," the NPS added several Lakota and Dakota bands, the Kootenai, Coeur d'Alene, Northern Arapaho, Gros Ventres, Assiniboine, Northern Cheyenne, Confederated Colville, and Confederated Umatilla tribes to its list of tribes known to possess a history intertwined with the Yellowstone Plateau.[16]

For many of the tribes, their use of the park proved quite temporary. In any event, their presence as inhabitants vanished following an 1882 treaty negotiated by acting park superintendent Colonel Norris, United States Army. Remembering the unpleasant encounter some tourists had with Nez Perce combatants during the Nez Perce War of 1877, Norris believed that Indians detracted from the tourist experience. Therefore, he wanted them evicted.[17] With that, traditional existence in Yellowstone ended for Native Americans, but their association with the region did not terminate nor did their collective memory of it as a stronghold for the buffalo nation.

As the Yellowstone bison herd grew, park officials faced the prospects of disposing of excess animals. Live shipments such as those to private individuals or public institutions accounted for some of the disposal. As documented earlier in this book, a few shipments of live bison also helped establish tribal herds for the Crow and Lakota nations. However, carcass shipments also helped alleviate perceived buffalo population pressures within the park. Park records indicate that between 1925 and 1948, Yellowstone National Park shipped 2,263 bison carcasses and 1,910 bison hides out of the park. From those shipments, 1,880 carcasses and 1,457 hides went to Indian agencies. In 1949 and 1951, no shipments occurred, but in 1950 and 1952 the shipping to Indian agencies returned. Native Americans received 161 carcasses and 121 hides from the 162 animals slaughtered in 1950. In 1952, the agencies acquired 239 carcasses and 240 hides of the 242 slaughtered bovids. The carcasses typically went to either reservation headquarters or schools. For example, records from 1948 and 1950 show that the Fort Belknap, Flathead, Standing Rock, Fort Berthold, Crow Creek, Cheyenne River, Turtle Mountain, and Blackfeet agencies received shipments, while school recipients included Pierre Indian School, Flandreau Indian School, Haskell Institute, and the Phoenix Indian School. Shipments became far more sporadic in the period leading up to the implementation of the natural regulation policy in 1967, often going first to slaughterhouses in Livingston before distribution to tribes. The preponderance of the slaughter and distribution activity in this time period probably occurred in the three to four years preceding 1967.[18]

Although receiving carcasses of bison from Yellowstone National Park offered a far different connectivity with the bison than traditional hunting and butchering, it did provide a link for a significant number of Native Americans.

The strength of the bond increased in the 1990s as park personnel allowed Native Americans to participate in the slaughter process with ceremonial field butchering. This meat went to reservations, educational organizations such as the Montana State University Indian Club, or intertribal organizations represented, for example, by the Helena Indian Alliance. With bison restoration more of a concern than bison harvesting in Indian country, the field butchering offered a method for continuing to interact with the bison resource even though it was less desirable than taking live bison for seed stock. Nonetheless, the perceived sacrilege of the volume and manner of execution of the 1996–1997 slaughter in many ways precipitated the Yellowstone bison crisis. After all, in terms of biological carrying capacity, which changes over time, the park possessed too many bison to survive a difficult winter as the rain and snow began to arrive late in 1996.[19]

The biological carrying capacity of Yellowstone for bison did not concern Native Americans nearly as much as the treatment of those buffalo seeking to flee the park and its unavailable forage. This concern largely stemmed from the fact that many Native people saw the buffalo and its plight as a mirror of their own. For them, killing the buffalo too much resembled the death of Native Americans. Fellowship as the "last survivors" between the Indian nation and buffalo nation of Yellowstone sparked strong rhetoric.[20]

"They're killing us again, there's no separation. That's how people feel, that's how I feel," stated Lakota activist Rosalie Little Thunder in reflecting on the Yellowstone winter slaughters of the late 1990s. Reminiscent of Lakota bison savior Mary Ann Dupuis, Little Thunder emerged as a leader in the bison restoration movement surrounding the Yellowstone controversy. Active at the killing fields, in several environmental organizations, and as the defender of the Yellowstone bison, she demonstrated extraordinary skill as an orator and nonviolent social protestor. She helped forge the coalition between the Buffalo Nation bison activist group led by Michael Mease and Native American protestors into a new group known as the Buffalo Field Campaign. Calling the slaughter an "act of genocide" in a 2000 interview reflected her contention that "the buffalo are victims of pathological politics" and that shooting them equated to "outright racism."[21]

Little Thunder did not stand alone, as her affiliation with several organizations including the ITBC made clear. Cooperative president Louis LaRose echoed her comments about the killing when he stated that it "likened to the gatling guns at Wounded Knee." He added, "You're killing the answer to our elder's prayers that the buffalo would return." A young Lakota man named Nathan Chasing Horse attacked the political economy behind the slaughter at a pilgrimage that ended in Yellowstone National Park's northern range in 1999: "Brucellosis is a myth [as a valid reason for the slaughter]. They should kill the myth not the buffalo." Winona LaDuke (Anishinabe), Little Thunder's colleague in Honor the Earth and eventual 2000 Green Party candidate for vice president, poignantly asked in a televised interview, "Is not America done killing buffalo? How could this happen again?"[22]

LaDuke posed the vexing questions. Little Thunder added the observation, "The one thing that really makes a difference is prayer." Spoken two years after Caleb Shields's speech describing the spiritual link with the bison, Little Thunder's words resonated as much as Shields's. In fact, she became a symbol for the Native American effort to end the Yellowstone slaughter when she was arrested while offering prayers for a freshly shot buffalo less than a mile from a vigil held on the National Day of Prayer on March 6, 1997, near Gardiner, Montana, at the entrance to the northern range of Yellowstone National Park. On that day, across the nation, Indian people prayed for the Yellowstone bison. On Capitol Hill, ITBC spiritual advisor Rocke Afraid of Hawk, Lakota, led an assortment of tribal representatives. More than two thousand miles away, Lakota chief and keeper of the Sacred White Buffalo Calf Pipe Arvol Looking Horse conducted the ceremony at Gardiner within earshot of Montana Department of Livestock agents gunning down bison moving from the park onto private property. Little Thunder left the ceremony when she heard the shots so she could pray over the fallen bison. Law enforcement officials reluctantly placed her under arrest.[23]

Speaking of her experience that day, Little Thunder remarked: "It was horrifying. The slaughter itself is so disturbing. I wonder why they did it in such close proximity to our ceremony." She added: "I just wonder how they can kill the buffalo. I think when people look at a buffalo they automatically think of Indians. I wonder what they are thinking." She did go on to clarify that she did not hold the National Park Service at fault. The crux of the matter were the responsibilities thrust on the park by the judicial system to halt the spread of brucellosis. "They [NPS personnel] participated in our prayers. They are so unhappy to see the killing of the buffalo too," she said.[24]

While the slaughter diminished over the next two comparatively mild winters, to approximately 150 animals taken from spring 1997 to spring

1999, the commitment of a select group of Native Americans did not waver. In 1999, forty Lakota men and women led by Rosalie Little Thunder—carrying the Sacred White Buffalo Calf Pipe Bundle—walked and rode horseback 507 miles from South Dakota to Roosevelt Arch at the entrance to the northern range of Yellowstone Park. Sixty other Native Americans from tribes, including the Apache, Nez Perce, Southern Ute, and Tuscarora, joined as well. At times braving wind-chill temperatures down to twenty-five degrees below zero, the pilgrims concluded their sacrificial and symbolic migration with a ceremony on February 28, 1999, in which more than 300 Native American activists as well as officials from the National Park Service were present. The culminating event of the march to the arch occurred when Lakota spiritual leader Gary Silk performed an age-old buffalo skull ceremony. Assistants pierced the skin on the Lakota man's back and attached two bison skulls with a cord. Blowing a traditional whistle, Silk dragged the skulls through the brush and finally grasped a horse's tail. The combined force tore Silk's flesh as onlookers cried and prayed. Little Thunder encapsulated the moment: "This is how much we care."[25]

As emotions and spirituality gripped Native Americans during the late 1990s in response to the continued slaughter of Yellowstone bison, they also persisted in seeking a way to develop alternative solutions to save the Yellowstone bison and even use them as seed stock for bison restoration. Gary Silk elucidated the Native mindset on the issue: "If the government doesn't want them, we'll take them and bring them home." Using almost identical words, Rosalie Little Thunder stated: "They are not wanted here. We'll take them home." For his part, Louis LaRose made it clear where Native people could look for leadership in the process: "We're the herd bull, ITBC—the herd bull."[26]

When the ITBC and NWF signed their memorandum of understanding in 1997 they initiated the Buffalo Recovery Project. The agreement laid the groundwork for a more fully articulated plan largely governed by both sentiment and science. At the 1999 annual conference, Tim Wapato of the Colville Confederated Tribes, the executive director of the ITBC, explained the cooperative's salient points of the ITBC's alternative plan to the organization's membership. First and foremost, the ITBC sought the treatment of bison as wildlife, with wildlife officials making the policy decisions affecting the park buffalo. Second, the existing slaughter needed to stop. Instead, hazing was to continue. Third, captured animals were to receive disease testing. Seral positive animals would require slaughter, and seral negative animals would be placed under the protection and transportation network of the ITBC so captured animals could be quarantined at either the Choctaw facility or Fort Belknap, which offered to harbor the refugee bison. Fourth, the tribes demanded a place in the environmental impact statement (EIS) process. Fifth, the infirmity of brucellosis was to be handled as a park disease issue and not just a bison issue. Also, tribal colleges and Native American scientists were to collaborate in the research on the disease. Sixth, several facets concerning herd size required reconsideration, including the idea that park carrying capacity should be three thousand animals, that animals deserved the right to wander outside the limits of the park, that winter roads required closure, and that treaty rights should be restored allowing aboriginal bison hunting on adjacent lands. Seventh, with respect to bison-cattle interaction, adjustments such as vaccinations and the timing of placement on overlapping ranges would be made by the livestock interests and not the bison. If bison wandered onto private property, then the ITBC would round up the animals for quarantine. As the organization developed this plan it also lobbied on the political front, delivering to Governor Racicot a 10,000-signature petition supporting the Buffalo Recovery Project.[27]

Meanwhile, the ITBC's alternative plan to that of the NPS became part of the formal alternative known as the Citizen's Plan. Endorsed by the ITBC and NWF, the Citizen's Plan maintained the integrity of the Buffalo Recovery Project and ITBC plan, with the addition of some points addressing compensation of private landowners for bison damage and cooperation with bison-friendly landowners in the bison range. Aside from the ITBC-NWF partnership, sponsors of the plan included the Greater Yellowstone Coalition, Gallatin Wildlife Association, Jackson Hole Conservation Alliance, Montana Audubon Society, Montana River Action Network, National Resource Defense Council, Defenders of Wildlife, National Parks Conservation Association, and the Wildlife Federations of Montana, Idaho, and Wyoming. During the National Park Service's comment period on its EIS for the Yellowstone bison, twelve alternatives existed. When the Park Service tallied the comments, 47,751 comments favored the Citizen's Plan, with the second-most-favored plan receiving 4,842 comments, the third receiving

1,653 favorable comments, and the fourth only 754, the downward trend continuing through the rest of the proposals.[28]

Through the buildup into the comment period and then the interval before the park's new bison policy was imposed, Native Americans had reason to be optimistic about the future of the Yellowstone bison and, by association, themselves. South of the park, federal and state departments devised plans for hunting bison that frequented the National Elk Refuge. Although the hunt failed to materialize when a federal judge decided that it violated the aesthetic rights of tourists, tribes had received a guarantee of 30 percent of the permits. This established an important precedent toward restoring aboriginal hunting of animals in public domain in accordance with treaty rights. Game official and Blackfeet tribal spokesman Buzz Cobell voiced elation that this type of hunt on federal property "recognizes cultural heritage" and noted that it was superior to the Indian-bison interaction allowed at Yellowstone. To the north in Yellowstone National Park, federal agencies acquired eight thousand acres of adjacent land on winter range for bison habitat. National Park Service official Barbara Sutteer attended the 1999 annual conference of the ITBC and declared: "Stewards—you certainly are." Showing the commitment behind her statement, the NPS agreed to let Indian people into the decision-making process through tribal consultations. It warrants consideration that not all federal bureaucrats endorsed Native participation as readily as Sutteer. This became evident by the time the "rump" tribal consultation convened in August 1998, to which only a select few tribes received invitations. Six tribal councils passed resolutions demanding their right to be consulted in accordance with federal policy. This political maneuver resulted in the scheduling of another consultation in the spring of 1999.[29]

The tribal consultation process of 1999 presented challenges and opportunities for Native Americans. Proceedings bogged down at the initial consultation in May 1999 when a rather eclectic group of Native people sought to implement their agendas. Blackfeet cultural consultant Curly Bear Wagner afterward expressed concern that "urban Indians" who often did not represent any tribe took up much of the agenda. Both Tim Wapato and Louis LaRose expressed similar concerns. Wapato worried about the influence of "State House Indians." LaRose remarked, "One of the difficulties with these issues is that it pits Indian against Indian." Calling on legal tradition, the two ITBC officers responded by insisting on government-to-government or nation-to-nation negotiations between state and federal agencies on the one side and Native people on the other so as to focus the agenda. Noting that "buffalo is the cement that can bypass our division," Rosalie Little Thunder also advocated "keeping the tribal voice legally strong." In fact, even before the May meeting, she sent out, on behalf of Honor the Earth, memoranda to myriad tribal councils imploring them to send official representatives to the meeting. Reflecting on the May consultation and anticipating the October 1999 consultation led ITBC President Louis LaRose to state in September of that year that the ITBC must serve as the "herd bull" in the process to unify the Native front on the issue.[30]

By the end of 1999 and into 2000, the Yellowstone bison had enjoyed comparatively mild winters for two years. Native hunting of bison in the federal domain of part of the greater Yellowstone ecosystem had received consideration by various government entities. The NPS was consulting Native people about the Yellowstone herd. A bison-friendly alternative endorsed by Native Americans existed to guide future policies on the Yellowstone bison. A new federal EIS appeared to be "88–90 percent" like the Citizen's Plan. Indeed, the people had spoken up overwhelmingly for the Citizen's Plan. The ITBC and NWF issued a joint statement: "The Citizen's Plan and its overwhelming support by the American public are all that stand between the Indian people and another, perhaps final, assault on their culture."[31] The people had spoken, but then again in the year 2000 so did the court system.

A federal court decision in 2000 on brucellosis abrogated the EIS and alternatives process. The court simply ordered a "2000 Management Plan" under which the National Park Service would manage bison and the park to maintain a herd of three thousand animals. Montana would allow up to one hundred bison that tested negative for brucellosis to wander outside the park. The court mandated that hazing would be the first choice for excess bison moving out of the park. After that, capture, test, and slaughter would dominate the scene once again. The court also required the NPS to assist Montana in this process. Protections for bison outside the park would be removed if the number of animals rose above three thousand.[32]

A great irony exists in this application of the law. Canadian biologist Valerius Geist analyzes wildlife law in North America and finds it a "powerful model based on local, populist wildlife harvest and management." He adds,

"The policies governing the laws of North America's wildlife conservation are essentially 'tribal' in nature." He explains the tribal nature of the wildlife law as communal ownership outside of market forces, allocated by elders, and under local direction. Geist qualifies his assessment: "The quality of decisions in the North American system depends not only on science, but also on an enlightened public and the political power of special interest groups."[33] Thus, it would seem that tribes affiliated with the park—and backed by millions of people in special interest groups represented by officials who rely on research and scientific data to develop wildlife policies—ought to get their way. Yet, for all the cases where Geist's analysis adequately characterizes fish and game programs across the United States and Canada, it simply does not describe the Yellowstone situation.

Regardless of jurisdictions or political machinations, bison possess an instinct to move with the natural rhythms of their environment. Between 1997 and 2003, the winter environment of Yellowstone never became as severe as in 1996–1997. For most of those years, fewer than 100 bison perished at the hands of agents slaughtering bison out of the park, although in the 2002–2003 cold season, agents killed 202 animals through late January. Still, as the herd survived past the winter and toward spring, it again approached 4,000 members. The groundwork for another crisis similar to that of 1996–1997 existed. As Yellowstone bison expert Mary Meagher stated, "A lot of times, things look pretty good until all of a sudden they go to hell."[34] Native Americans would call it an "apocalypse" both for them and the buffalo. Their vision of the landscape remained unfulfilled, but hope endured.

For many years through the 1990s and into 2003, Curly Bear Wagner of the Blackfeet tribe in Browning, Montana, prayed. He offered his pipe in a sacred circle highlighted by the four compass points and the landmarks he knew. To the north, he acknowledged Chief Mountain in Waterton Park; to the east, the Sweetgrass Hills; to the west, the mountainous spine of the continental divide; and to the south, Yellowstone. Wagner explained his act of supplication the same both in 1999 and 2003: "When I pray, I offer my pipe last to the south, to Yellowstone, because that is where the buffalo always have been, and that is from where again they will come."[35]

Fig. 19: A few survivors: Yellowstone National Park bison, 1896. Photo by Nat Little. Courtesy Montana Historical Society, Helena.

Fig. 20: Winter and the Yellowstone bison. © William Campbell, Homefire Productions, Inc.

Fig. 21: Yellowstone: a home where the buffalo must roam. © William Campbell, Homefire Productions, Inc.

Fig. 22: Yellowstone bison in 1997: a free-ranging herd? © William Campbell, Homefire Productions, Inc.

(Opposite top) Fig. 23: Native Americans field dressing slaughtered Yellowstone bison, 1997. © William Campbell, Homefire Productions, Inc.

(Opposite bottom) Fig. 24: Rosalie Little Thunder bearing the skull of a bison leads the 1999 pilgrimage into Yellowstone. © William Campbell, Homefire Productions, Inc.

(Bottom) Fig. 25: Rosalie Little Thunder, ITBC Vice President Carl Tsosie, and ITBC President Louis LaRose (left to right) at the 1999 ITBC annual conference on the Yellowstone bison issue. Photo by author.

6. A Comparative Perspective on Canada's Native Restoration of the Bison

The bison look after me as I look after them. Something good will happen, and this will occur in the future. It's been tough but I know that down the road, this will help the people.

Harley Frank (1999)

A comparison between the bison restoration effort of Canada and that of the United States yields similarities as well as differences. On the surface, the overall plight and salvation of the bison appears the same. The European hegemony extended over the indigenous countryside, resulting in a marginalized existence for the aboriginal people and a landscape largely devoid of bison. Subsequently, a few people saved bison, and the observer can find them today in ever increasing numbers on ranches, growing by an estimated 25 percent per year, on reserves and in parks. However, focusing on the Native aspect in this bison recovery reveals some differentiating nuances that show the indigenous effort in Canada at once both more advanced and more fractured than that of the United States.[1] Government cooperation with the Native bison stewards rose to a high level while the degree of coordination among the First Nations lagged that established by the Intertribal Bison Cooperative in the United States.

Before launching into any discussion of Canadian bison restoration, we must first make an important clarification regarding bison speciation and subsequent policy. Historically, bison of Canada consisted of two groups. The first group wandered across the plains and prairies and appeared quite similar in all aspects of existence to the bison of America's Great Plains. These bison numbered into the millions together with their counterparts farther south. The second group inhabited the boreal forest and meadows of the north country in present-day northern Alberta, southwestern Northwest Territories, northeastern British Columbia, and northwestern Saskatchewan. This woodland group probably numbered between 112,000 and 168,000. For many years, leading scientists in Canada considered these northern bison to be a subspecies known as "Wood Bison" (*Bison bison athabascae*) as opposed to "Plains Bison" (*Bison bison bison*). These northern bison tend to grow a bit larger, possess a darker pelage, and show less distinction between fore-quarters pelage and the rest of the body than the southern bison.[2] Leaders in the field of contemporary bison conservation believe that no subspecies exist because of genetic similarity and experiments showing that either type of bison can develop similar characteristics in a given environment. Nevertheless, Canadian policies continue to treat the two variations as different. For our purposes here, "Wood Bison" will refer to the northern bison as distinguished by Canadian policy, and "Plains Bison" will refer to those bison more dominant to the south. For example, Plains Bison are considered a domestic species in the prairie provinces while Wood Bison are considered wildlife in all provinces except Manitoba.[3] Thus, the two bison receive segregated treatment from government officials since they often fall under the jurisdiction of different agencies.

However defined, both populations of bison plummeted with the approach of the twentieth century. The last of Canada's plains bison succumbed to the killing field straddling the forty-ninth parallel in the 1880s. Meanwhile, the more isolated northern bison dipped to a low of 250 animals between 1896 and 1900. The Buffalo Protection Act (1877) had failed to protect either population. An act to preserve the wood buffalo in 1893 reversed the trend of annihilation, but not until the Mounties of the Royal Canadian Mounted Police began protecting bison in 1897 did the future of the animals seem secure. In 1911, the government appointed six full-time buffalo rangers to the northern bison's home range. Under their vigilance, the northern herd increased to 500 in 1914 and between 1,500 and 2,000 in 1922 when Canada established Wood Buffalo National Park.[4]

As the Dominion of Canada saved its northern bison, it augmented its few exhibition plains bison at Banff with the mass purchase of the Pablo-Allard herd. As noted earlier, this herd exploded in population, quickly outgrowing its temporary pasture at Elk Island Park and even its more spacious park area in Wainwright. Reduction became imperative and herd managers sought an outlet for their problem. This resulted in the controversial transfer of these plains bison into Wood Buffalo National Park.[5] At this point, the histories of the two bison populations became one again, and the parameters for future restoration efforts were established.

Between 1925 and 1928, Canadian officials transferred 6,673 bison from Wainwright to Wood Buffalo National Park (WBNP). As many wildlife scientists feared, the plains bison quickly mingled with the northern bison, resulting in disease transfer and the hybridization of what had been perceived as pure "Wood Buffalo." The park's bison population shot up to 12,000 in 1934. However, the population declined over the next sixty years to 2,000 by 1994. During the decline, scientists confirmed the presence of disease in the park herd, including anthrax, tuberculosis, and brucellosis. The animals, weakened from anthrax and tuberculosis, succumbed more readily to predation, habitat loss, and severe environmental conditions such as floods and fire. Disease eradication efforts failed miserably, leading conservation biologist Valerius Geist to later characterize the entire situation as an "adventuresome history of mismanagement."[6]

Still, the retention of a pure "Wood Bison" herd remained important to policymakers. Thus, excitement grew around the late 1950s discovery of a remote herd in the Nyarling River area of the northwest section of Wood Buffalo National Park. Tests confirmed the "purity" of the herd genetically and the absence of disease. Thus, officials instituted a capture program in the early 1960s, in which animals were caught and moved to Fort Smith. Program managers bottle-raised captive-born calves and slaughtered the parents in order to develop a disease-free herd. A restoration program using these progeny took shape in 1963 when wildlife officials introduced eighteen of the animals to the region west of the Great Slave Lake, an area that soon become known as the Mackenzie Bison Sanctuary, and another twenty-three to Elk Island National Park, where they were separated from the plains bison already on site. The Elk Island "Wood Bison" became the seed stock for later herds, including the Nahanni-Liard herd of the southwestern Northwest Territories, the Nissling River herd in the Yukon, and Waterhen Wood Bison Ranch in Manitoba, in addition to others. By 1994, the Canadian government began to make Wood Bison available to private herd owners, and the Mackenzie Bison Sanctuary totaled two thousand animals.[7]

Indeed, it was through the establishment and management of herds such as some of those just mentioned that the heavy collaboration between Natives and government emerged. In the United States the government had excluded the aboriginal people from the national park lands and subsequently allowed them to assume only consultative roles, for example, in Yellowstone National Park. In contrast, Canada often embraced Native co-management of parks, refuges, and bison restoration efforts in the government domain.[8] However, winning such rights took patience and perseverance along with an adherence to traditional lifestyle while remaining cognizant of the importance of sustainable economic development.

For their part, members of the First Nations in Canada, just like some Native groups in the United States today, always sought the preservation of the bison landscape so as to preserve their way of life. Evidence of such interest comes from treaty negotiations by Native leaders in which they sought to retain their aboriginal hunting, fishing, and foraging rights as well as the participation by some Cree tribal members in the Northwest Rebellion of 1885.[9] Native studies scholars Theresa Ferguson and Clayton Burke link wildlife management with the treaty negotiations and cite Treaty Eight on the range of the northern bison as an example:

> From the local Native perspective, this concern for the right to manage wildlife is of long standing. Native spokespersons stressed the point strongly in the Treaty Eight negotiations (1899). As a result, the Treaty included a clause which guaranteed that Native people had "the right to pursue their usual vocations of hunting, trapping and fishing" with the proviso that this was "subject to such regulations as may from time to time be made by the Government of the country" [Treaty No. Eight, made 21 June 1899, and Adhesions, Reports etc. (Ottawa: Queen's Printer, 1966), 12]. The intent of this proviso is clarified in the written comments on the negotiations by the Treaty Commissioners. These comments indicate that the Treaty Commissioners had assured the people that "only such laws as to hunting and fishing as were in the interest of the Indians and were found necessary in order to protect the fish and fur-bearing animals would be made, and that they would be free to hunt and fish after the Treaty as they would be if they never entered into it" (Treaty No. Eight, made 21 June 1899, and Adhesions, Reports etc., 6).[10]

Clearly, Natives sought retention of their lifestyles and the landscape that produced their modes of production.

Also, some record exists of direct action and rhetoric by First Nations to maintain their bison-based existence. For example, in 1857, the Plains Cree formed a grand council to attempt to impose a collective policy that forbade white men from killing bison on Cree hunting grounds. Approximately twenty years later, Sweetgrass, a Cree Chief, pleaded with the British North American government to protect the bison.[11] Both efforts failed. Like their brethren to the south, Canada's Native people became marginalized and impoverished while enduring the assimilationist whims of the dominant European-originating culture.

Although it is difficult to tie the Canadian Native effort to restore the bison population to the cycle of federal legislation, as can be done in the United States, certainly Canadian government policies on its indigenous people drastically impacted the efforts of Natives to restore a landscape complete with bison. It's worth noting, for example, that the seeming liberalization of Native policy allowing greater autonomy occurred in Canada in the 1980s, roughly concurrent with the effects of American legislation in the 1970s such as the Indian Self-Determination Act (1974) and the American Indian Religious Freedom Act (1978). Specific to bison restoration, the Canadian government made three separate exemplary agreements with Native groups that stipulated joint aboriginal-government agency management of wildlife. The Native Canadians received the right to make decisions, as opposed to simple consultation. In 1986, the Canada and Alberta Fort Chippewyan Cree Band Settlement extended to the Cree of Fort Chippewyan, located just east of Wood Buffalo National Park, the right to participate in wildlife management, which impacted the park's bison. Two years later, a separate agreement, known as the Comprehensive Land Claim Agreement in Principle between Canada and the Dene Nation and the Metis Association of the Northwest Territories, empowered Natives just north of Wood Buffalo National Park to become co-managers of area bison. About the same time, in 1987 the Dene Band near Fort Providence in the form of the De Gah Goh Tie Betterment Corporation received back part of its age-old hunting culture when management agreements allowed the band to resume subsistence hunting and some trophy-hunt guiding of the bison living in the Mackenzie Bison Sanctuary.[12]

These settlements and rights to restore aboriginal subsistence capitalized on an existing policy known as the National Recovery Plan for Wood Bison in Canada. The plan, entered into by federal, provincial, and territorial governments in 1975, possessed four objectives: first, to re-establish free-roaming "Wood Bison;" second, to maintain the genetic integrity of the "Wood Bison;" third, to restore herds in order to contribute to aesthetic, cultural, economic, and social well-being for rural communities through sustainable development; and fourth, to build long-term cooperative management with local communities and aboriginal populations. Specifically, the plan originally called for three free-roaming herds of at least two hundred animals each. In succeeding years, managers upgraded their goals to four herds of two hundred animals, and eventually they agreed to a goal of four free-roaming herds of at least four hundred animals each.[13]

As part of the plan, the Wood Bison Recovery Team sought the assistance of First Nations. Two First Nations bison projects opened in 1984. The first project involved the Waterhen First Nation in the northern Interlake region north of Winnipeg, Manitoba. The Ojibway band took animals from various sites, including Elk Island National Park, in 1984. With a successful captive breeding program in place, the band released thirteen animals into a more remote location on Chitek Lake. The bison stewards released nine more animals in 1996, and by 1999 they declared their transfer successful, with eighty bison occupying the area.[14]

The second project unfolded far to the north and west in northwestern Alberta near Habay. A 1982 range assessment by the Canadian Wildlife Service (CWS) and the Alberta Environmental Protection Natural Resources Service (AEP-NRS) near Hay and Zama Lakes found a suitable site for reestablishing bison in the area. The Alberta agency set up a liaison with the Dene Tha First Nation and established a Bison Management Agreement ratified by both groups in 1985. Meanwhile, twenty-nine "Wood Bison" arrived from Elk Island National Park in February 1984. Upon their arrival, one tribal elder remarked: "I am very happy that the buffalo are returned today. The wildlife is decreasing. Hopefully, the buffalo will breed and increase in numbers." The project managers accommodated the bison in a temporary enclosure with the intent of releasing all of them over five to six years beginning in two years. However, after five years the herd still totaled only twenty-nine animals and just thirty-one animals the next year.[15]

Despite the fact that the Dene Tha won concessions from tribal members to protect the herd and refrain from using it for subsistence, herd managers in 1990 still felt that the low level of reproduction combined with the threat of disease from free-ranging bison necessitated retaining the bison in their three-square kilometer enclosure. Nonetheless, in 1993, the enclosure partially collapsed, and forty-eight bison wandered out, becoming Alberta's first successfully reintroduced, disease-free, and free-ranging Wood Bison herd. The provincial government declared a bison protection zone bounded by the provincial borders to the north and west. Any bison except those of the Hay-Zama herd in the bison protection area were considered wildlife and thus subject to hunting in accordance with provincial regulations, including aboriginal hunting rights. Moreover, the agreement between Alberta and the Dene Tha made it clear that when the Hay-Zama herd reached 250 members, it would be subject to reductions by hunting, with the Dene Tha receiving one-half of all quotas. Presumably, the protection against harvesting afforded by the tribal accords offered good stewardship. By 1999, the herd increased to 100 and continued expanding its range, particularly toward the north and toward the political boundary of the Northwest Territories and physical boundary of the Mackenzie River. Thus, success was the result of the joint management effort by provincial agencies and First Nations people to restore a free-ranging bison population to northern Alberta.[16]

A third project developed when the Northwest Territories government and Fort Smith Hunters and Trappers Association, an ethnically mixed community interest group, agreed in 1990 to create a bison facility on the Slave River lowlands. They created the Hanging Ice Bison Ranch, which by 1994 possessed 120 bison and became a source of meat and employment for local residents.[17]

With its increasing participation in wildlife management, First Nations felt a greater sense of stewardship over their resources. For example, the Little Red River Cree maintain resource use areas as part of their indigenous rights on the western and southern boundaries of Wood Buffalo National Park. In the winter of 1998–1999, Cree tribesmen confronted Euro-Canadian hunters led by a guide. The hunters sought unprotected bison in the Caribou Mountains area. The Cree stopped the hunt. Such cooperation between indigenous people surrounding the park in managing the moving bison resource led park official Peter Lamb to state in 1999: "I expect to see continued progress in working toward a cooperative management regime with our numerous aboriginal partners in and around Wood Buffalo National Park. Formal negotiations are underway with First Nations and Metis Associations with respect to Treaty Land Entitlements, land claim issues and park management activities."[18] The restoration of free-ranging bison in Canada was underway, and Native people fully participated in the remarkable success story.

Nonetheless, in 1990 Natives had had to persevere to win a hard-fought battle that made possible these successes of the 1990s. The issue arose over Agriculture Canada's approved proposal to create a disease-free Wood Bison herd in and around Wood Buffalo National Park. In the interest of eradicating disease to promote the status of Canadian cattle but under the guise of helping the bison, Agriculture Canada proposed slaughtering all wild buffalo in the region and then reintroducing disease-free bison out of captive breeding programs. Natives responded vehemently to the proposal. Representing the Deninu Kué First Nation comprised of Chippewyan and Métis members, Elder Fred Dawson of Fort Resolution (on the shores of the Great Slave Lake just north of the park) expressed his despondency over Agriculture Canada's proposal: "It breaks my heart to hear you talk about the buffalo like this." His words represented his people, who defended their right to participate in the decision-making concerning the bison and felt that the government infringed on the treaty rights for subsistence.[19]

During 1990, a Federal Environmental Assessment and Review Office (FEARO) panel presented the Agriculture Canada proposal in Canada's Indian country. The resulting discussions defined the positions of the adversarial parties and hearkened to the ongoing struggle of indigenous people worldwide to maintain a subsistence lifestyle without being absorbed into the modern world system of nonrenewable resource development. Proponents of the plan forwarded by Agriculture Canada defined the bison of Wood Buffalo National Park and surrounding areas as "transmitters of disease," tainted with "genetic impurity." For their part, Natives opposed wholesale slaughter. After all, only about one-third of the bison suffered from tuberculosis or brucellosis. Much like their Native American brethren in the Yellowstone crisis, the Native Canadians emphasized that discrimination against bison resembled racism. They warily viewed the attempt to manipulate resources in the park as a step toward much further development in logging or agriculture. Additionally, they noted that agreements existed with the government regarding the Native influence in effectuating wildlife policy and that these proceedings would violate their rights to wildlife stewardship.[20] Ultimately, the confrontation occurred over different visions of the landscape. First Nations sought an environment relatively free of manipulation, with bison maintaining their own autonomy. Agriculture and development interests sought a heavily manipulated landscape.

Ultimately, the Minister of the Environment intervened, and the decision-making process fell to a newly created Northern Buffalo Management Board. The board consisted of seventeen members, including nine community representatives, five government agency representatives, and three representatives from nongovernmental organizations. Two co-chairpersons would preside, with one receiving an appointment from the government while the other hailed from the First Nations. Upon taking office, Chairman George Kurszewski, representing the Dene-Métis First Nation, stated: "This is a victory for us. We stopped the slaughter. We're a majority in this management board." Chairman Kurszewski described the management plan as "one in which the rights of the aboriginal people are recognized."[21]

As a measure of the commitment of the Northern Buffalo Management Board to the input of the Native community, the Research Advisory Committee (RAC) also reflected a Native presence in its eight-member constituency. Four community members, such as trappers, elders, or chiefs, joined two government scientific advisers, one nongovernmental environmentalist organization representative, and a member of the scientific community such as a veterinarian. They plainly stated their goal of integrating traditional and scientific knowledge for a more "holistic approach" to bison management. Avoiding wholesale slaughter as an alternative and keeping alive the possibility for "free-ranging bison," the RAC supported the Northern Buffalo Management Board's policy advocating a compromise no- buffalo zone south of the Mackenzie Bison Sanctuary, north of British Columbia and Alberta, and west of Wood Buffalo National Park. Officials intended for this zone to prevent contact between diseased animals, namely, carriers of tuberculosis and brucellosis, and disease-free animals.[22]

Further evidence of Native participation in restoring Canadian bison came from the Hook Lake Recovery project, originally proposed by the Denin Kué in 1991. The following year, the First Nations teamed with the Northwest

Territories Department of Resources, with funding from the federal coffer and the Canadian Wildlife Federation, to begin an ambitious plan to reverse a disturbing trend affecting the wild Hook Lake northern bison herd. Ranging in the Slave River lowlands north of Wood Bison National Park, the herd, once numbering 1,700, dropped to fewer than 500 due to anthrax, tuberculosis, brucellosis, and predation before the implementation of the Denin Kué plan. The plan possessed five objectives: to create a healthy herd, preserve genetic diversity, salvage healthy bison, enhance the Hook Lake ecosystem, and develop economic opportunities for local people. To implement the plan, the bison handlers caught calves and tested them. Those youngsters that tested positive for disease went back into their wild herd. Those that tested negative traveled by helicopter back to the Denin Kué community at Fort Resolution. There, the handlers used test and slaughter methods to ensure that the calves would become disease-free. The program utilized separation by cohort peer groups to monitor the generations in anticipation of the disease-free generation that could roam the backcountry repopulating the countryside. By 1998, the captive herd contained more than forty females, thereby producing optimism about the future of the program.[23]

Let's now turn to a more in-depth examination of a northern bison management program to gain insights into the policy, structure, implementation, and cultural effect of First Nations bison restoration in Canada. The program is situated in the Mackenzie Bison Sanctuary located north of the Mackenzie River and west of Great Slave Lake. The Dene Got ie First Nation with its band headquarters at Fort Providence, Northwest Territories, manages one of the most significant bison herds in the world because of its size—nearly 2,000 animals in 1999—and its status as a purebred northern bison herd that free ranges without tuberculosis or brucellosis.[24]

As part of its plan to establish a free-roaming disease-free Wood Bison herd, the Canadian government established the Mackenzie bison herd in 1963 with eighteen animals from Elk Island National Park that had Nyarling River herd blood coursing through their veins. While the herd grew in size, its management passed to the local Hunters and Trappers Association, which consisted of local residents of varied ethnicity. However, in 1993 the Fort Providence Resource Management Board formed and took over management of the herd. By design, the constituency of the board gave Natives a voting majority, with three Dene seats, two Metis seats, and two at-large seats for community members. Developing a management plan, an organic document responding to fresh data accumulated continually, became a top priority.[25]

Challenges arose immediately for the Native managers. Anthrax spores, believed to have come from birds, infected the herd and caused unforeseen mortality. Unfortunately, anthrax-infected animals tend to abort and become more vulnerable to predation. Thus, the bison management team tasked its field hands and trappers to begin collecting anthrax data collection; implementing a vaccination program, using both salt blocks and helicopter darting; and curbing the wolf population. The anthrax outbreak caused the managers to burn 173 bison carcasses and spend countless hours in the field monitoring the bison. Treatments helped alleviate the effects, but the issue stayed unresolved through the 1990s.

Greg Nyuli, chairman of the Resource Management Board, characterized the wolfing program as "not wiping out wolves, just keeping a balance." Eighty-two-year-old Art Look, a Euro-Canadian trapper and outdoorsman raised by the Cree, became a wildlife consultant for the board. In a 1999 interview he explained that curtailing wolf predation of bison does not require taking many wolves. The trapper must simply get the adult leaders since they serve as the pack's repository of knowledge for slaying bison. Eliminating the leaders forces the pack to re-learn the skill and temporarily takes the predatory pressure off the bison. Chairman Nyuli noted that older community members would not trap wolves because they felt a spiritual link to it, but younger community members expressed far less hesitation.[26]

The herd's population was safeguarded through treatment for anthrax, predator reductions, and range management in which prescribed burning was initiated to enhance grazing. As a result, in the latter part of the 1990s, the management board implemented a hunt. With forty-seven tags allotted, twenty went to Dene and Metis community members, three went to members of the Dogrib band, nine went to guided hunts with private clientele, and sixteen went into a drawing for Northwest Territories residents.[27]

Chief Nyuli explained that these hunts gave enhanced prestige to the bison project for many community members. Prior to the hunts, some local hunters believed that the bison chased away the moose, and the huntsmen remained bitter about it. Such disgruntlement subsided when hunting seasons opened and the people became reconnected with the buffalo. Nyuli explained some of the reconnection process: "We lost our history and we need to consult further with our elders." He added, "This used to be our resource and was wiped out and the government putting back bison is pay-back more than anything, for our resources."[28]

The people's feeling of connection with the bison occurred through influ-ence in the decision-making process on behalf of the Dene Got ie. In 1999, Chief Nyuli described future projects for his community and the bison. He believed the band could stage elite trophy hunts for Safari Club Inter-national. He also entertained the possibility of a separate bison ranch to produce meat both for the people and for sale. Also, he hoped to capital-ize on the eco-tourism industry by offering a safari experience featuring bison creeps to view and photograph one of the largest wild bison herds in the world. Others in the community apparently shared his vision since Chief Nyuli maintained that the bison management scenario enjoyed 90 to 95 percent support from the community.[29] Thus, perhaps as much as any group of people in North America, the Dene Got ie have become reassoci-ated with their age-old contemporary, the bison. Their experience reveals both the bonds of the past and the bridges to a future where the modern world meets a more nostalgic counterpart. In the end, however, the tribe enjoys the benefits of seeing free-ranging bison, largely unfettered by the restrictions of the Europeanized landscape imposed on North America be-ginning a half millennium ago.

The restoration of the northern bison under the aegis of First Nations and often in collaboration with various Canadian government entities produced at least three significant similarities and three major differences with the restoration efforts in the United States. The first similarity is the feeling of the indigenous peoples that bison roaming as freely as possible is a cul-tural goal. The second similarity is the role of disease in prompting often heavy-handed policy by government entities, policies often rejected by the Indian people. This proved true both with Yellowstone and Wood Buffalo National Parks: agents of the government either destroyed or intended to destroy large numbers of bison while Native Americans and Native Cana-dians protested. The third similarity is the acquisition of surplus bison for seed stock from national parks: Wind Cave National Park or Theodore Roosevelt National Park in the United States and Elk Island National Park in Canada. This signifies some degree of cooperation between the governments and their aboriginal people.

The differences begin with the level of support offered by the respective governments. The Canadian government ensured that Natives possessed management rights, while the American government offered to entertain consultation at most. Another difference involves free-roaming bison. Canadians indicated a readiness to allow open range for bison, at least in the northern range, albeit with the exception of bison protection areas, which are not in any case major avenues of movement. By contrast, policies in the United States, as illustrated by Yellowstone, reflect a hesitancy to allow free-ranging buffalo. As a result, Natives of Canada can witness bison occupying a niche not unlike that of ages past. Finally, intertribal collaboration in Canada lags behind that in the United States. While coordination between the government and local First Nations occurs, for many Canadian Natives their bison restoration experience is quite singular since no indigenous umbrella organization coalesces the effort.

While the discussion so far has concerned efforts to restore the northern bison, a significant effort has been made for the plains bison in Canada as well. This bison restoration effort warrants consideration and comparison, though a lack of pan-Native coordination is readily apparent. Nothing like the ITBC exists in Canada and subsequently Canada's indigenous bison restoration effort remains quite fractured. Nonetheless, five case studies of Native bison programs offer fertile ground for comparing Canadian efforts with those of the United States. Ranging from north to south, the Kikino Métis Settlement, Whitefish Lake First Nation, Okanese First Nation, Piikani (Northern Piegan) First Nation, and Blood First Nation offer insights into the plains bison recovery underway in Canada over the past quarter century.

Located in Alberta northeast of Edmonton, the Kikino Métis bison enterprise commenced in 1978 with the acquisition of twenty-four plains bison from Elk Island National Park. The Kikino Council sought to establish a herd on its landholdings so as to provide employment opportunities and utilize a land base that lent itself well to bush pasture. Thus, the Kikino bison restoration effort began under circumstances different than most Native American attempts in the United States where traditional spiritual and cultural affinity, far more than economics, provided the impetus for bringing back the buffalo. However, in the case of the Métis, a people born out of the mixed-blood relations steeped in the fur trade, economic use of the bison resource to enter into the larger economy is quite traditional.[30]

Regardless of motives, the Kikino Métis proved themselves able bison stewards, as their herd grew to 167 breeding cows by 1999. They utilized three sections of grazing, but the lower-quality bush pasture necessitated supplemental feeding, including grain for younger animals. Meat production encouraged herd managers to use grains when supplementing. The settlement sells or donates all bulls except those maintained for breeding stock each year. For the most part, the bison managers utilized a hands-off approach and offered some guided hunts during the 1990s. Ceremony was not part of the harvests whether during the hunts or in the butchering to provide senior citizens with meat.[31] Comparing the Kikino Métis bison program with that of Native Americans below the border demonstrates that economics has played a greater role in the development of the Kikino Métis herd. This raises a question: whether the Métis's intricate involvement in the fur trade created a more rationalist economic value for bison than that associated with other indigenous people.

The Whitefish Lake First Nation provides one possible answer to this question. Located quite close to Kikino, the Plains Cree also possess a fur trade history, though not to the extent of the Métis. Much like Kikino, Whitefish Lake used bush pasture for its herd, which started from fifty plains animals bought from the Alexander band in 1991 though originating in Elk Island National Park. By 1999, the herd totaled more than three hundred bison ranging on four sections, with plans for expanding grazing area by 200 percent. The operation easily paid for itself through the sale of excess stock and meat. Donations of excess animals occurred early in the herd's residency at Whitefish Lake, but the band council minimized them so as to maximize profits. Herd managers supplemented feed about six months of the year and concerned themselves with meat production. A proposal to bring in northern bison was met with enthusiasm by some elements of the population due to the slightly better meat production potential vis-à-vis plains bison. This quite possibly would balance out in a couple generations as morphotype developed in alignment with environmental constraints, although one herd manager remarked that the northern bison looked like a "great feedlot animal."[32]

Yet despite the fact that bison managers make it clear that "this ranch is a business," some Cree community members hold the bison range to be sacred. Herd steward Darryl Steinhauer remarked in 1999 that the "community people have a fascination with bison." Many mornings he observed one tribal elder performing rituals at the bison pasture, leaving burnt sweetgrass braid offerings as a reminder of the ceremony. Also, people gathered rocks from the bison pasture to use in their sweat lodges. Steinhauer explained: "This is a live relationship, as Natives we respect these sites."[33] These spiritual and nostalgic overtures toward the bison reflect the same commitments witnessed in many American Indian bison restoration programs, but the overshadowing concern with economics here is the exception rather than the rule.

The Okanese First Nation located northeast of Regina, Saskatchewan, marks a departure from the Whitefish Lake First Nation and Kikino Métis Settlement in that its bison restoration effort resembles that of an ITBC member tribe more than do other Canadian efforts. The Plains Cree community acquired a pair of bison in 1996 from a local rancher, and the next year augmented the acquisition with additional animals from Elk Island, a Métis settlement, and later even from the Cheyenne River Lakota. The herd increased to thirty animals in 2003 and grazed on 500 acres. The bison stewards minimally managed the herd and some years the environment did not require feed supplementation. The tribe committed to bison restoration with a balance of cultural and economic motives, and many of the early advocates came from the cattle industry, which offered them a standard of comparison for working with bison. Spiritual ceremonies accompanied all harvests, and the program contributed bison for cultural activities such as the Sun Dance. The First Nations also planned to initiate a bison-based health and diet program.[34]

The features surrounding the Okanese bison restoration program in many ways equate with those of ITBC tribes. However, one other important consideration emerges from the Okanese story. In Canada, Native bison stewards have utilized the Canadian Bison Association or in Saskatchewan, the Saskatchewan Bison Association as their institutional affiliation. In Saskatchewan, at least fifteen First Nations or Native owners ran bison in early 2003. Out of those ranks, a nascent movement started to take shape in 2002 and 2003 in which First Nations, sometimes disenchanted with the commercial bison industry, started talking about forming a Native organization of bison producers sensitive to the cultural aspects of bison restoration. Thus, the foundation for a northern version of the ITBC may have started to take form on the prairies of Saskatchewan even though at the time, little call for a vast bison landscape existed. It's worth noting that another nascent organization, similar in size and function, formed in Manitoba: the Manitoba Elk and Bison Council. The Council organized as early as 1999 but continued to define its mission while remaining far behind the development of the ITBC.[35]

Near Head-Smashed-In buffalo jump in southwestern Alberta, the Piikani (Northern Piegan) First Nation runs a herd of bison established in the early 1980s with about thirty head acquired from Parks Canada. The band promoted its bison population for the spiritual connection, and the herd never grew large, rising to just above fifty members in 2003. Ceremonies accompanied all harvests, and the tribe sold excess animals. The herd grazed over 800 acres and required some supplementation during environmentally difficult times. However, the tribe practiced a hands-off style in interacting with the herd. The bison steward, Edwin Small Legs, has managed the herd with a high level of support from both the tribal council and the community.[36] In short, the Piikani program mirrors those south of the forty-ninth parallel with the exception that it does not enjoy the networked support of an organization akin to the ITBC.

Sometimes, however, conditions simply required the Natives to go it alone. Such was the case for Harley Frank, the former chief of the Blood Nation, who tried to bring bison back to his people in 1992. Raised on the Blood Reserve in an agricultural family near the American border in southwest Alberta, the idea of reintroducing bison to his people became fixed in Frank's mind in 1987. During that year, he found an *iniskim*, a bison-shaped rock of great importance to members of the Blackfeet Confederation. Reflecting much on the spiritual and material benefits of bison during the day, Frank had a vivid dream one night showing him a bison skull buried on his property. He went with his children to the spot of the dream, and, sure enough, his daughter found a horn that led them to uncover the skull. The experience stuck with Frank, and five years later he ran for tribal council on the platform that he would return the bison to the area.[37] However, in many ways, the romance of the story ends at that point.

After winning election, Frank traveled to South Dakota in 1993 and purchased eighty yearling bison from a large private ranch. Upon his return to
Canada, protestors met his caravan. The protestors were Blood, and tensions
ran high as counter-protestors also met the caravan. At one point, protestors
lay across the road to stop passage of the bison, but elder women from the
Buffalo Women Society, hearkening back to the great historical contributions
of women in saving bison, simply brushed the bodies aside as the Royal Canadian Mounted Police watched. Protestors threatened Frank, shoved him,
and even spat on him. Frank asked for passage from the Mounties, and his
supporters secured his route. With that, the bison came back to the Blood
Reserve. Yet, within a year, Frank lost election and bought out half the herd.
He provided stewardship in the bison restoration effort on his own by keeping forty animals, which he raised according to hands-off principles. After
all, for Frank, he stated, "It's more about the spiritual sense."[38]

In the narrative of bison restoration by North America's indigenous people
Frank's story is quite exceptional. The reasons behind the tensions were
fear of change and of the allocation of resources from existing areas into
the bison project. Some of the Blood Nation simply was not ready to bring
back buffalo. Frank's perseverance in bringing back the bison against un-
believable opposition mirrors that of Indian people in overcoming the difficult conditions of hundreds of years of Euro-American or Euro-Canadian
oppression. For Frank's story, however, there is a happy denouement. In
1995, Frank put down one of his bison cows during birthing because she
broke her hip. He delivered the calf, which subsequently took him to be her
mother. From then on, the two became virtually inseparable. Harley Frank
communed with the buffalo virtually every day he remained at home. He
also returned to the tribal council in 2004.[39]

Comparing the Canadian and U.S. bison restoration efforts by indigenous
people produces a few salient points. First, the Native American effort to
restore bison knows no geopolitical boundaries—efforts exist on both sides
of the forty-ninth parallel. Second, government collaboration can result in
a free-roaming bison herd, though sparsely populated northern Canada is
less problematic as a buffalo commons than are more populous areas to
the south. Third, Native wildlife stewardship can offer effective ecosystem
management. Fourth, the effects of the fur trade may still determine rational
economic behavior in contrast to substantive, non-market related behavior:

Natives more intertwined with the fur trade concern themselves more with the financial rewards of bison restoration than do non-fur-trading tribes. It's worthy noting, however, that bison-restoring tribes of today that were less involved with the centuries-old fur-bearing animal-skin trade probably had life ways based entirely on bison—they were people of the plains not of the woodlands. Fifth, the ITBC lends synergy to bison restoration in the United States. Canada's effort lags behind in unity because no umbrella organization coordinates or represents First Nations buffalo restoration. Indeed, the legitimacy conferred by an intertribal group supporting a bison-raising effort could well have helped Harley Frank's cause as he sought to bring the bison back to his people.

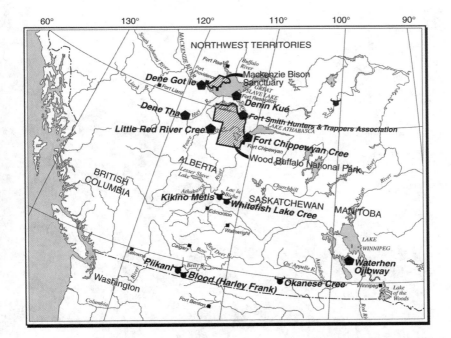

Map 3: Select First Nations and Canadian Bison.
Source: Roe, *North American Buffalo* appendix map.

KEY

Federal Park/Refuge
w/ Native Mgmt. of Bison

Native Mgmt. Group
of/with bison.

Native Owned Bison Herd

Fig. 26: Alex Ayotte, Charles Allard Jr., and Howard Douglas (left to right) ensured the negotiation, roundup, and purchase of Pablo's bison to bring plains bison back to Canada. Photo by Norman K. Luxton. Courtesy Montana Historical Society, Helena (1908).

Fig. 27: The northern bison and its habitat (1999). Photo by author.

Fig. 28: The Little Red River Cree participate in bison management on federal lands. Photo by author (1999).

Fig. 29: The Denin Kué quarantine facility near Fort Resolution, Northwest Territories. Photo by author (1999).

Order Number: 3903

seven day promise

Jason Rabant
516 Center Street

Huron, OH USA 44839
Day: 440-315-4414 Eve:
Fax:
Email:

TOTAL DEPOSIT: 0.00
Pre-Pay Tender:

Borders Books & Music
4314 Milan Road
Sandusky Mall
Sandusky, Oh 44870
Phone: 419-626-1173
Fax: 419-626-1145

QTY	TITLE	AUTHOR	PRICE*	CODE	PUB.	TITLE NUMBER	T/E
1	Buffalo Nation: Amer	Zontek, Ken	19.95	QP	Universi	0803299222	N RESERVED

Pickup at BORDERS BOOKS & MUSIC

*Publisher Prices And Times May Vary Due To Availability

BORDE... **order form**

4/12

SY

FIRELANDS AUDUBON@
AOL.COM

▶ Date eligible titles will
for pickup (mark X if n

▶ Bookseller initials

Pickup date is the same da
the item will be available
week later. For example: Or
Tuesday at 5:00 PM.

The Promise Guarantee ter
apply only to orders place
store, and are void if then
order, marked as "RESERVE
the reverse side of this doc
subject to verification.

Call or stop by the store
pickup date. If your order
store within seven days
present this form to the ca

...red at time of redemption)

...card. If your order qualifies
...offer, present this card to the
...s picked up.

...as available from our primary distributors, ordered for in-
...e for pickup within seven days, then present your Borders
...d have been in our store, available for pickup. Please note
...later. The seven-day calculation excludes Thanksgiving,
...ments are delayed as a result of a natural disaster or other
...maximum of 30 days. The store is not obligated to notify you
...le store anytime after 5:00 PM on the " available for pickup
...order will be free (up to a maximum of $50.00 per order). To
...ase visit the Information Desk. Offer applies to orders placed
...ate Sales orders, and Special Orders.

Borders Cashiers: Ring items, select S1, select S4,
scan or enter certificate #0336783200000000,
enter price of item (or $50, whichever is less), and
proceed.

Borders Express Cashiers: Scan or key ISBN on
each title, enter retail price of each title, and use
Item. Discount and Discount Code #31 to
discount the free item for the full amount.
Validate the Special Order form.

...in stores only. Excludes not-yet-published...

1590117000000000000

Fig. 30: Field hand Lester Antoine,
Chief Greg Nyuli, and biologist
Darren Campbell represent the
Dene Got ie and Integrated Resources Management Team in managing the Mackenzie Bison Sanctuary. Photo by author (1999).

Fig. 31: Bison steward Darrell Bellerose and one of the Kikino Métis bison. Photo by author (1999).

Fig. 32: Harley Frank and his companion bison (1999). Photo by author.

7. Conclusion

Contemporary Indian people have debated the issue of how bison can be
sacred on one hand, yet still be used in a way that can boost their economy.
It could be argued that both points of view can be achieved if done with
the proper amount of moderation, respect for, and ethical treatment of,
the buffalo.

Jim Garrett (2001)

Perhaps the most striking example of the indigenous effort to restore the
bison landscape comes from the range of the northern bison. When the
various layers of government and local constituents join with Native people
as advocates for the buffalo nation, then free-ranging wild bison can exist.
Already, this occurs in northern Canada. Many Native Americans hope that
it can occur to the south as well, all the way to the southern plains. They
long for the opportunity to bring back the bison.

Optimism exists in Indian country for bison restoration, and the accelerated acquisition of bison and bison range in the 1990s offers positive proof.
Indeed, much of this book hinges on dates in the 1870s or 1880s when the
bison was saved from extinction and dates in the 1970s, 1980s, or 1990s
when bison herds were restored on reservations. However, for many Indian
people, these dates possess little meaning in bison history. Rather, for them
the relatively recent births of white buffalo are far more significant to the
cosmology of North American Native people. "Miracle" became the name
of the first of these calves born, which occurred in 1994. The first Native
American pilgrim arrived less than twenty-four hours later and seventy-five
thousand other visitors appeared in the first two years of the calf's existence. Native people everywhere interpreted the event differently, with one

Lakota medicine man likening the birth to the "second coming of Christ." Two years later, two more white bison calves entered the world in the town of Michigan, North Dakota, and a fourth white youngster, born on the Pine Ridge Reservation, joined them in 1996. Regardless of interpretations, for Native Americans the prevailing theme suggested by these births was the dawning of a new age, one often symbolized by the return of the buffalo nation.[1]

Two features of the white buffalo's birth require explanation. First, whether or not the buffalo is a true albino and changes colors as it matures does not diminish the spirituality of the birth for Native American spiritual leaders. In fact, for the Lakota, the color phase change is paramount, symbolizing the color changes of the White Buffalo Calf Woman who originally made the covenant between the buffalo and Lakota nations. Second, statistical significance is important. White buffalo births occur very infrequently; therefore, the increase in such births most likely reflects growth in the bison population, a key step in bison restoration.[2]

Many Native American spiritual leaders feel the time is right for the return of their bison brethren. As demonstrated by Canada's return of the northern bison, other entities must join with the indigenous people to effectuate the return of the buffalo. This requires inculcating the idea that a buffalo landscape is a good thing, and it probably also requires acceptance on three planes—aesthetic, ecological, and economic—across a wide spectrum of government agencies and elements of the population.

The first point, aesthetics, finds easy acceptance within society. Bison are an icon of American and Canadian society. They appear as government symbols such as the Department of Interior's seal in the United States and the Royal Canadian Mounted Police's seal in Canada or as cultural phenomena such as team mascots, for example, the Buffalo Bills of the National Football League. National parks feature bison. The public outcry over the Yellowstone slaughter occurred because of the displeasure felt by many people at the sight of agents gunning down an American icon. The Academy Award–winning film *Dances With Wolves* (1990) featured bison, and the buffalo landscape helped the film win the award for best cinematography. Few people of any ethnic background appear to oppose the notion that bison should run on the North American landscape at least in some capacity.[3]

Moreover, some key factors indicate that some influential non-Native citizenry seek a return of the buffalo. Most notably, Ted Turner, the cable news mogul, accumulated a virtual bison empire over the course of the 1990s, vowing that aesthetics and ecology reigned as his primary concerns, with economics second. By 1996, his ranches, equivalent in extent to those of the ITBC, ran 12,300 bison on 1.3 million acres spread across Montana, New Mexico, and Nebraska. His land total equaled that of the Nature Conservancy, a group committed to aesthetic and ecological health, which itself boasted a bison restoration project. Centered on its 37,000-acre Tallgrass Prairie Preserve in Pawhuska, Oklahoma, the project's land stewards expect the original herd of 300 to reach 2,000. Turner and the Nature Conservancy achieve notoriety because of their ubiquity, but they certainly do not stand alone. For example, a former Montana rancher forged an organization in the late 1980s and 1990s called the Big Open Project. The project, originated by Bob Scott, aimed to restore 39,000 square kilometers in central Montana to bison range. Also, the Great Plains Restoration Council created a broad coalition of individuals and groups as part of its Million Acre Project to restore the buffalo landscape on a million acres as a first step toward a broader restoration on the western plains.[4]

These commitments warrant analysis in light of a statement once made by Lakota Chief Luther Standing Bear:

> The white man does not understand America. He is too far removed from its formative processes. The roots of the tree of his life have not yet grasped the rock and soil. The white man is still troubled by primitive fears; he still has in his consciousness the perils of this frontier continent. The man from Europe is still a foreigner and an alien. And he still hates the man who questioned his path across the continent. But in the Indian the spirit of the land is still vested: it will be until other men are able to divine and meet its rhythm. Men must be born and reborn to belong. Their bodies must be formed of the dust of their forefathers' bones.[5]

Perhaps the fear has subsided and longevity on the continent facilitates a desire to enjoy the Native landscape. Will others join the Native people in sufficient numbers to allow the buffalo to roam?

People concerned with ecology often banter about the benefit of bringing buffalo back to the landscape. Observers utilizing anecdotal research often cite that when Europeans arrived they found a bountiful landscape rich in flora and fauna managed by Native American stewards—the buffalo landscape of the plains contained a rich fertile sod that became the breadbasket of the world. As part of the hegemonic process, agriculture and ranching replaced the buffalo. Hence, much of the debate about the ecology of the plains rests on whether or not cattle can graze and retain a healthy range like bison. Apparently, cattle can graze sustainably on the North American grasslands. However, they require intensive management. Much of cattle's detrimental effect on the landscape stems from its habituation around water sources, which requires mitigation to avoid "ecological costs." As journalist William Stolzenburg stated in a 2000 article: "No longer is the blame for the beaten range to be pinned solely on the four-legged beast of burden. Rather, the solution ultimately lies with the two-legged keeper walking behind it."[6] However, it is cattle's comparatively high maintenance cost on the North American range that has encouraged many individuals to concede that bison better fit the range, and perhaps the finances of range utilization as well.

Regarding the economics of bison, one rancher stated it quite clearly: "What it comes down to is this: bison are half the work and twice the money." Thus, many ranchers have jumped from cattle into bison. By 1993, bison ranching had become the top growth industry in Alberta. In 1995, bison meat fetched twice the value on the market as beef. That same year, the North American Bison Cooperative (not to be confused with the ITBC) opened markets in Europe and across the United States for USDA-inspected bison meat. Thus, the following summer, when North Dakota ranchers lost money on cattle sales, they doubled their money on bison returns. Such statistics spurred the commercial bison industry. By 1998, 300,000 bison existed around the globe. The number grew to more than 350,000 in less than two years and inspired projections of one million buffalo by 2010.[7]

Nonetheless, in much of the western plains, the benefits of the bison industry cannot save economies dwindling as a result of the mechanization of agriculture, low prices, overproduction, environmental degradation, and the globalization of agricultural competition. Geographers Frank and Deborah Popper characterized the suffering human populations in the western Dakotas, Nebraska, Kansas, Oklahoma, and Texas along with those in eastern Montana, Wyoming, Colorado, and New Mexico as being in "land distress," meaning the loss of 10 percent of the population, fewer than four people per square mile, a median age in excess of thirty-five years, and a poverty rate higher than 20 percent. In 1987, the Poppers published their data and added that perhaps the western plains would function best as a federally sponsored buffalo commons where people could live in a sustainable environment. People of the plains initially responded quite negatively to the Popper's buffalo commons proposal. However, over the years, attitudes softened, and by 1999, Frank Popper announced to the ITBC that "the Buffalo Commons is happening, more creatively and less federally." He was referring to the piecemeal buffalo commons effectively being patched together by reservations, government parks and grasslands, environmental organization landholdings, and bison-friendly real estate tycoons. In 2000, Frank Popper went on to call the commons a "done deal" as the forces working toward coalescence around a bison landscape advanced.[8]

One theme that pervades some bison restoration literature is that easterners saved the bison through their efforts to establish parks and refuges for the buffalo. The famed work of characters such as William Hornaday, Teddy Roosevelt, and their colleagues in the American Bison Society do indicate such a trend. Careful analysis of these restoration efforts, however, reveals that the easterners' restoration concept did not embrace a widespread bison landscape, unlike that recently envisioned by the Poppers. Rather, these bison advocates sought a conservation component to their vision of a progressive landscape dominated by Euro-American industry and agribusiness, a place where individuals could take respite in a countryside that preserved remnants of the indigenous flora and fauna. Indeed, they relegated this sample of former America to sites for tourism and safari zones for recreational and trophy hunting.[9]

Further examination shows that these eastern efforts ultimately capitalized on the work of westerners, such as those saviors of bison who propagated the species from its nadir. As well, the Native Americans involved in this early and ongoing restoration always maintained a vision of a free-roaming bison landscape, and they did all they could to implement their vision on as wide a scale as possible. Thus, westerners not only saved the bison, but kept alive the idea of providing the aegis for bison to roam as bison.

Parallels to these East-versus-West origins for restoration more than a century ago have also occurred in the recent past. Thus, the Poppers from New Jersey provided intellectual support for a buffalo commons, Ted Turner from Georgia continued acquiring lands and buffalo for bison ranching, and the Nature Conservancy based in Virginia augmented the effort with the acquisition of land and bison in the West. But meanwhile, western Native Americans were quietly concentrating their work to realize the buffalo commons they had envisioned for generations, a vision shared by many mainstream Americans in contemporary society. For example, Lakota scholar Edward Valandra offered his quite focused data that suggested the possibilities for a bison commons in western South Dakota as a vanguard for a larger buffalo commons of the western plains. An expert on indigenous landscape restoration, Valandra claimed four criteria were necessary for a buffalo commons: sufficient acreage on the order of at least 10,000 to 20,000 acres; land available outside reservation boundaries; an intact ecosystem, preferably a watershed; and an area traditionally habituated by bison. For Valandra, the nineteen counties of western South Dakota present the opportunity to synthesize these four criteria for a buffalo commons. Private entrepreneurs own 60 percent of the region, with federal government agencies including the Bureau of Land Management and Department of Agriculture, proprietor of the national grasslands, dominating the other 40 percent with some small area under state control. Moreover, the average ranch size in the region stands at more than 3,000 acres. This would facilitate the consolidation of significant landholdings with minimal land transfer legalities involved given the comparatively few sales required to aggregate the land.[10]

Moreover, the western South Dakota counties possess a recent history of fairly severe land distress. Population decreased from 1970 to 2000 in fourteen of the nineteen counties. Thirteen of the nineteen counties contained fewer than four people per square mile by 2000. The average age of ranch owners exceeded fifty-two years, and the region's population decreased by fifty thousand young people in the 1990s. Soil scientists contend that soil distress due to erosion plagues more than a third of the counties. Meantime, the poverty rate had risen to nearly 20 percent by the end of the 1990s, while one-fourth of the ranches made less than $10,000 income annually at the turn of the new millennium. For Valandra, this data indicated a "bison conducive" area ready for reintroduction. Valandra's fellow Lakota scholar Professor Joseph Dupris, a direct descendant of Mary and Frederick Dupuis, has reinforced Valandra's stance by explaining the necessity for bison programs to function as public service venues. He stated: "The tribe needs to make a commitment to the people at the same time as the buffalo."[11]

Another attempt to facilitate the bison commons came with the 1999 "Tribal Alternative," proposed for the northern Great Plains management plan's environmental impact statement process. Written by Jim Garrett, the tribal alternative possessed four salient points: the elimination of the present grazing lease permit system; the adoption of native species and a bison refuge system philosophy along with implementation of the refuge system; the adoption of co-management responsibilities between the U.S. Forest Service and tribal colleges; and the adoption of the grasslands as tribal college field research facilities and laboratories.[12] Notably, the plan contained elements not unlike those in successful programs in Canada, where First Nations assist in policy-making and the management of bison landscapes. Ultimately, the Department of Agriculture did not endorse the plan, although it gave it consideration.

All the while reservations on the western plains began creating their own comparatively larger-scaled buffalo grazing ranges, awaiting a possible future conjunction with other bison areas so as to form a greater grasslands bison commons. These reservations already met the majority of Valandra's criteria even without extending the bison range off the reservation. For example, the Crow tribe built their herd in the 1990s to well over one thousand animals on 22,000 acres. To the north, the Assiniboine–Gros Ventres of Fort Belknap grew their herd of more than four hundred animals on the same amount of acreage. To the east, the Cheyenne River Lakota increased their tribe's herd to more than two thousand animals grazing more than 30,000 acres, with the idea of creating a tribal park. Their fellow Lakota from the Rosebud Reservation committed their reservation to the same type of large-scale operation and offered to become part of a conglomerate bison commons with grasslands, parks, and private landholdings, just as envisioned by Valandra.[13]

Native Americans have shown the resolve to bring back the bison unilaterally if necessary, but the likelihood of success in restoring the largest possible buffalo commons has hinged on collaboration between both Native and non-Native entities. Indeed, the contemporary efforts of these Native westerners could stand alone like the initial bison-saving efforts of their ancestors in 1870s and 1880s until federally ordered land allotments ended any hope of a continuous relationship with relatively free-ranging bison. The cooperation of other groups better ensures the restoration of the bison landscape. For example, Ted Turner owns 172,000 acres in western South Dakota, which indicates the possible area that mergers of bison territory could ensnare. The Turner land managers have a positive record for working with Indians. Regarding his work in New Mexico with Turner's workers, Richard Archuleta of Taos commented in 1999: "The Turner people are great." At the same time, a consortium of ranchers in the Great Plains Buffalo Association endorses the reintroduction of buffalo as wildlife. Of course, environmental organizations such as the National Wildlife Federation, Defenders of Wildlife, and the Nature Conservancy, with millions of members, all participate in ecological restoration involving bison as a keystone species.[14]

Regarding Native and non-Native cooperation toward aboriginal management of bison, a significant development in the United States began to occur in 1994. In that year, the Confederated Salish and Kootenai Tribes capitalized on an innovative interpretation of the Indian Self-Determination Act (1974), identifying a federal government concession that would allow tribes to participate in the management of Department of the Interior resources on tribal lands possessing geographic, historic, or cultural significance. The fauna and flora—namely, the buffalo—of the National Bison Range, an enclave within the reservation, easily qualified as "significant" to the leadership of the Salish and Kootenai. They argued that they could accommodate the intent of Congress with respect to federal wildlife refuges. They also made other important contentions including these three: the taking of 18,500 acres from the Flathead Reservation for conversion into the National Bison Range contradicted the 1855 Hellgate Treaty allotting the land to the Salish and Kootenai Tribes, and, therefore, they held at least a legal historic relationship to the land; over a century and a quarter ago tribal members such as Walking Coyote and Sabine caught and successfully increased the ancestral herd of the Range's bison until land expropriation forced Michel Pablo to sell the herd; and, finally, the Confederated Salish and Kootenai Tribes already possessed, by 1994, a distinguished record for environmental stewardship on the reservation. Thus, the tribes launched a publicity campaign arguing that tribal management for the Range's bison was sensible and that supporters of the movement should "join the herd."[15]

By 2004, the effort toward indigenous management of the National Bison Range successfully resulted in an Annual Funding Agreement draft between the United States Fish and Wildlife Service and the Confederated Salish and Kootenai Tribes. The agreement went into a comment period late in 2004 with consideration of adoption scheduled for 2005. The draft's provisions included the retention by the Fish and Wildlife Service of the ownership and management authority over the lands of the National Bison Range. The Salish and Kootenai would meanwhile perform activities in several "categories," most notably, the biological program and visitor services.[16] If adopted, the agreement would fall short of the management latitude afforded First Nations in Canada at the Mackenzie Bison Sanctuary and Wood Buffalo National Park, but certainly the agreement would comprise a monumental step toward Native input in the management of bison in the public domain. The implications of such acknowledged stewardship could loom large in the potential conversion of any federal lands into a bison commons, especially those immediately adjacent to reservations where range restoration is a priority.

At the same time, scientists and Native Americans find themselves in agreement over land management. Bison acting as bison, and not being manipulated like cattle, ultimately benefit the landscape. This marriage of indigenous culture and Western science offers a powerful alternative to current land-use practices in much of the former buffalo country, particularly in the western plains. The key lies in allowing the bison to live as native bison in a natural setting where they can roam with the rhythms provided by their habitat. Valerius Geist posits this notable insight: "Conservation requires the preservation of environments that continually challenge the adaptations of the species conserved." Otherwise, deterioration occurs. Other scientists, such as Mary Meagher and Jim Shaw, also warn of the deleterious effects of intensive management and restriction of movement, which "eventually convert a wild species into another form of livestock." For their part, Native Americans offer the same view, with slightly varied diction. Louis Larose explains: "One thing we know, Grandfather meant for bison to be wild. We must constantly remind ourselves that we must maintain its nature and do everything in our power to do that."[17] Carla Rae Brings Plenty adds: "The buffalo are the real stewards of this land, the caretakers of all animals, plants and people. The buffalo have been and always will be, better for this land than any 'slow elk' (cattle) will ever be. Many Native people were killed trying to get this point across a hundred years ago."[18]

As we noted in the first chapter, two debates still linger, constituting a virtual trial of the Native American role as stewards of the landscape. The first debate rages over the Pleistocene extinctions. Overkill advocates contend that North America's aboriginal inhabitants destroyed the vast majority of the megafauna through overharvesting. Overchill advocates maintain that environmental change spelled doom for the megafauna and that, at most, Paleo-Americans slightly accelerated a foregone conclusion: the megafauna could not survive the climatic changes associated with the onset of the Holocene epoch. The second debate considers the role of Native Americans in annihilating the bison population during the nineteenth century. Scholars and supporters who argue that Indians killed off the buffalo point to the high volume of the robe trade and pemmican industries and that the robe trade focused on killing females, thereby exponentially reducing the reproductive capability of the bison herds. The opposition to this overharvesting argument maintains that millions of bison continued roaming the American West until the arrival of the American buffalo runners following the Civil War. These men destroyed the last of the buffalo herds.

However, the future should introduce a third argument over Native American land stewardship and bison conservation: what was the role of Native Americans in bringing back the bison? Suffice it to say that they have led the way in bison restoration. From the capture of the original herds to their growth in a free-ranging environment, North America's Native people have sought to maintain the buffalo nation. Moreover, Indians have worked to allow their animal brethren to fulfill their inherent tendencies and to share in the dynamics of the landscape. In part, as well, this acknowledgment that Native Americans began saving the buffalo even before its demise ought to vindicate them from guilt cast on them by proponents of the argument that Native Americans caused the destruction of the bison. After all, Native people have demonstrated through their actions that they always sought a home for the buffalo to roam, a landscape capable of again nurturing the prolific herds. Indians have demonstrated phenomenal cultural perseverance—spanning more than 125 years—in reinstating the bison once again as part of a sacred symbiosis.

Fig. 33: Bison visionaries Jim Garrett, Fred DuBray, and Rocke Afraid of Hawk (adults in back row, left to right) share a bison harvest ceremony with Lakota youth. © William Campbell, Homefire Productions, Inc.

Fig. 34: "Big Medicine," a white buffalo that lived on the National Bison Range in the mid-twentieth century, presaged the birth of several white calves near the close of the century. Courtesy Montana Historical Society, Helena (undated).

(Opposite top) Fig. 35: Floyd Fisher reconciled his cattle experience with his affinity for the buffalo to become the Northern Cheyenne bison steward. Photo by author (1999).

(Opposite bottom) Fig. 36: Travelers through Indian country find increasing numbers of tribal herds as well as private herds, such as that found here on the Flathead Reservation (1999). Photo by author.

(Above) Fig. 37: Flathead Reservation sign, 2004. Photo by author.

8. Cheyenne River Lakota: Photo Essay

Buffalo Nation, we need you. We're depending on you. We're depending on you again. Today is a sacred day. So, Grandfather, hear my prayers.

Rocke Afraid of Hawk (*Return of the Native*, 1995)

Image 1: "Welcome" provides an apt description for the bison on the Cheyenne River Lakota Reservation, South Dakota. The presence of the bison there symbolizes, at least to some degree, the answer to the prayers of the participants in the Ghost Dance ceremony: the restoration of the buffalo nation, Pte Oyate. Photo by author (2004).

Image 2: The Cheyenne River Reservation contains the largest Native American buffalo herd on the continent, with more than three thousand animals running on approximately 40,000 acres.[1] This reservation offers one of the few places where the observer can witness a teasing glimpse of the past when bison herds once stretched to the horizon. Photo by author (2004).

Image 3: The origins of the Cheyenne River herd lie in the 1880s when members of the Dupuis family brought calves into a Lakota hunting camp similar to that depicted here. Family tradition attributes both the impetus and success for the bison recovery effort to Good Elk Woman, also known as Mary Ann Dupuis or Marian Dupree, a contemporary of these Lakota women.[2] Photo courtesy of the South Dakota State Historical Society—State Archives (undated).

Image 4: The Dupuis family nurtured its bison herd on a ranch along the Cheyenne River just a few miles downstream from this similar contemporary settlement located on Cherry Creek.[3] Like the residents of this area, the Dupuis family also clung to a traditional lifestyle as the country around them was transformed. Photo courtesy of the South Dakota State Historical Society—State Archives (ca. 1880s).

Image 5: The paramount importance of the bison to the Dupuis (Dupree) family becomes obvious when one views the gates to the family cemetery on the ranch where the bison herd first found its refuge on the reservation. The three figures most intimately connected with bringing the calves to the reservation, Good Elk Woman, Frederick Dupuis, and Pete Dupuis, lie buried beneath the prairie grasses on their graves found here.[4] Photo by author (2004).

Image 6: A direct descendant of Good Elk Woman and Frederick Dupuis, Jim Garrett stands on the breaks of the Cheyenne River on the Dupree Ranch where his ancestors began saving the bison. Garrett helped complete the circle of bison restoration through his efforts to implement a bison stewardship program at the tribal community college and bring a small bison herd to a reservation school district located along Cherry Creek.[5] Photo by author (2004).

Image 7: The Cheyenne River bison left the reservation under the aegis of Scotty Philip and his Cheyenne wife, Sarah (Laribee) Philip, in 1901. The herd prospered on the Philip Buffalo Ranch and became seed stock for several succeeding herds, most notably that of Custer State Park in 1914.[6] Photo courtesy of the South Dakota State Historical Society—State Archives (undated).

Image 8: These bison in Custer State Park share virtually the same bloodline as those of the Cheyenne River Reservation. According to reservation sources, a donation of bison originating in Custer State Park brought buffalo back to the Cheyenne River Lakota circa 1975 and formed the nucleus of the present reservation herd.[7] This acquisition of public herd bison by the tribe heralded much of the growth in Native American bison programs across the West. Photo by author (2004).

Image 9: The National Park Service (NPS) has facilitated the resurrection of the buffalo nation in Indian Country. Bison donations from Wind Cave National Park, Theodore Roosevelt National Park, and Badlands National Park (pictured here) have augmented the Cheyenne River herd. In fact, a full circle of bison on the reservation can be traced through the following route via the NPS: Dupuis's to Philip (1901) to Custer State Park (1914) to Fort Niobrara Wildlife Refuge (1935/1937) to Theodore Roosevelt National Park (1956) and back to Cheyenne River (ca. 1975).[8] Any possible future "buffalo commons" will require such collaboration between Native and non-Native, government and nongovernment sectors. Photo by author (2004).

Image 10: Whether or not the bison can be restored to Indian country is no longer a question. Successful stewardship produces ample herd growth, as this stocky calf nursing on Lakota pasture demonstrates. Rather, the present dilemma is how best to bring the bison back with "dignity" while meeting the demands of the modern world, symbolized by the fence in the background. Photo by author (2004).

Image 11: Cheyenne River Lakota tribal member and Intertribal Bison Cooperative (ITBC) President Fred DuBray states: "Each tribe must decide how best to restore the buffalo to tribal lands." The Cheyenne River tribal council elected to place control of its bison program into the tribe's Game, Fish, and Parks Department. Thus, the stewardship of the herd fell on the shoulders of director Dennis Rousseau (at right, white shirt), pictured here with members of his staff. Two to four tribal members work with the herd on a full-time basis.[9] Photo by author (2004).

Image 12: The tribe made their intentions clear regarding the importance of its bison herd when it bought the 22,000 acre VE Ranch (seen here) as the heart of its bison range. In alignment with traditional beliefs of landscape conservation and communalism, the Lakota created a tribal park and commenced several projects that were complementary to bison reintroduction and integral to prairie restoration, such as the black-footed ferret release program and preventing the eradication of the prairie dog.[10] Photo by author (2004).

Image 13: The reservation also contains other bison pastures, such as the "lower pasture" depicted here along the banks of Lake Oahe. However, acquiring range for the bison herd costs money and vexes herd managers and tribal decision-makers as they seek to maintain a "hands-off" bison program to the extent possible while attempting to make the bison program self-funding. By 2004, despite large debt from the purchase of the VE Ranch, the program experienced a net profits through live sales, meat sales, tourism, and hunting.[11] Photo by author (2004).

Image 14: In some years, calf sales alone have financed the herd, especially when mild winters negate the need for any supplemental feeding and no land debt exists. Meanwhile, live bison prices fluctuate wildly from as low as a few hundred dollars to $2,000 per head. Environment and market conditions therefore produce tenuous profit margins from live sales, at best. Thus, the tribe seeks other sources of cash income such as guided hunts. Either of these two bulls could fetch $2,000 in a guided hunt for a client who is neither a reservation resident nor tribal member, and $1,000 for a reservation resident or tribal member.[12] Photo by author (2004).

Image 15: The Cheyenne River Sioux Tribe Game, Fish & Parks Department—Tourism Division also offers tours of the tribal park that feature visits to the bison herd found anywhere within the confines of the 22,000-acre enclosure. In 2004, the tours required at least eight participants, with the cost starting at $36 per person. Tourists received packaged options including interacting not only with the bison but with the tribe's elk and wild horse populations.[13] Photo by author (2004).

Image 16: The tribe's live sales and meat sales necessitate roundups and manipulation of the herd. Native visionaries of bison restoration grudgingly acknowledge the need to handle the bison. The tribe's bison stewards seek to manipulate the herd no more than twice in a year, although some years a third or fourth roundup occurs because of the need to get bison to market. As shown here, the Game, Fish, and Parks Department utilizes vehicles to move the herd.[14] Photo by author (2004).

Image 17: Once the drivers bring the bison off the range, they then drive them down a chute into sorting corrals. Thundering hooves and the heave of hard breathing punctuate the experience as the bison rely on their age-old defense mechanism of running from perceived danger. Many of these bison will become meat sales as part of a tribal industry that generated nearly 1 million dollars by 2004 without significantly diminishing the tribal herd due to a high fertility rate.[15] Photo by author (2004).

Image 18: While the hunts and tours tend to spawn few misgivings due to the limited manipulation of the bison herd as a whole during these interactions, other methods for raising money with the bison cause more concern. The look of this bison in the sorting pen runs contrary to the vision of the founders of the contemporary bison herds in Indian country.[16] Yet economic realities transform these bison, bound for butchering in a slaughter facility, into sacrificial members of their bison community. They will die in the tribal slaughterhouse so the rest of the herd can maintain its existence on the range. Photo by author (2004).

Image 19: The Cheyenne River Lakota brought bison back to the reservation for spiritual and cultural reunification under the idea that it would be a "dignified" return.[17] Toward that end, those bison who must be herded and sorted find themselves manipulated by quietly working individuals who use black flags on long poles to "buffalo" the bison into moving through the maze of gates and chutes. The bison do not have to endure a host of cattle prods and "yee-haw" yells. Photo by author (2004).

Image 20: While the Cheyenne River Sioux Tribe is fairly unique in possessing its own slaughter facility, it remains similar to other tribes in holding spiritual ceremonies each time members kill a bison. Each morning a bison is killed at the facility, the shooter conducts a sage smudge and tobacco offering ceremony to bless the process.[18] Thus, the Lakota grapple with blending spiritual respect and economic exigency. Photo by author (2004).

Image 21: Roy Lemmon, the slaughter facility manager, married into the Lakota tribe. He finds the work of the slaughterhouse consistent with the bison traditions of his adopted home. Utilizing a formula provided by South Dakota State University, Lemmon estimates that reservation butchering of the tribe's bison and contracts for cattle amounts to $1.4 million in revenue for the tribal community with an economic impact of between $10 million and $20 million. He states: "The bison was Wal-Mart. It provided everything. Here, we're doing the same thing. The difference is that we're giving jobs." In 2004, the facility increased its workforce from two to twenty-six people and could not keep pace with the demand for bison beef.[19] Photo by author (2004).

Image 22: Consistent with the ITBC goal of bringing health back to Indian communities through bison beef, the Cheyenne River Sioux Tribe markets its bison at low cost. For example, in 2004, a customer could purchase a twelve-ounce bison sirloin steak grilled at this mobile food counter on the reservation for five dollars. Photo by author (2004).

Image 23: Like virtually all other tribes in the ITBC, the Cheyenne River Lakota provide bison for ceremonies. And as with many of the member tribes, the Cheyenne River bison program provides bison beef for the elderly nutrition program and to augment the reservation's school lunch program.[20] Photo by author (2004).

Image 24: The symbolism of these bison heading out of sorting corrals on the Cheyenne River Reservation remains strong. On this day, these bison were taken off the range; subjected to very alien treatment including forced movement and restriction; survived a harvest process that would soon kill several of their cohorts; and then lived to gain their freedom and autonomy back on their home range. It is little wonder that Indians work with bison with respect and some trepidation and that Native Americans see the plights of themselves and the bison as intertwined past and present. Indeed, Lakota Jim Garrett is correct when he calls the Indian-buffalo relationship a "sacred symbiosis." [21] Photo by author (2004).

Appendix

ITBC Bison Program Survey Results

- 35 tribes surveyed, 1999–2003
- Not all tribes responded to each question
- All categories reported by tribe, e.g., 1 ITBC member tribe established its current herd in the 1930s

Herd Origins

	Established Current Herd [28 respondents]	Joined ITBC [25 respondents]
1930s	1	
1960s	2	
1970s	3	
1980s	3	
1990	1	
1991	1	
1992	1	14
1993	3	3
1994	5	3
1995	4	1
1996		1
1997	1	1
1998		2
1999		
2000	2	
2001		
2002	1	

Bison Sources

	Original Herd [26 respondents]	Herd Additions [23 respondents]

Many tribes report more than one source for original herd or additions.

	Original Herd	Herd Additions
Private	6	7
State Government	2	4
National Parks [unidentified]	1	4
Badlands N.P.	3	4
Ft Niobrara Natl. Wildlife Refuge	1	3
Natl. Bison Range		1
Theodore Roosevelt N.P.	5	1
Wichita Mtns. Natl. Wildlife Refuge	4	5
Wind Cave N.P.	7	6
Tribes [unidentified]	1	2
Assiniboine/Gros Ventres	3	1
Crow	2	1
Kalispel	1	
Taos	2	2

Program Rationale

Reasons for Establishment [30 respondents]

	Primary	Secondary
Spiritual/Cultural	22	2
Health & Diet	8	3
Financial		2
Ecological		1
Novelty		1

Reasons for Continued Stewardship [30 respondents]

	Primary	Secondary
Spiritual/Cultural	22	2
Health & Diet	7	5
Financial		8
Ecological	1	4
Novelty		

Stewardship Style [28 respondents]

Hands-Off   27
Manipulative   1

Feed [27 respondents]

Range Only   6
Range/Limited Supplement   12
Irrigated Pasture/Lim. Supp.   5
Limited Range/Heavy Supp.   3
Pens/Full Supplement   1

New Stock Selection [21 respondents]

Enhance Gene Pool   17
Appearance   3
Meat Production   1

Financially Self-Supporting Program [10 respondents]

Yes   5
No   5

Harvesting and Culling [26 respondents]

Community Distribution of Products   22
Harvest for Ceremonies   16
Live Donation   5
Live Sale   10
Products Sale   7

Ceremony/Prayer Accompanies All Harvest [21 respondents]

Yes   16
No   5

Support Level Perceived

From Tribal Government [28 respondents]

Very High	13
High	6
Medium	8
Low	1
Very Low	

From Tribal Community [28 respondents]

Very High	9
High	14
Medium	5
Low	
Very Low	

Perceived Future of the Bison Program [25 respondents]

Very Optimistic	10
Optimistic	14
Cautious	1
Pessimistic/Very Pess.	

Bison Numbers [35 respondents]

0	6
1–10	2
11–25	4
26–50	2
51–100	10
101–200	4
201–350	3
351–500	3
501–1000	
1,001–2,000	
2,001+	1

Acres of Pasture [25 respondents]

0–99	2
100–199	1
200–299	1
300–399	3
400–499	5
500–999	2
1,000–4,999	6
5,000–9,999	2
10,000–19,999	1
20,000–29,999	
30,000+	2

Appendix Sources

Richard Archuleta (Taos), interview by author, 18 January 1999, Taos, New Mexico.

Wayne Azure (Fort Belknap, Gros Ventres/Assiniboine), interview by author, 19 August 1999, Harlem, Montana.

Douglas Broyles (Caddo), telephone interview by author, 16 January 2003.

Ervin Carlson (Blackfeet), telephone interview by author, 17 January 2003.

Alonzo Coby (Fort Hall, Shoshone-Bannock), telephone interview by author, 9 January 2003.

Butch Denny (Santee Sioux), survey correspondence with author, 27 June 2000.

Mike Durglo (Salish-Kootenai), e-mail correspondence with author, 19 June 2000.

Mike Durglo (Salish-Kootenai), e-mail correspondence with author, 17 January 2003.

Ray Entz (Kalispel), interview by author, 22 June 1997, Usk, Washington.

Mike Faith (Standing Rock Sioux), telephone interview by author, 22 January 2003.

Kade Ferris (Turtle Mountain Band of Chippewa), telephone interview by author, 10 January 2003.

Lloyd Finley (Kalispel), interview by author, 21 June 2000, Usk, Washington.

Floyd Fisher (Northern Cheyenne), interview by author, 29 June 1999, Lame
    Deer, Montana.

Phil Follis (Modoc), telephone interview by author, 21 January 2003.

Monty Ford (Spokane), interview by author, 20 June 2000, Wellpinit,
    Washington.

Cecil Garvin (Ho Chunk), survey correspondence with author, 20 June
    2000.

Shaun Grassel (Lower Brule Sioux), survey correspondence with author,
    20 June 2000.

Tracy Hames (Yakama), interview by author, 14 January 2003, Toppenish,
    Washington.

James Holt (Nez Perce), telephone interview by author, 21 January 2003.

Robert Krantz (San Juan), telephone interview by author, 16 January 2003.

Lamont Laird (Eastern Shawnee), survey correspondence with author, 20
    July 2000.

Louis LaRose (Winnebago), e-mail correspondence with author, 20 January 2003.

LeRoy Lovato (Sandia), telephone interview by author, 10 January 2003.

Mike Mithlo (Comanche), telephone interview by author, 21 January 2003.

Gary Moquino (Tesuque), telephone interview by author, 16 January 2003.

Mark Morey, "Yakima Bison Herd Still Growing," *Wenatchee World*, 3 February 2002.

Muscoda Bison Herd Web-Site (Ho Chunk), www.muscodabison.com, 26
    January 2003.

Robert Nygard (Sault Ste. Marie Tribe of Chippewa), survey correspondence
    with author, 12 July 2000.

Dustin Olds (Miami), telephone interview by author, 16 January 2003.

Chris Olguin (Southern Ute), telephone interview by author, 16 January
    2003.

Alan Pahmahmie (Prairie Band of the Potawatomi), telephone interview by
    author, 16 January 2003.

Valentine Parker (Omaha), telephone interview by author, 10 January
    2003.

Jack Pate (Choctaw), survey correspondence with author, 19 June 2000.

Tim Pickner, telephone interview by author, 17 January 2003.

Danyelle Robinson, "Shoshone-Bannock Build Culture of the Buffalo," *Indian Country Today*, 3–10 March 1997.

Larry Thompson (Yankton Sioux), survey correspondence with author, 19 June 2000.

Carl Tsosie (Picuris), comments at the Second Annual ITBC Conference, 21 September 1999, Polson, Montana.

Leonard Two Eagle (Rosebud Sioux), telephone interview by author, 21 January 2003.

Suzanne Westerly, "Thoughts of Bison Roaming and Free over the Land," *Canku Ota*

(Many Paths), online newsletter,

http://www.turtletrack.org/Issues02/Co02232002/CO_02232002_Bison, 21 November 2002.

Ben Yates (Nambe O-Ween-Ge), telephone interview by author, 16 January 2003.

Curley Youpee (Fort Peck, Assiniboine/Sioux), telephone interview by author, 16 January 2003.

Notes

Introduction

1. *Indian Country* denotes areas in which Native Americans live and is commonly used, especially in the American West. See Mathiessen, *Indian Country*, and Louis LaRose (Winnebago), comments at the ITBC Second Annual Conference, 21 September 1999, Polson, Montana.

2. Associated Press, "Indians Work to Restore Buffalo to Tribal Lands," *News-Review* (Roseburg, Oregon), 27 January 1993. See also, Garrett, "A Case Study of an American Indian Economic Development Project," 6–7.

3. For an explanation of the term *buffalo nation* as a reference to the bison species, see Garrett, *The Cheyenne River Tribal College Tatanka Management Program*, 2–3, and Geist, *Buffalo Nation*, 28–29. For analyses of the writing of Native American history, see Fixico, "Ethics and Responsibilities in Writing American Indian History"; Mihesuah, *So You Want to Write about American Indians?*; and Mihesuah, "Voices, Interpretations, and the 'New Indian History.'" For analyses of Native American oral history, see Lagrand, "Whose Voices Count?", and Wilson, "American Indian History or Non-Indian Perceptions of American Indian History?"

4. See Zontek, "Hunt, Capture, Raise, Increase"; Zontek, *Saving the Bison*; and Zontek, *Sacred Symbiosis*.

5. For comments on ethnohistory, see Brown, "Ethnohistorians: Strange Bedfellows, Kindred Spirits"; and Hoxie, "Ethnohistory for a Tribal World." For analysis of the complexity of Native American history and the considerations necessary in writing that history, see Ortiz, "Some Concerns Central to the Writing of 'Indian' History."

6. Robinson, *West from Fort Pierre*, 191–97.

7. See Robbins, "Historians Revisit Slaughter on the Plains," F3, for an overview of revisionist and counterrevisionist viewpoints on the involvement of Native Americans in the destruction of the bison.

8. For arguments over the assessment of Native Americans as environmentalists, see Waller, "Friendly Fire."

9. For analysis of contemporary Native American society in the historical context, see Lewis, "Still Native."

10. *Reports of the Commissioner of Indian Affairs*, 1879, 90; Young to Commissioner of Indian Affairs, 1 March 1878, Indian Office Records, in Ewers, *The Blackfeet*, 295.

1. A Relationship from Time Immemorial

1. *Bison* and *buffalo* will be used interchangeably in this manuscript. *Bison* is the correct taxonomic term for *Bison bison*, but *buffalo* serves as a vernacular term. The etymology of the term *buffalo* remains somewhat obscure. It probably originated with the French term for bison, "les boeufs," which English settlers adopted. By the mid-nineteenth century Americans used *buffalo* as the accepted term, derived from variants such as "boffle," "buffler," and "buffilo." See Danz, *Of Bison and Man*, 6; and Sample, *Bison*, 10.

Two bison species survive today: the American bison, *Bison bison*, and the European bison, *Bison bonasus*, known as the *wisent*. No indigenous "true buffalo" exist in North America as their home ranges include parts of Asia and Africa. Both true buffalo and bison belong to the bovid family and the ox-like tribe of the bovinae subfamily along with their relative, wild cattle. See Danz, *Of Bison and Man*, 6–7; Garrett, *The Cheyenne River Tribal College Tatanka Management Program*, vi–vii, 19; Hasselstrom, *Bison*, 81; and Roe, *North American Buffalo*, 3–5.

Although the term *Indian* in reference to the native people of the Americas stands as a classic historical error dating back to Christopher Columbus, this manuscript will interchangeably use the terms *Native American*, *American Indian*, and *Indian*. The justification for this is the vernacular usage and understanding of these terms as well as the comfort Native Americans have in referring to themselves as "Indian," both in academic and nonacademic settings. When referring to the native people of Canada, I will frequently use the term *First Nations* in compliance with the vocabulary utilized in Canada. See Giago, "Indian or Native?"

Often, the Native belief structure assigns equal status to humans and animals. For example, the Lakota refer to the bison as Pte Oyate, the buffalo nation. The concept of "bison brother" remains quite familiar to many Native Americans. See Geist, *Buffalo Nation*, 28–29; Garrett, *Cheyenne River Tribal College Tatanka Management Program*, 2–3; and Hodgson, "Buffalo: Back Home on the Range," 69, 89.

2. Arvol Looking Horse, guest address, Bison Conference 2000 hosted by the University of Nebraska, Lincoln, 7 April 2000. The "dignity" of the buffalo, meaning a nondomesticated status, is a priority for Native Americans involved in bison restoration. Much of the rhetoric at the Intertribal Bison Cooperative's annual conference in September 1999 at Polson, Montana (whose theme was the future of the Yellowstone herd) aimed at describing the need for bison to remain wild and to experience maximum space and range conditions when in captivity.

3. Hodgson, "Buffalo: Back Home on the Range," 89. Undeniably, bison command a large presence in literature. Arthur's bibliography, *A Buffalo Round-Up*, lists more than twenty-five hundred titles. Significant works in bison historiography include the following: Allen, *American Bisons*; Hornaday, "Discovery, Life, History, and Extermination of the American Bison"; Seton, "American Bison or Buffalo"; Garretson, *American Bison*; Soper, "History, Range, and Home Life"; Roe, *North American Buffalo*; Haines, *The Buffalo*; McHugh, *Time of the Buffalo*; Meagher, *Bison of Yellowstone National Park*; Dary, *Buffalo Book*; Barsness, *Heads, Hides and Horns*; Foster, Harrison, and MacLaren, *Buffalo*;

Geist, *Buffalo Nation*; Danz, *Of Bison and Man*; Isenberg, *Destruction of the Bison*; and Lott, *American Bison*.

4. Hasselstrom, *Bison*, 25. For a discourse on change in nature, see Botkin, *Discordant Harmonies*.

5. Guthrie, "Bison Evolution and Zoogeography"; Guthrie, "Bison and Man in North America"; Garrett, *Cheyenne River Tribal College Tatanka Management Program*, 19–22; McDonald, *North American Bison*, 236–58; and Meagher, "Evolutionary Pathways and Relationships" (chapter draft), 1–2. For comments on the overabundance of nomenclature associated with bison evolution, see Wilson, "Problems in the Speciation of American Fossil Bison," 178; Speer, "Bison Remains," 126; and Guthrie, "Bison and Man in North America," 55. Skinner and Kaisen's "The Fossil Bison," is an oft-cited landmark study. The bison monographs usually cover bison evolution: Barsness, *Heads, Hides and Horns*, 27–30; Danz, *Of Bison and Man*, 6–12; Dary, *Buffalo Book*, 5–6; Haines, *The Buffalo*, 7–18; McHugh, *Time of the Buffalo*, 27–38; and Sample, *Bison*, 22–24. See also Pielou, *After the Ice Age*, for a general overview of flora and fauna colonization and recolonization associated with glacial North America.

6. Wilson, "Bison in Alberta," 10. See also, Guthrie, "Bison and Man in North America," 70; Voorhies, "Hooves and Horns," 75–79; Wilson, "Archaeological Kill Site Populations."

George Frison and Waldo Wedel stand as the "giants" in the field of bison and paleo-American archeology, especially in the present-day Great Plains. Consult their monographs, Frison, *Prehistoric Hunters of the High Plains*, and Wedel, *Prehistoric Man on the Great Plains*.

7. Discussion of "creation" warrants consideration of Native American religion and/or philosophy. See Deloria, *God Is Red*; Harrod, *Renewing the World*; Harrod, *Becoming and Remaining a People*; Harrod, *Animals Came Dancing*; Kellert and Wilson, *Biophilia Hypothesis*; Hultkrantz, "Water Sprites"; and Brown, *Animals of the Soul*.

8. Barsness, *Heads, Hides and Horns*, 78–80; and Harrod, *Renewing the World*, 51–52. For guidance in analyzing indigenous oral traditions, see Erdoes and Ortiz, *American Indian Myths and Legends*, xii, 8–11. For the Lakota tradition, see Johnson, *Book of Elders*; and Garrett, *Cheyenne River Tribal College Tatanka Management Program*, 2–3. For Wolf Smoke, see his "Bison Love Their Children Too," lecture presentation at the Bison Conference 2000 hosted by the University of Nebraska, Lincoln, 7 April 2000.

9. For thoughts by Pawnee tribal historian Roger Echo Hawk on collaboration between scientists and oral traditions, see "Working Together," 138, and "Working Together—Exploring Ancient Worlds." See also Evers and Toelken, *Native American Oral Traditions*; and Wilson, "Power of the Spoken Word," for arguments supporting the importance of considering Native American oral traditions. For early bison behavior, see Geist, "Relation of Social Evolution and Dispersal"; Geist, *Buffalo Nation*, 22, 29–30, 40–41; and McDonald, *North American Bison*, 265–66. For contemporary bison behavior, see Geist, *Buffalo Nation*, 40–41.

For the Arikara story, see Harrod, *Animals Came Dancing*, 55–56. For the Blackfeet tradition, see Grinnell, *Blackfeet Lodge Tales*, 137–44; Wilson, "Bison in Alberta," 1; and

Barsness, *Heads, Hides and Horns*, 75–85. Barsness also describes the Cheyenne beliefs on the aggressive bison of antiquity. For another rendition of the Cheyenne stories, see Grinnell, *Cheyenne Indians*, I:244–52; and "The Great Race," in Erdoes and Ortiz, *American Indian Myths and Legends*, 390–92.

10. For the Blackfeet explanation, see McHugh, *Time of the Buffalo*, 130–31. Isenberg relates the Cheyenne story in *Destruction of the Bison*, 75. Valerius Geist garnered the Lakota story related in *Buffalo Nation*, 34, from Judson, *Myths and Legends of the Great Plains*. For the emergence of archery, see Thomas, *Exploring Ancient America*, 58–59.

11. For the arid West, see Guthrie, "Mosaics, Allelochemics and Nutrients," 267. For the other megafauna, see Cohen, *Food Crisis in Prehistory*, 181; and Geist, *Buffalo Nation*, 18–19. See also Guthrie, *Frozen Fauna of the Mammoth Steppe*, for a thorough analysis of Pleistocene and early Holocene fauna, which also conveys information derived from the analysis of "Blue Babe," a steppe bison dated to 36,000 BP.

On the Paleo-American hunters, see Sauer, "Geographic Sketch of Early Man"; Guthrie, "Bison and Man in North America"; Strong, "Plains Culture in Light of Archaeology," 283; and Wheat, "A Paleo-Indian Bison Kill," 44. The Clovis and Folsom labels refer to lithic technology. See Reeves, "The Southern Alberta Paleo-Cultural," 21–25; Pielou, *After the Ice Age*, 289; Cohen, *Food Crisis in Prehistory*, 170–71; Thomas, *Exploring Ancient America*, 10–12; Wheat, "A Paleo-Indian Bison Kill," 47; Claiborne, *Emergence of Man*, 48–49; and Pickering, "Natural History and Human Interaction," 14–15.

12. Dan Flores, "Bison Past, Bison Present," keynote address at the Bison Conference 2000 hosted by the University of Nebraska, Lincoln, 6 April 2000.

13. For works addressing the "overchill vs. overkill" debate, see Martin and Klein, *Quaternary Extinctions*; Martin, *Pleistocene Extinctions*; Cohen, *Food Crisis in Prehistory*, 184–87; Pielou, *After the Ice Age*, 251–66; and Susan Okie (*Washington Post*), "Rethinking Extinction: Clovis, Climate or Germ?" *Wenatchee World* (Wenatchee, WA), November 16, 2001. For the Flores quotation, see Flores, *Caprock Canyonlands*, 17.

14. McDonald, "Reordered North American Selection Regime," 245–49, 265–66, and 404–39. See also Shay, "Late Prehistoric Bison and Deer Use," 194.

15. Guthrie, "Mosaics, Allelochemics and Nutrients," 259–98. For an analysis of the impact of climate change on terrestrial productivity, see Bryson, "A Perspective on Climatic Change."

16. For a study describing the grazing-versus-browsing capabilities of bison, see Waggoner and Hinkes, "Summer and Fall Browse Utilization." For "Great Bison Belt," see Guthrie, "Bison and Man in North America," 68. For the ebb and flow of prehistoric bison populations, see Dillehay, "Late Quaternary Bison Population Changes"; Flores, "Bison Ecology and Bison Diplomacy," 469; McDonald, *North American Bison*, 250; West, *Way to the West*, 80; and Wedel, *Central Plains Prehistory*, 72–80.

For Flores's "dwarf weed species," see Flores, "Bison Ecology and Bison Diplomacy," 469; and Flores, *Caprock Canyonlands*, 16. For the ability of bison to disperse into various ecological niches, see Epp, "Way of the Migrant Herds." For the dynamic nature of the effects of prehistoric bison populations on human organization, see Reeves, "Communal Bison Hunters of the Northern Plains"; and Bamforth, *Ecology and Human Organization on the Great Plains, passim.* See also Reher, "Buffalo Population and Other Deterministic Factors."

17. For an assessment of arguments over Native American harvesting ethics as "outlasting their usefulness," see White, *Roots of Dependency,* xiii. Still, the crux of the matter is the facts that laws and policies for Native Americans often emerge from historic and prehistoric resource use and that the environmental movement derives a model and symbol from Native Americana. For Barsh, see Barsh, "Forecasting Bison Migration: An Illustration of Indigenous Science," presentation at the Bison Conference 2000 hosted by the University of Nebraska, Lincoln, 7 April 2000.

Dunsmore, *Earth's Mind,* 107. Dunsmore examines relations between human hunters and animal prey in general.

18. Geist, *Buffalo Nation,* 63–67; and Barsh, "Forecasting Bison Migration." See Keyser and Knight, "Rock Art of Western Montana," 6, for Native American rock art depicting the use of canines in hunting on the northwestern plains and evidence of the paramount role of bison to Natives who did not dwell on the plains. For a monograph on human-wolf relations, see Lopez, *Of Wolves and Men.* See also Fox, *Concepts in Ethology,* 45–49, for a comparison of human and animal hunting societies. "Verged on pastoralism": Wilson, "Bison in Alberta," 13.

19. Fraser, *Bear Who Stole the Chinook,* 109–11, 125–29, in Isenberg, *Destruction of the Bison,* 80. Typically, Americans use the term *Blackfeet* while Canadians use the term *Blackfoot.* Both refer to the Algonquian speakers of the northern plains and Rocky Mountains. For Head-Smashed-In estimates, see Pringle, *In Search of Ancient North America,* 150–55; Frison, *Prehistoric Hunters of the High Plains,* 217–20. For a "must read" for anyone interested in prehistoric humans and bison on the plains of North America, see the November 1978 issue of *Plains Anthropologist* (vol. 23, number 82, booklet 2). Editors Leslie Davis and Michael Wilson devoted the entire issue to a symposium on bison procurement and utilization. See also Bryan, *The Buffalo People.* For predictability of bison movements, see Arthur, *Introduction to the Ecology,* 20–30; Harrington and Harman, "Climate and Vegetation in Central North America," 110–11; Frison, *Prehistoric Hunters of the High Plains,* 140–41; and Mitchell, "The American Indian." See also Dickinson, "Changing Times," which describes the co-evolution of Holocene cultures and landscapes.

20. Guthrie, "Bison and Man in North America," 71. For the larger size of bison eaters, see Gill, "Human Skeletal Remains on the Northwestern Plains." For Blackfeet *natapi waksin,* see Johnston, "Man's Utilization of the Flora of the Northwest Plains," 110. See also Hasselstrom, *Bison,* 42, where "real food" receives translation as *nitani-waksim.* For the ubiquity of bison in varied Native American cultures, see McDonald, *North American Bison;* Wilson, "Bison in Alberta," 13; Van Vuren, "Bison West of the Rocky Mountains"; Spielmann, "Late Prehistoric Exchange"; and Anfinson, "Prehistoric Subsistence-Settlement Patterns in the Prairie Lake Region." See Keyser and Knight,

"Rock Art of Western Montana," for evidence of the paramount role of bison to Natives who did not dwell on the plains.

21. Garrett, *Cheyenne River Tribal College Tatanka Management Program*, 3–4; McHugh, *Time of the Buffalo*, 83–109; Barsness, *Heads, Hides and Horns*, 65–74; Allen, *American Bisons*, 191–201; Garretson, *American Bison*, 156–69; and Hasselstrom, *Bison*, 44–49. Frison, *Prehistoric Hunters of the High Plains*, 10, describes the plains as a preindustrial living environment. See also Ewers, *The Blackfeet*, 9.

22. Hough, "The Bison as a Factor in Ancient American Culture History," 315.

23. For the meat yield of bison, see Wheat, "A Paleo-Indian Bison Kill," 52. For daily caloric intake provided by bison meat, see Lundwickson, "Historic Indian Tribes," 140–41. For the "dog days," see Walker, "The Seasonal Nature of Post-Altithermal Communal Bison Procurement," 3; Wheat, "A Paleo-Indian Bison Kill," 52; Frison, *Prehistoric Hunters of the High Plains*, 329; Reeves, "Communal Bison Hunters of the Northern Plains," 169–71; and Ewers, *Indian Life on the Upper Missouri*, 8–9.

24. For "small-group and individual hunting," see Frison, *Prehistoric Hunters of the High Plains*, 155. For hunting techniques, see Geist, *Buffalo Nation*, 39, 41; and McHugh, *Time of the Buffalo*, 60–82. For hunting implements, see Frison, *Prehistoric Hunters of the High Plains*, 170. For theorists on hunters' proficiency, see Kay, "Aboriginal Overkill and Native Burning"; and Kay, "Aboriginal Overkill: The Role of Native Americans." For criticism of Kay's work, see Yochim, "Aboriginal Overkill Overstated." Yochim's work faults Kay's methodology on the magnitude of "overkill" but does not negate the arguments on aboriginal hunting efficiency.

25. For the communal hunting arsenal, see Frison, *Prehistoric Hunters of the High Plains*, 155–56; Geist, *Buffalo Nation*, 38–48; Walker, "The Seasonal Nature of Post-Altithermal Communal Bison Procurement," 23; and Reeves, "Communal Bison Hunters of the Northern Plains," 174–75. Archeological evidence shows that most communally harvested herds consisted of females and young. See Frison, *Prehistoric Hunters of the High Plains*, 170; and Stanford, "Bison Kill by Ice Age Hunters." See Geist, *Buffalo Nation*, 42–48, for an explanation of the rationale governing the harvest at communal hunting sites. For "poundmasters," see Frison, *Prehistoric Hunters of the High Plains*, 171–72; Wedel, *Central Plains Prehistory*, 87–94; Dobak, "Killing the Canadian Buffalo," 50; and Medicine Crow, "Notes on Crow Indian Buffalo Jump Traditions," 249. For an excellent lay reader's essay and illustrations highlighting the study of one communal hunting site, see Stanford, "Bison Kill by Ice Age Hunters."

26. For a landmark work addressing human organization and the buffalo from prehistory into the historic period, see Bamforth, *Ecology and Human Organization on the Great Plains*. For models and graphics depicting the interaction of environmental productivity and cultural complexity over time, see Reeves, "Communal Bison Hunters of the Northern Plains," 187–91. See also Bozell, "Culture, Environment, and Bison Populations," 145–63. For equal harvest distribution and for moisture and forage on the plains, see Ewers, *Indian Life on the Upper Missouri*, 8–9. See also Bamforth, "Historical

Documents and Bison Ecology on the Great Plains." For the more numerous tribes of the northeastern plains, see Hanson, "Bison Ecology in the Northern Plains." Hanson agrees with the conclusions of Bamforth in his "Historical Documents and Bison Ecology on the Great Plain," but he emphasizes unpredictability as a defining characteristic of human organization based on bison.

27. For the Algonkian and Siouian speakers, see Schilz and Schilz, "Beads, Bangles, and Buffalo Robes." For the south and west, see Huebner, "Late Prehistoric Bison Populations in Central and Southern Texas"; and Speth, *Bison Kills and Bone Counts*. Archeologists do not always agree on the exact season when prehistoric Native Americans most likely congregated in response to aggregate bison herds. See Reeves, "Communal Bison Hunters of the Northern Plains," 170–71; Walker, "Seasonal Nature of Post-Altithermal Communal Bison Procurement"; Frison, "Paleo-Indian Winter Subsistence Strategies on the High Plains"; Frison, "Animal Population Studies"; Quigg, "Winter Bison Procurement in Southwestern Alberta"; Arthur, *Introduction to the Ecology*; and Speth, *Bison Kills and Bone Counts*. On the impact of fluctuating bison population on human settlement, see Bamforth, *Ecology and Human Organization on the Great Plains*, 160–61; and Frison, *Prehistoric Hunters of the High Plains*, 12. For growing bison-hunting sophistication over time, see Guthrie, "Bison and Man in North America," 70; and Frison, *Prehistoric Hunters of the High Plains*, 211. For works reflecting the continuity between prehistoric and historic bison culture, see Pringle, *In Search of Ancient North America*, 157; Ewers, "The Last Bison Drives of the Blackfoot Indians"; and Lehmer, "The Plains Bison Hunt—Prehistoric and Historic."

28. For the Columbian Exchange, see Crosby, *The Columbian Exchange*. "Discordant harmony" is borrowed from the title of Daniel Botkin's book, *Discordant Harmonies*. The term describes the complex dynamism of nature well beyond the simplistic models that suggest predictable equilibria. The term aptly describes the presence/absence of bison throughout prehistory in various locales. See also Botkin, *Our Natural History*. For a more specific discussion to the grasslands, see Keeler, "Grasslands: An Introduction"; and Isenberg, *Destruction of the Bison*, 11. Regarding the application of similar theories to historic bison studies, see Malin, *The Grassland of North America*, 436–40.

For general worldwide discussion on the impact of the penetration of one population on another, see Crosby, *Germs, Seeds, and Animals*; and Diamond, *Guns, Germs, and Steel*. For focus on the Americas, see Crosby, *The Columbian Exchange*. More specific to the present United States, see Jacobs, *The Fatal Confrontation*. "Day before America": MacLeish, *The Day Before America*.

29. For the range of pre-Columbian bison, see Shaw and Meagher, "Bison," 450; Roe, *North American Buffalo*, 257–333; Haines, *The Buffalo*, 8–9; Warren, "Altitudinal Limits of Bison"; Fryxell, "The Former Range of the Bison in the Rocky Mountains"; Kingston, "Buffalo in the Pacific Northwest"; Van Vuren, "Bison West of the Rocky Mountains," 65–69; Butler, "Bison Hunting in the Desert West before 1800"; Agenbroad, "Buffalo Jump Complexes in Owyhee County, Idaho"; Ricklis, "The Spread of a Late Prehistoric Bison Hunting Complex"; and Shay, "Late Prehistoric Bison and Deer Use," 194–212. For the

impact of European influence on bison's distribution, see Cronon and White, "Ecological Change and Indian-White Relations," 422. It's worth noting that bison eventually would also suffer the deleterious effects of Old World disease, namely, anthrax and brucellosis to a lesser degree. However, these diseases apparently did not check the bison expansion witnessed after 1500. See Owens and Owens, "Montana Commentary—Buffalo and Bacteria"; and Flores, "Bison Ecology and Bison Diplomacy," 481.

For the buffalo's expanded range in the East, see Belue, *Long Hunt*, 7–8. Belue's work provides the best glimpse into bison east of the Mississippi River in the historic period. See also, Haines, *The Buffalo*, 37–39; and Roe, *North American Buffalo*, 228–56. For the expansion of the bison's range west of the Atlantic seaboard, see Belue, *Long Hunt*, 10.

30. Belue, *Long Hunt*, 27, 55, 25, 29, 30.

31. Belue, *Long Hunt*, 37–41, 18–21, 44. See also Henderson, "The Former Range of the Buffalo"; and Lehmer, "The Plains Bison Hunt—Prehistoric and Historic," 211–17.

32. Belue, *Long Hunt*, 46, 98–99, 154, 160. See also Goff, "The Buffalo in Georgia," 19–28. For a description of war zones as buffer zones creating animal refuges, see Martin and Szuter, "War Zones and Game Sinks in Lewis and Clark's West." See also Cronon and White, "Ecological Change and Indian-White Relations," regarding animal refugia as a product of the Columbian Exchange.

33. Belue, *Long Hunt*, 163–64; and Seton, "American Bison or Buffalo," 405.

34. For the archeological and historical record, see Van Vuren, "Bison West of the Rocky Mountains," 65; and Butler, "Bison Hunting in the Desert West before 1800," 106–12. For specific western tribes, see Haines, *The Buffalo*, 4–5, 48–57, 61; Lupo, "The Historical Occurrence and Demise of Bison in Northern Utah"; Kingston, "Buffalo in the Pacific Northwest," 164–71; and Isenberg, *Destruction of the Bison*, 34.

35. Clark Wissler, Francis Haines, John Ewers, and Frank Gilbert Roe stand as the giants in the historiography of the horse's arrival into western North America. Their seminal works include Wissler, "The Influence of the Horse in the Development of Plains Culture"; Haines, "The Northward Spread of Horses among the Plains Indians"; Haines, "Where Did the Plains Indians Get Their Horses?"; Haines, *Horses in America*; Haines, *The Plains Indians*; Ewers, *The Horse in Blackfoot Indian Culture* ; Ewers, "Were the Blackfeet Rich in Horses?"; and Roe, *The Indian and the Horse*. See also Holder, *The Hoe and the Horse on the Plains*; Carlson, *The Plains Indians*; and Osborn, "Ecological Aspect of Equestrian Adaptations in Aboriginal North America." For the eastward movement of tribes, see Haines, *The Plains Indians*, 20, 25, 40, 41; Dobak, "Killing the Canadian Buffalo," 39–40; and Isenberg, *Destruction of the Bison*, 7, 34. See also Roe, *North American Buffalo*, 742–803, for an in-depth presentation of Native American populations with respect to buffalo hunters.

36. For the buffalo in the Great Plains in the nineteenth century, see Flores, "Bison Ecology and Bison Diplomacy," 466; and Shaw and Meagher, "Bison," 448. For the "genesis" argument, see Isenberg, *Destruction of the Bison*, 33. "Cultural whole previously formed": Wissler, "The Influence of the Horse in the Development of Plains Culture," 25. See also Reeves, "Communal Bison Hunters of the Northern Plains," 68; and Guth-

rie, "Bison and Man in North America," 72. For the horse and "effective density," see Osborn, "Ecological Aspect of Equestrian Adaptations in Aboriginal North America," 584–85. For aggregation into bands, see Bamforth, *Ecology and Human Organization on the Great Plains*, 97–128; and Isenberg, *Destruction of the Bison*, 43, 69. For the Plains Indian "high culture" peak, see Wissler, "The Influence of the Horse in the Development of Plains Culture," 15. "Poetry and life of the prairie": Jackson and Spence, *The Expeditions of John Charles Fremont*, 1:185.

37. Linderman, *American*, 252.

38. "Dead ones have all come to life": Jacob Halsey to Pratte and H. Chardon, 6 October 1834, *Ft. Pierre Letter Book*, 267, in Clow, "Bison Ecology," 267. "Buffalo in such multitudes": Thwaites, *The Original Journal of the Lewis and Clark Expedition*, 1:153. "Almost countless herds": Catlin, *Letters and Notes*, 1:249. "A million is a great many": Greeley, *An Overland Journey*, 72–73. "A monstrous moving brown blanket": Goodnight et al., *Pioneer Days in the Southwest*, 236.

39. For historians' guesses, see Barsness, *Heads, Hides and Horns*, 1–36; Danz, *Of Buffalo and Man*, 15–41; Dary, *Buffalo Book*, 28–29; and Haines, *The Buffalo*, 32–33. For Seton's estimate, see Seton, "American Bison or Buffalo," 386, 402. For McHugh, Flores, and Isenberg, see McHugh, *Time of the Buffalo*, 13–17; Robbins, "Historians Revisit Slaughter on the Plains," F3; Flores, "Bison Ecology and Bison Diplomacy," 470–71; and Isenberg, *Destruction of the Bison*, 24–25. For Shaw, Meagher, and Geist, see Shaw and Meagher, "Buffalo," 447–48; Shaw, "How Many Bison Originally Populated Western Rangelands?"; Robbins, "Historians Revisit Slaughter on the Plains," F3; and Meagher, interview with the author, 26 June 1999, Mammoth Hot Springs, Yellowstone National Park. "No other large mammal": Shaw and Meagher, "Buffalo," 447.

40. Botkin, *Our Natural History*, 115, 116; McDonald, *North American Bison*, 262; Martin and Szuter, "War Zones and Game Sinks in Lewis and Clark's West," 36; Flores, *Bison Ecology and Bison Diplomacy*, 475–76; and West, *Way to the West*, 61–65. "Comments from early observers": West, *Way to the West*, 52. See also Roe, *North American Buffalo*, 345.

41. For the argument that Native Americans did not waste, see Hunter, *Manners and Customs of Indian Tribes*, 237; and Wilson, *The White Indian Boy*, 35, 74. For the opposing argument, see Rylatt, *Surveying the Canadian Pacific*, 165; and Doane and Pease, *Report to the Commission of Indian Affairs*. "There never was a greater mistake": "The Buffalo," *Forest and Stream*, 22 January 1874. "The Indian kills many times": "Destruction of Buffalo," *Forest and Stream*, 30 April 1874. For the larger historical process of Euro-American hegemony, see Henderson, "The Former Range of the Buffalo," 97; and Seton, " "American Bison or Buffalo," 404. "That the twentieth century America": Burlingame, "The Buffalo in Trade and Commerce," 290. For Wallerstein and Braudel, see Wallerstein, *The Modern World System*; and Braudel, *Civilization and Capitalism*. Significant works on the bison robe trade include Burlingame, "The Buffalo in Trade and Commerce," 262–91; and Dobak, "Killing the Canadian Buffalo," 41–47. See White, *Roots of Dependency*, xv–xix, for a description of the "culture of dependency"; Isenberg, *Destruction of the Bison*, 44–61,

92–123, for a portrayal of the "ascendancy of the market" that Native Americans could not resist; Ewers, "The Influence of the Fur Trade upon the Indians of the Northern Plains," for the poverty caused by the end of the fur trade; Kardulias, "Fur Production as a Specialized Activity in a World System," for further arguments on the empirical evidence of dependency; and Tough, "Indian Economic Behavior Exchange and Profits in Northern Manitoba," 385–401, for comparative analyses of Native American and Euro-Canadian primary sector producers and resulting dependency.

For works that address the effects of the biotic invasion and climatic variation on the demise of the bison, see Dobak, "Killing the Canadian Buffalo," 37–39; Flores, "Bison Ecology and Bison Diplomacy," 478–84; Isenberg, *Destruction of the Bison*, 32–33, 83–84; Koucky, "Buffalo Disaster of 1882," 23–30; and Meagher, interview, 26 June 1999.

42. Works describing the Euro-American harvesting of bison include Barsness, *Heads, Hides and Horns*, 86–132; Dary, *Buffalo Book*, 69–120; Flores, *Bison Ecology and Bison Diplomacy*, 467; Garretson, *American Bison*, 79–155; Haines, *The Buffalo*, 89–199; McHugh, *Time of the Buffalo*, 39–49, 247–90; and Roe, *North American Buffalo*, 367–488. For a good overview of the issues concerning the evaluation of Native American interaction with the environment, see Krech, *The Ecological Indian*. See also Axtell, "The Ethnohistory of Native America"; Butzer, "The Americas Before and After 1492"; Cronon and White, "Ecological Change and Indian-White Relations," 417–29; Denevan, "The Pristine Myth"; Gray, *Wildlife and People*; Hughes, *American Indian Ecology*; Vecsey and Venables, *American Indian Environments*; White, "American Indians and the Environment"; and White, "Indian Peoples and the Natural World." For works focusing on environmental consciousness as a function of religion, see Albanese, *Nature Religion in America*; Bierhorst, *The Way of the Earth*; Booth and Jacobs, "Ties that Bind"; Gill, *Mother Earth*; and Hultkrantz, *Belief and Worship in Native North America*.

Richard White offers solid historiography addressing arguments over Native Americans as environmentalists and involvement in the fur trade. See White, "Native Americans and the Environment." See also Callicott, "American Indian Land Wisdom?" Historiographers tend to separate historians into two camps with respect to analysis of aboriginal motives in the fur trade: the formalists who view decision-making as a product of empirical analysis associated with western political economy and the substantivists who view decision-making more as a product of unique cultural constructs. For a basic explanation of this division, see Whelan, "Dakota Indian Economics and the Nineteenth Century Fur Trade"; and Peterson and Anfinson, "The Indian and the Fur Trade," in Swagerty, *Scholars and the Indian Experience*, 223–58. For a more detailed discussion, see Gudeman, *Economic Anthropology*.

43. Flores, "Bison Ecology and Bison Diplomacy," 467n, 478–84; Dary, *Buffalo Book*, 68; Robbins, "Historians Revisit Slaughter on the Plains," F3; and White, *Roots of Dependency*, 197–211.

44. Flores, "Bison Ecology and Bison Diplomacy," 478–84; Isenberg, *Destruction of the Bison*, 193; and Dobak, "Killing the Canadian Buffalo," 52. For another work on the southern plains, see Sherow, "Workings of the Geodialectic." "Native Americans did

not grasp": Flores, "Bison Past, Bison Present." Robbins, "Historians Revisit Slaughter on the Plains," F3;

45. Isenberg, *Destruction of the Bison*, 2–3, 83–85, and Robbins, "Historians Revisit Slaughter on the Plains," F3. See also West, *Way to the West*, 66.

46. Dobak, "Killing the Canadian Buffalo," 35. For a succinct summary of a similar argument specific to the Canadian West, see Foster, "The Metis and the End of the Plains Buffalo in Alberta," 66. For an explanation of the term *Métis* as opposed to *métis*, which designates mixed-blood Euro-Americans and Native Americans in general and is not specific to the Plains, see Brown, "The Métis: Genesis and Rebirth." For a description of the Métis bison culture, see Foster, "The Metis and the End of the Plains Buffalo in Alberta." See also Peterson and Brown, *The New Peoples*, and Ray, "Reflections on Fur Trade Social History and Métis History in Canada." On the robe trade encouraging Natives to take more animals, see Dobak, "Killing the Canadian Buffalo," 49, 52. See also Foster, "The Metis and the End of the Plains Buffalo in Alberta," 72–74, for the impact of Métis hunting. "Native" receives capitalization here since it includes both Métis and First Nations peoples, which makes "Native" an ethnic designation in Canada. On exclusion of competition as a conservation tool, see Dobak, "Killing the Canadian Buffalo," 51.

47. Dobak, "Killing the Canadian Buffalo," 33–52; Ostler, "They Regard Their Passing as *Wakan*"; Cronon and White, "Ecological Change and Indian-White Relations," 417–29; and Flores, "Bison Past, Bison Present." See also Whelan, "Dakota Indian Economics and the Nineteenth Century Fur Trade," 247, 261. On Indian beliefs about the bison's relationship to the earth, see Bowers, "Crows Heart's Reminiscences and Personal Experiences," 28; Dobak, "Killing the Canadian Buffalo," 49; Dorsey, *Traditions of the Skidi Pawnee*, 36–38; Geist, *Buffalo Nation*, 26; Harrod, *Renewing the World*, 47; Hasselstrom, *Bison*, 17; Isenberg, *Destruction of the Bison*, 76; Linderman, "Plenty Coups: Chief of the Crows," 250; McHugh, *Time of the Buffalo*, 134–35; Roe, *North American Buffalo*, 644–45; Pickering, *Seeing the White Buffalo*, 15–16; Flores, *Bison Ecology and Bison Diplomacy*, 485; and Erdoes and Ortiz, *American Indian Myths and Legends*, 490–91.

48. Goff, "Buffalo in Georgia," 278; Smits, "The Frontier Army and the Destruction of the Buffalo," 321; Ostler, "They Regard Their Passing as *Wakan*," 485, 476; Dary, *Buffalo Book*, 68; *Reports of the Commissioner of Indian Affairs*, 1879, 90; Young to Commissioner of Indian Affairs, 1 March 1878, Indian Office Records, quoted in Ewers, *The Blackfeet*, 295; and Linderman, *American*, 227.

49. Ostler, "They Regard Their Passing as *Wakan*," 488; and McWhorter, "Yellow Wolf," 191.

50. Robbins, "Historians Revisit Slaughter on the Plains," F3; and Garrett, *Cheyenne River Tribal College Tatanka Management Program*, 33. "They told us not to drink whisky": Linderman, *American*, 227. "For the western world": Valandra, *Lakota Buffalo Theology*, 34. See also Shaw, "How Many Bison Originally Populated Western Rangelands?" 148–50; and Shaw and Meagher, "Bison," 447–66.

51. White, *Roots of Dependency*, xiii; Flores, "Bison Ecology and Bison Diplomacy," 467.

52. Tuan, "Thought and Landscape," 89; and Schama, *Landscape and Memory*, 61. Bison play a significant role in this work by Schama in the form of the wisent, European bison, which parallels the bison-Indian-land relationship through the role it plays in the spirit of the Polish people. Reflecting on Polish history, Schama writes, "For as long as the beast [wisent] and its succoring forest habitat endured, it was implied, so would the nation's martial vigor" (p. 41). For changing perceptions based on the culture of the observer, see also Meinig, "The Beholding Eye."

53. Momaday, "Native American Attitudes toward the Environment," 80.

54. See Utley, *The Indian Frontier of the American West*; Hagan, "United States Indian Policies, 1860–1890"; Kvasnicka, "United States Indian Treaties and Agreements"; Prucha, "United States Indian Policies, 1815–1860"; and Utley, "Indian–United States Military Situation, 1848–1891." "Yearning for an ideal and humane habitat": Tuan, "Thought and Landscape," 101.

For treaty rights to chase buffalo, see Isenberg, *Destruction of the Bison*, 124–28; Ostler, "They Regard Their Passing as *Wakan*," 484–89; and *Death Wind on the Plains* (video). "The Wasichus came": Black Elk (ca. 1875), quoted in Berger and Cunningham, *Bison*, 23. ""The white man is still troubled": Standing Bear, *Land of the Spotted Eagle*, 248. For a work examining the central plains and Rockies from the perspective of historical landscape, see West, *The Contested Plains*.

55. For discussion of buffer zone refugia, see Martin and Szuter, "War Zones and Game Sinks in Lewis and Clark's West."

56. *Death Wind on the Plains* (video); Smits, "Frontier Army and the Destruction of the Buffalo," 312–38; Barsness, *Heads, Hides and Horns*, 126–32; and Dary, *Buffalo Book*, 127–28. "The best thing which could happen": "History of Buffalo Legislation," *Forest and Stream* 18 (6 April 1882), 890.

57. For general works on the hide hunters, see Branch, *The Hunting of the Buffalo*; Gard, *The Great Buffalo Hunt*; Gilbert, *Getting a Stand*; Robinson, *The Buffalo Hunters*; and Sandoz, *The Buffalo Hunters*. For the history and technology of processing buffalo hides, see Isenberg, *Destruction of the Bison*, 130–43; Hasslestrom, *Bison*, 64; Barsness, "The Bison in Art and History," 20; and Smits, "Frontier Army and the Destruction of the Buffalo," 326. On the end dates of the buffalo nation, see Dary, *Buffalo Book*, 114–20.

58. Owens and Owens, "Montana Commentary—Buffalo and Bacteria," 65–67; and Koucky, "Buffalo Disaster of 1842," 23–30. For the agricultural transformation of the American West, see Knoblock, *The Culture of Wilderness*. For an analysis of Native Americans and the impact on them of agriculture, see Lewis, *Neither Wolf Nor Dog*.

59. "It was a decimation of race": Garretson, *American Bison*, 184. Typically, the Native people of the Siksika nation refer to themselves as Blackfoot in Canada and Blackfeet in the United States. On the Blackfoot starvation, see Roe, *North American Buffalo*, 478; and Ewers, *The Blackfeet*, 295. On the Blackfeet starvation, see Ewers, *Indian Life on the Upper Missouri*, 173; and McHugh, *Time of the Buffalo*, 284–86.

60. "Poverty that still exists": Ewers, "Influence of the Fur Trade upon the Indians of the Northern Plains," 58–60. For the Plenty Coups quotations, see Linderman, *American*, 252, 311. "A cold wind blew": *Death Wind on the Plains* (video).

61. "[It] removed far more": Wilson, "Bison in Alberta," 14. Ostler, "They Regard Their Passing as *Wakan*," 489–95; McHugh, *Time of the Buffalo*, 287–90; and Garrett, *Cheyenne River Tribal College Tatanka Management Program*, 7. For comprehensive works on the Ghost Dance and Lakota religion, see Mooney, *The Ghost Dance Religion and the Sioux Outbreak of 1890*; DeMallie, "The Lakota Ghost Dance"; and DeMallie and Parks, *Sioux Indian Religion*.

62. Dary, *Buffalo Book*, 198–99; Hornaday, "Discovery, Life, History, and Extermination of the American Bison," 525; Hasselstrom, *Bison*, 91, 98; and Rorabacher, *The American Buffalo in Transition*, 49–54.

2. Saving the Buffalo Nation

The Duncan McDonald epigraph is from "Legend of the Red Buffalo Leader," page 7. In this passage, McDonald refers to Samuel Walking Coyote and the descendants of his herd, who became the nucleus of the Pablo-Allard herd. The regionally renowned McDonald first told the story for the Old Timer's Club in 1904, and the *Daily Missoulian* published it on August 28. Olson compiled the story and other material for the WPA Writer's Project (*McDonald* is often spelled as *MacDonald*).

1. See Barsness, *Heads, Hides and Horns*, 147–48; Danz, *Of Bison and Man*, 118–22; Geist, *Buffalo Nation*, 103–11; Isenberg, *Destruction of the Bison*, 176–82; Rorabacher, *American Buffalo in Transition*, 51–60; and Zontek, "Hunt, Capture, Raise, and Increase." Parts of this chapter first appeared in Zontek, "Hunt, Capture, Raise, and Increase."

2. Hebbring Wood, "The Origin of Public Bison Herds in the United States"; and Coder, *The National Movement to Preserve the American Buffalo*, 40–42, 76–84. Coder's unpublished dissertation remains the single best work detailing the initial efforts to save bison. For a more contemporary assessment of early efforts to save the bison and validation of the captive breeding programs' importance, see Grinnell, "The American Bison in 1924."

3. White, *"It's Your Misfortune and None of My Own,"* 216–19; Barsness, *Heads, Hides and Horns*, 152–57; and McHugh, *Time of the Buffalo*, 304–14.

4. Hornaday, "Discovery, Life, History, and Extermination of the American Bison," 502, 525; and Barsness, *The Bison in Art*, 121.

5. For the destruction of the Jackson Hole herd, see Clifford, "Bison Hunting," 261. For the fifty-two Texas bison, see Hornaday, "Discovery, Life, History, and Extermination of the American Bison," 502. On Yellowstone herd, see Meagher, *Bison of Yellowstone National Park*, 21, 26; Coder, *The National Movement to Preserve the American Buffalo*, 98–106; Barsness, *Heads, Hides and Horns*, 154–56; and Geist, *Buffalo Nation*, 98. On the 1925 Gallatin Valley incident, see Martin Garretson to Dick Adams, 1 July 1925, American Bison Society Files (Conservation Center Library, Denver, Colorado), quoted in Barsness, *Heads, Hides and Horns*, 157. On the Peace River herd, see Harper, "Letter to the Canadian Field

Naturalist," 305. See also Geist, *Buffalo Nation*, 98. On the 1912 hemorrhagic septicemia outbreak, see Grinnell, "The American Bison in 1924," 399.

6. See Dary, *Buffalo Book*, 241–44; Haines, *The Buffalo*, 213–19; Roe, *North American Buffalo*, 707; Barsness, *Heads, Hides and Horns*, 147, 186–87; and Smith, "Roping Buffalo Calves," 147.

7. Murphy, *Sporting Adventures in the Far West*, 165–66.

8. "This number does not include": Charles Jesse Jones to Charles Goodnight, 18 April 1917, Charles Goodnight File. Jones claimed that he captured eighty-nine calves in this letter; however, other sources fixed his actual total to approximately fifty-six animals, e.g., see Coder, *National Movement to Preserve the American Buffalo*, 38; and Isenberg, *Destruction of the Bison*, 176. On the McKoy brothers, see Dary, *Buffalo Book*, 233–34.

9. See Haley, *Charles Goodnight*; Hamner, *The No-Gun Man of Texas*; and Inman, *Buffalo Jones' Adventures on the Plains*.

10. Haley, *Charles Goodnight*, ix; Hamner, *No-Gun Man of Texas*, 251.

11. Haley, *Charles Goodnight*, 438; Dary, *Buffalo Book*, 229.

12. Goodnight, *Pioneer Days in the Southwest*, 28. See also Dary, *Buffalo Book*, 229, 227. See also Coder, *National Movement to Preserve the American Buffalo*, 7–15.

13. Hamner, *No-Gun Man of Texas*, 133; Goodnight, *Pioneer Days in the Southwest*, 21.

14. Haley, *Charles Goodnight*, 422, 80; Hamner, *No-Gun Man of Texas*, 11, 4–5.

15. Hamner, *No-Gun Man of Texas*, 240, 226; Haley, *Charles Goodnight*, 464; and Dary, *Buffalo Book*, 229–31.

16. See Barsness, *Heads, Hides and Horns*, 173–79; Dary, *Buffalo Book*, 271–78; Haines, *The Buffalo*, 213–16; and Rorabacher, *American Buffalo in Transition*, 95–105.

17. John Henderson, "The Former Range of the Buffalo," 80.

18. Edmund Seymour to Charles Goodnight, 19 March 1917, Charles Goodnight File. It is worth noting that in this letter Seymour makes it clear that Goodnight favored spelling *catalo* as "cattalo." Buffalo Jones favored the more widely adopted "catalo." Seymour's interest in this business stemmed from his position as an official in the American Bison Society. He eventually became president of the organization.

19. "Great possibilities": Goodnight to Seymour, 1 March 1917, Charles Goodnight File. See also Jones to Goodnight, 18 April 1917, Charles Goodnight File. For the Goodnight-Seymour correspondence, see Goodnight to Seymour, 24 February 1917; Seymour to Goodnight, 19 March 1917; Jones to Goodnight, 3 April 1917; and Goodnight to Seymour, 28 August 1917 (Charles Goodnight File). On the hybrid's program's fate, see Dary, *Buffalo Book*, 274–75; and Rorabacher, *American Buffalo in Transition*, 96.

20. Inman, *Buffalo Jones' Adventures*, 37; Barsness, *Heads, Hides and Horns*, 143; and McHugh, *Time of the Buffalo*, 298–99.

21. Inman, *Buffalo Jones' Adventures*, 58–65, 76–82.

22. Hough, "A Buffalo Hunt Indeed," quoted in Inman, *Buffalo Jones' Adventures*, 133, 135; and Barsness, *Heads, Hides and Horns*, 145.

23. Inman, *Buffalo Jones' Adventures*, 222–23, 219.

24. Inman, *Buffalo Jones' Adventures*, 235.

25. Inman, *Buffalo Jones' Adventures*, 24, 22, 50, 25, 49.

26. See note 19 in this chapter.

27. McHugh, *Time of the Buffalo*, 296; and Coder, *National Movement to Preserve the American Buffalo*, 89–93.

28. For the best synopsis and analysis of the McKay's bison-saving effort and subsequent dissemination of his small herd, see Coder, *National Movement to Preserve the American Buffalo*, 2–7. Judith Hebbring Wood also elucidates the record in her "Origins of Public Bison Herds," 168. See also Burns, "Bison: Back from the Brink," 19; Dary, *Buffalo Book*, 225–26; Garretson, *American Bison*, 216–17; Haines, *The Buffalo*, 220; and Roe, *North American Buffalo*, 708. For a biography of McKay, see McCarthy Ferguson, *The Honorable James McKay of Deer Lodge*. Three works on the Red River hunting brigades include Dobak, "Killing the Canadian Buffalo," 33–52; Foster, "The Métis and the End of the Plains Buffalo in Alberta"; and Ens, "Dispossession or Adaptation?"

"We talked it over": Charles V. Alloway, interview by T. W. Leslie, Buffalo Preservation file (Hudson Bay Library, Winnipeg, Manitoba), quoted in Coder, *National Movement to Preserve the American Buffalo*, 4. For Alloway's account of the bison-saving program's inception, see Coder, *National Movement to Preserve the American Buffalo*, 2–5. For Alloway's quotations Coder utilized an untitled article that he referred to only as "*Winnipeg Tribune*, June 24, 1925." See Coder, *National Movement to Preserve the American Buffalo*, 48nn10–18.

29. Coder, *National Movement to Preserve the American Buffalo*, 5–7; and Hebbring Wood, "Origins of Public Bison Herds," 168.

30. Coder, *National Movement to Preserve the American Buffalo*, 2.

31. Aubrey, "Natural History: Montana's Buffalo," 6. Grinnell published the story on two more occasions. See Aubrey, "The Edmonton Buffalo Herd"; and Grinnell, "The American Bison in 1924," 356–411. See also Isenberg, *Destruction of the American Bison*, 166–67. For a work on hunter conservationists in general, see Reiger, *American Sportsmen and the Origins of Conservation*.

According to the originally published story, Samuel Walking Coyote and his wife hailed from the Upper Pend d'Oreille tribe (Aubrey, "Natural History: Montana's Buffalo"). However, the area's Native Americans considered the Flathead and Upper Pend d'Oreille people culturally inseparable and therefore referred to themselves collectively as Salish ("Duncan McDonald," *Phillips County New and the Enterprise*, Malta, Montana, 1). For clarification of the term *Salish*, see Chalfant, "Aboriginal Territories of the Flathead," 5. To trace the etymology of the term *Flathead* (which did not involve the deformation of infant heads), see Thwaites, *The Original Journals of the Lewis and Clark Expedition*, 4:184; and Cox, *The Columbia River*, 142.

For conflicting accounts of the origins of the Flathead Valley herd, see Ronan, "Annual Report to the Commissioner of Indian Affairs, 1888," 158; Merriam, *Frontier Woman*, 119; Barsness, *Heads, Hides and Horns*, 182–83; and Howard, "The Men Who Saved the Buffalo," 123. For validation of the story as presented by Charles Aubrey, see Zontek, *Saving the Bison*. For critical proof of the veracity of Aubrey's story in light of the confusion over names, see Stinger interview. See also Que-que-sah interview and Bartlett, "The Pablo-Allard Herd," 70–82.

32. Grinnell, "American Bison in 1924," 371. For biographical information on Monroe, see the Jack Burton Monroe File, Montana Historical Society Collections, Helena. For biographical information on Aubrey, see "Charles Aubrey," *Forest and Stream*, 371; Aubrey, "Memories of the Buffalo Range," *Forest and Stream*; and Aubrey, "Memories of an Old Buffalo Hunter," *Forest and Stream*.

33. To read the story in its entirety, see Aubrey, "Natural History: Montana's Buffalo," 6.

34. For Joseph Attahe, see Duncan McDonald interview, "Duncan McDonald," 2–3.

35. Aubrey, "Natural History: Montana's Buffalo," 6.

36. Aubrey, "Natural History: Montana's Buffalo," 6. "Bought from the Indians": Charles Allard to George Bird Grinnell, 23 February 1889, quoted in Grinnell, "The American Bison in 1924," 370.

For Duncan McDonald's recollections, see Duncan McDonald interview. For Joseph McDonald's account, see Joseph McDonald interview, 3. For Morigeau's recollection, see Antoine Morigeau, interview by Bon I. Whealdon, "Diminishing Herds in the Judith Basin," 8 September 1941, quoted in Bigart, *"I Will Be Meat for My Salish,"* 112.

37. Que-que-sah interview; Palladino, *Indian and White in the Northwest*, 177–78.

38. Aubrey, "Natural History: Montana's Buffalo," 6; Que-que-sah interview, 1–2; Green and Allard, "The Life and Times of Joe Allard," 181; Bartlett, "The Pablo-Allard Herd," 77–82; and Allard to Grinnell, 23 February 1889, quoted in Allard, "The Life and Times of Joe Allard," 183.

39. Dupree, "The First Dupree into South Dakota," 1, 8; and Dupuis, "The Dupuis Letters."

40. Dupree, "The First Dupree into South Dakota," 2–3.

41. See Dary, *Buffalo Book*, 231; Deland, "Basil Clement (Claymore)," 384–85; Philip, "James (Scotty) Philip," 391, 393; Hebbring Wood, "Origin of Public Bison Herds," 169; and Riggs, "Sunset to Sunset," 228–30, 240–41.

42. Philip, "James (Scotty) Philip," 391, 393. See also, Robinson, *West from Fort Pierre*.

43. Deland, "Basil Clement," 384–85.

44. C. Stanley Stevenson, "Buffalo East of the Missouri in South Dakota," *South Dakota Historical Collections* (Pierre SD: Hipple Printing, 1912), 6:392, quoted in Coder, *National Movement to Preserve the American Buffalo*, 25; Robinson, *West from Fort Pierre*, 124–26; and "Dupree Was No Dude," *Pierre Free Press*, 29 May 1890. "Only authority [they] acknowledged": Deland, "Basil Clement," 270. For the oral tradition, see Jim Garrett (Lakota), interview by author, 20 September 1999, Polson MT. Joseph Dupris (Lakota), interview by author, 6 April 2000, Lincoln, Nebraska. Both Garrett and Dupris, cousins, are direct descendants of Frederick and Mary Dupuis. For renditions of the Lakota's White

Buffalo Calf Woman story, see "White Buffalo Woman," 47–52; Lone Man, interview by Frances Densmore, *Teton Sioux Music* (Washington DC: Bureau of American Ethnology, 1918), quoted in Geist, *Buffalo Nation,* 28–29; Ostler, "They Regard Their Passing as Wakan," 479–80; and Pickering, *Seeing the White Buffalo,* 16–20. The traditions of other tribes also explain the key roles played by women in establishing primary links with the bison. For the Blackfeet, see Clark, *Indian Legends of the Northern Rockies,* 275–76. For the Cheyenne, see Jackson Penney, *Tales of the Cheyennes,* 7–14. For the Hidatsa and Mandan, see Harrod, *Becoming and Remaining a People,* 70, 74–76.

3. Indians and Buffalo, 1890–1990s

1. Jim Garrett, quoted in *American Buffalo: Spirit of a Nation* (video).

2. Lewis, "Native Americans and the Environment," 423.

3. Looking Horse, guest address, Bison Conference 2000.

4. For overviews of United States Indian policy, see Hagan, "United States Indian Policies, 1860–1900," 51–65; and Kelly, "United States Indian Policies, 1900–1980," 66–80. See also Fixico's bibliographic piece, "Twentieth Century Indian Policy," 123–61. For an analysis of the reform movement pursued to "correct" the "Indian problem," see Hoxie, "The Curious Story of Reformers and the American Indians."

5. The Blackfeet Confederacy consists of the Blackfeet (proper), Piegan, and Blood tribes. Therefore, reporting that someone was "Blackfeet" often can indicate ancestry from any of the three related tribes. For Pablo's ties to the Flathead Valley, see Bigart, "I Will Be Meat for My Salish," 260. For Agathe's influence, see Barsness, *Heads, Hides and Horns,* 161; Coder, *National Movement to Preserve the American Buffalo,* 20–21; and Holterman, *Pablo of the Buffalo,* 1–2, 6–7. For the establishment of the ranch and purchase from Walking Coyote, see Coder, *National Movement to Preserve the American Buffalo,* 20–21; and Holterman, *Pablo of the Buffalo,* 1–2, 6–7.

6. Coder, *National Movement to Preserve the American Buffalo,* 21–22; and Howard, "Men Who Saved the Buffalo," 124.

7. Barnaby interview, 1.

8. Coder, *National Movement to Preserve the American Buffalo,* 22, 39–40; Holterman, *Pablo of the Buffalo,* 8; Hebbring Wood, "Origin of Public Bison Herds," 167–68; Barsness, *Heads, Hides and Horns,* 159; Dary, *Buffalo Book,* 224–25; and Haines, *The Buffalo,* 222–24. See also Bartlett, "The Pablo-Allard Herd," 77–82.

9. Coder, *National Movement to Preserve the American Buffalo,* 171–72; Dary, *Buffalo Book,* 224–25; Haines, *The Buffalo,* 222–24; Hebbring Wood, "Origin of Public Bison Herds," 167–68; and Holterman, *Pablo of the Buffalo,* 9.

10. Coder, *National Movement to Preserve the American Buffalo,* 84–85; Howard, "Men Who Saved the Buffalo," 125; Que-que-sah interview; and Barnaby interview, 2.

11. Dixon, "To Establish a Permanent National Bison Range," 2; Dary, *Buffalo Book,* 224–25; and Hebbring Wood, "Origin of Public Bison Herds," 167–68. For a summary of United States land policies toward Indians, see Gibson, "Indian Land Transfers," 211–29. See also Kelly, "United States Indian Policies, 1900–1980," 66–70. For the best

account of the sale and transport of Pablo's herd, see Coder, *National Movement to Preserve the American Buffalo*, 171–251.

12. Barnaby interview, 2.

13. Coder, *National Movement to Preserve the American Buffalo*, 180; Howard, "Men Who Saved the Buffalo," 125; Dary, *Buffalo Book*, 224–25; Hebbring Wood, "Origin of Public Bison Herds," 167–68; "Pablo Buffalo Sale," 893; and Elrod, "The Flathead Buffalo Range," 16.

14. Barsness, *Heads, Hides and Horns*, 164; Coder, *National Movement to Preserve the American Buffalo*, 199–200, 205, 208; and Bigart, "I Will Be Meat for My Salish," 239. For works describing Native American cowboys and cattle culture, see Iverson, *When Indians Became Cowboys*; Iverson, "When Indians Became Cowboys," 16–31; Dyck, "Does Rodeo Have Roots in Ancient Indian Traditions?"; and Lewis, "Native Americans and the Environment," 425.

15. Charles M. Russell to Fiddleback (Bertrand W. "Bill" Sinclair), 12 January 1910, quoted in Dippie, *Charles M. Russell*, 130–31; Coder, *National Movement to Preserve the American Buffalo*, 206, 222–24, 227–28; Elrod, "The Flathead Buffalo Range," 16; Barsness, *Heads, Hides and Horns*, 165, 168; Dippie, *Charles M. Russell*, 109–10; Dary, *Buffalo Book*, 224–25; Hebbring Wood, "Origin of Public Bison Herds," 167–68; and Howard, "Men Who Saved the Buffalo," 126. See also Barsness, *Heads, Hides and Horns*, 165, 168.

16. Perhaps most notably, Charles Marion Russell sent two postcards "hot off the press" in 1908 to his wife, Nancy. The first card shows cowboys chasing bison while the second portrays a pair of local Salish gentlemen in traditional dress (Dippie, *Charles M. Russell*, 109). For photographs of the event, see Jones, *The Last of the Buffalo*, passim; Barsness, *Heads, Hides and Horns*, 166–67; and Dary, *Buffalo Book*, 226–27. For Russell's accounts, see Charles M. Russell to Friend Goodwin (Philip R. Goodwin), January 1909; Charles M. Russell to Fiddleback (Bertrand W. "Bill" Sinclair), January 1909; and Russell to Fiddleback (Bertrand W. "Bill" Sinclair), 12 January 1910, quoted in Dippie, *Charles M. Russell*, 112–13, 114–15, and 130–31.

17. Russell to Fiddleback, January 1909, quoted in Dippie, *Charles M. Russell*, 115, 112.

18. Russell to Goodwin, January 1909, quoted in Dippie, *Charles M. Russell*, 112–13.

19. Russell to Fiddleback , January 1909, quoted in Dippie, *Charles M. Russell*, 115.

20. "The Outlaw Buffalo," 778; and Barsness, *Heads, Hides and Horns*, 168.

21. Dary, *Buffalo Book*, 237–39; Dolph and Dolph, "The American Bison," 21; Garretson, *American Bison*, 202–3; Isenberg, *Destruction of the Bison*, 182; McHugh, *Time of the Buffalo*, 300; William T. Hornaday to Senator Moses E. Clapp, 30 March 1908, quoted in Dixon, *To Establish a Permanent National Bison Range*, 2; and "The Montana Bison Range," 689. See also Dolph and Dolph, "The American Bison," and "Montana Buffalo Preserve," 697. For details on the formation of the American Bison Society, see Coder, *National Movement to Preserve the American Buffalo*, 118–70. See also Dixon, "To Establish a Permanent National Bison Range"; and Dolph and Dolph, "The American Bison," 14–25. For an assessment of eastern interests in saving the bison, see Isenberg, *Destruction of the*

Bison, 177–78; and Coder, *National Movement to Preserve the American Buffalo*, 326. For the role of women in fundraising, see Dolph and Dolph, "The American Bison," 23; and Hebbring Wood, "Origin of Public Bison Herds," 157.

22. Hornaday, *Thirty Years War for Wild Life*, 250; Isenberg, *Destruction of the Bison*, 189; and William Hornaday to Morton Elrod, 1 July 1908, American Bison Society Letterbooks (New York: American Bison Society, 1908), 2, quoted in Isenberg, *Destruction of the Bison*, 183. For a general analysis of the establishment of federal parks at the expense of Native Americans, see Burnham, *Indian Country, God's Country*; and Spence, *Dispossessing the Wilderness*.

23. "Pablo's Montana Buffalo Formed Nucleus for Huge Canadian Herd of Bison," *Montana Standard*, 15 October 1933, 1; and Coder, *National Movement to Preserve the American Buffalo*, 228–29, 311.

24. Dary, *Buffalo Book*, 231–32; Lee, *Scotty Philip*, 231–34, 225–27; Philip, "James (Scotty) Philip," 394; Robinson, *West from Fort Pierre*, 126–27; and Hebbring Wood, "Origin of Public Bison Herds," 173–74. See also Lee, *Scotty Philip*, 242–43; Philip, "James (Scotty) Philip," 393–94; and Robinson, *West from Fort Pierre*, 194.

25. Robinson, *West from Fort Pierre*, 71; and Hebbring Wood, "Origin of Public Bison Herds," 173–74. For salient biographical details on Scotty Philip with respect to saving the bison, see Coder, *National Movement to Preserve the American Buffalo*, 25–27; "Dakota Images," 89; Robinson, *West from Fort Pierre*, 49–54, 71, 74; and Hebbring Wood, "Origin of Public Bison Herds," 173–74. It's worth noting that Ila Wiedemer, a local historian of Pierre, interviewed a friend of the Philips, Flora Huston Ziemann, years ago. Huston Ziemann knew daughter Olive and mother Sarah. They had told her that Sarah did indeed influence her husband to help save the bison. Huston Ziemann also shared her information on the origins of Philip's herd to South Dakota state archivist Ken Stewart, who relayed it to the author in an e-mail dated 27 June 2002.

26. Lee, *Scotty Philip*, 116; Philip, "James (Scotty) Philip," 379; Robinson, *West from Fort Pierre*, 71, 122; Deland, "Basil Clement," 270; Coder, *National Movement to Preserve the American Buffalo*, 26; and Hebbring Wood, "Origin of Public Bison Herds," 173–74. See also above note 25 in this chapter.

27. Philip, "James (Scotty) Philip," 393, 396, 372; and Robinson, *West from Fort Pierre*, 194.

28. Dary, *Buffalo Book*, 232; Robinson, *West from Fort Pierre*, 127, 129, 198; and Philip, "James (Scotty) Philip," 394–95. For a vision of such a park predating Scotty Philip, see Catlin, *Letters and Notes* 1:249, 251. For visions of a park or buffalo commons after Philip, see Popper and Popper, "The Great Plains"; and Frank Popper, comments at the Bison Conference 2000, 7 April 2000, Lincoln, Nebraska. See also Edward Valandra (Lakota), comments at the Bison Conference 2000, 7 April 2000, Lincoln, Nebraska.

29. Robinson, *West from Fort Pierre*, 198; and Hebbring Wood, "Origin of Public Bison Herds in the United States," 159–66, 175–77. See note 28 in this chapter for a discussion of a "buffalo commons."

30. Dary, *Buffalo Book*, 232; and Robinson, *West from Fort Pierre*, 191–97.

31. Population estimates for Native Americans are nearly as elusive as those for the bison population. Scholars often indicate 200,000 to 250,000 as the nadir. See Gibson, *The American Indian*, 515; and Faragher et al., *Out of Many*, 564. For a monograph on Native American population in the twentieth century, see Shoemaker, *American Indian Population Recovery in the Twentieth Century*. For a comprehensive bibliographic essay, see Dobyns, "Native American Population Collapse and Recovery."

For Native American views on the subjugation efforts stemming from the Dawes Act and boarding school movement, see Joseph Dupris, interview with the author, 6 April 2000, and Jim Garrett (Lakota), interview with the author, 6 April 2000, Bison Conference 2000, Lincoln, Nebraska. Lavina White, quoted in Johnson, *Book of Elders*; Garrett, *Cheyenne River Tribal College Tatanka Management Program*, 12. See also Hagan, "United States Indian Policies, 1860–1900," 56–64; and Connell Szasz and Ryan, "American Indian Education." 284–300.Szasz and Ryan term the damage from allotment and Indian education "immeasurable" (294). For an assessment of the blow to the environmental foundation of Native economies caused by the Dawes Act, see Cronon and White, "Ecological Change and Indian-White Relations," 426–27.

32. John (Fire) Lame Deer, *Lame Deer: Seeker of Visions*, with Richard Erdoes (New York: Simon and Schuster, 1972), quoted in Geist, *Buffalo Nation*, 128. Two monographs address the boarding schools as disease zones: Child, *Boarding School Seasons*, and Riney, *The Rapid City Indian School*.

33. For works explaining the benefits of the Meriam Report and subsequent Indian Reorganization Act, see Garrett, *Cheyenne River Tribal College Tatanka Management Program*, 6; Gibson, "Indian Land Transfers," 227; Kelly, "United States Indian Policies, 1900–1980," 70–74; and Szasz and Ryan, "American Indian Education," 294.

34. Rogers to National Park Service Director, 21 October 1937, Bison Shipments File, Yellowstone National Park Archives. For the acknowledgment of Robert Yellowtail's requests, see Edmund B. Rogers, superintendent of Yellowstone National Park, to National Park Service Director, 21 October 1937, Bison Shipments File, Yellowstone National Park Archives. For biographical information on Robert Yellowtail, see Edmunds, *The New Warriors*.

35. For a description of opinions among the Crow over reintroducing the bison, see Mary Meagher to John W. Grandy IV (Wildlife Administrative Assistant, National Parks and Conservation Association), 5 January 1973, Bison File, Yellowstone National Park Archives.

The concerns by various factions of Crow over reintroducing bison heralded friction on other reservations as well. See also Mary Meagher, interview notes, 28 September 1972, from an interview by Meagher of Glen Jackson, Bureau of Indian Affairs, Billings, Montana, 22 September 1972, Bison File, Yellowstone National Park Archives.

For Jeanne Eder's recollections, see moderator comments at the Coalition for Western Women's History Annual Conference (2000), 29 July 2000, Pullman, Washington; and Jeanne Eder, telephone interview by the author, 23 April 2003. For the development of the Crow's herd and range, see Meagher, interview notes, Jackson interview, 28 September 1972; Mary Meagher, interview notes, 28 September 1972, from an interview by Meagher of Helen Peterson (*Hardin Tribune Herald*), 7 and 11 September 1972, Bison File, Yellowstone National Park Archives; and Meagher to Grandy, 5 January 1973.

36. For a detailed analysis of this process, see Philip, *Termination Revisited*.

37. Newton B. Drury (Director, National Park Service) to Regional Director (Region Two), 18 August 1950, in Skinner and Alcorn, History of the Bison in Yellowstone National Park (1942–1951) File. For Tolson's announcement, see Hillory A. Tolson (Acting Director, Fish and Wildlife Service) to Dr. Charles F. Webb, 21 August 1950, in Skinner and Alcorn, History of the Bison in Yellowstone National Park (1942–1951) File.

38. Meagher, Helen Peterson interview notes, 28 September 1972; Meagher, Shipment of Live Bison, Yellowstone National Park Archives; and Meagher to Grandy, 5 January 1973.

39. Meagher to Grandy, 5 January 1973; and Meagher, Glen Jackson interview notes, 28 September 1972.

40. Hoyt-Goldsmith, *Buffalo Days*, 12–18, 32.

41. Danz, *Of Bison and Man*, 134–35; Bison Shipment File, Yellowstone National Park Archive; Callenbach, *Bring Back the Buffalo!*, 69; Hebbring Wood, "Origin of Public Bison Herds in the United States," 163; and Isenberg, *Destruction of the Bison*, 189–90.

42. Danyelle Robinson, "Shoshone-Bannock Build Culture of the Buffalo," *Indian Country Today*, 3–10 March 1997; Rudner, *Chorus of Buffalo*, 98; Wayne Azure (Fort Belknap, Assiniboine/Gros Ventres), interview by author, 19 August 1999, Harlem, Montana; Cotes, *The Kalispels*, 29; Ray Entz, interview by author, 22 June 1997, Kalispel Reservation, Usk, Washington; Yatchak, "A Population and Behavioral Study of the North American Buffalo (Bison bison)," 48; and Garrett, *Cheyenne River Tribal College Tatanka Management Program*, 38.

43. Dupris interview, 6 April 2000; and Garrett interview, 6 April 2000.

4. The Intertribal Bison Cooperative

1. Intertribal Bison Cooperative website; Intertribal Bison Cooperative, *1998 Annual Report*, 4; Intertribal Bison Cooperative, *Intertribal Bison Cooperative*, 1; Garrett, *Cheyenne River College Tatanka Management Program*, 40–41.

2. Meagher to Grandy, 5 January 1973; Garrett, *Cheyenne River College Tatanka Management Program*, 40–41; and *Return of the Native* (video).

3. Intertribal Bison Cooperative, *1998 Annual Report*, 4–5; and Intertribal Bison Cooperative, *Intertribal Bison Cooperative*, 1. See also Colman McCarthy, "The Buffalo Is Back," *Washington Post*, 14 September 1996, A25. Sources often vary on the numbers of tribes at any given point. Both numbers fluctuate as tribes join and sometimes leave the ITBC, while bison stewards often regulate herd numbers for multiple reasons such as available range, market prices, weather, and politics. For checkpoints of the ITBC's growth through the 1990s, see the following sources. For 1993, see Associated Press, "Indians Work to Restore Buffalo, *Roseburg News-Review*, 27 January 1993, 46 ." For 1994, see Popper and Popper, "The Buffalo Commons," 144. For 1995, see *Return of the Native* (video). For 1996, see Geist, *Buffalo Nation*, 124; and McCarthy, "The Buffalo Is Back,"

A25. For 1998, see Intertribal Bison Cooperative, 1998 Annual Report, 2. For 1999, see Intertribal Bison Cooperative, Intertribal Bison Cooperative, 1. For 2001, see Ricci, The Great Kinship between Native Americans and the Buffalo Nation, 20.

4. Garrett, Cheyenne River College Tatanka Management Program, 40–41; and Intertribal Bison Cooperative, Intertribal Bison Cooperative, 1.

5. Ricci, Great Kinship Between Native Americans and the Buffalo Nation, 20.

6. Intertribal Bison Cooperative, Intertribal Bison Cooperative, 1.

7. Intertribal Bison Cooperative website.

8. Intertribal Bison Cooperative website. See also Mark Morey and Ross Courtney, "A New Home to Roam," Yakima Herald Republic, 16 January 2003.

9. For a detailed study of the ITBC membership, see the appendix to this book. The Kalispel, Crow, Taos, and Assiniboine/Gros Ventres herds regularly contribute to the establishment or augmentation of other tribal bison herds (appendix). See also American Bison: Spirit of a Nation (video); Hoyt-Goldsmith, Buffalo Days, 18; Carl Tsosie, comments at the ITBC Second Annual Conference, 21 September 1999, Polson, Montana; Ervin Carlson (Blackfeet), telephone interview by author, 17 January 2003; and Susan Ricci, "Montana Tribes Demonstrate the Meaning of Cooperation," Buffalo Tracks (ITBC's quarterly newsletter), March 2001, 2.

10. Tracy Hames (Yakama tribal biologist, nonnative), interview by author, 16 January 2003, Toppenish, Washington. See also the appendix to this book.

11. Fred Dubray, quoted in Return of the Native (video); and Associated Press, "Indians Work to Restore Buffalo to Tribal Lands." See also Garrett, "A Case Study of an American Indian Economic Development Project," 6–7. The appendix to this book shows the answers to questions, verifying the hands-off, holistic approach pursued by most member tribes. Virtually all member tribes treat bison as much as possible as autonomous creatures and not as manipulated livestock.

12. Intertribal Bison Cooperative website.

13. Ernie Robinson and DuBray quotations from Return of the Native (video); LaRose, ITBC Second Annual Conference, 21 September 1999; Ben Yates (Nambe O-Ween-Ge), telephone interview by author, 16 January 2003. "Nambe O-Ween-Ge" is the full name of the tribe, although "Nambe" usually suffices in references found in the Southwest.

14. DuBray, quoted in Return of the Native (video); Associated Press, "Indians Work to Restore Buffalo to Tribal Lands"; Jim Robbins, "In the West, a Matter of the Spirit," New York Times (L), 21 January 1997; and Fred DuBray, comments at the screening of American Buffalo: Spirit of a Nation at the Bison Conference 2000, 8 April 2000, University of Nebraska, Lincoln.

15. Return of the Native (video); Mountain Tree Community School, The Gift of the Great American Bison, 1; and Associated Press, "Indians Work to Restore Buffalo to Tribal Lands."

16. Carl Tsosie, comments at the Second Annual ITBC Conference, 21 September 1999.

17. Callenbach, *Bring Back the Buffalo!*, 70; McCarthy, "The Buffalo Is Back," A25; Susan Ricci, "ITBC Takes Buffalo Restoration Movement to DC," *Buffalo Tracks*, winter/spring 1999, 1–2; Don Lake, "Department of Labor Funding for Education/Training," *Buffalo Tracks*, June 2000, 1, 4; Tony Willman, "Funding Proposal Deadline Draws Near," *Buffalo Tracks*, June 2000, 11; Tony Willman (ITBC Technical Services Director), e-mail to author, 31 January 2003.

18. Tony Willman, "Surplus Bison Proposals for ITBC Member Tribes," *Buffalo Tracks*, June 2000, 11; Ricci, "Montana Tribes Demonstrate the Meaning of Cooperation," 2; Rudner, *Chorus of Buffalo*, 110; Danz, *Of Bison and Man*, 185, 199; and Hebbring Wood, "Origin of Public Bison Herds in the United States," 158. See also Danz, *Of Bison and Man*, 185, 199; and Pickering, *Seeing the White Buffalo*, 119. For the leading federal donors, see the appendix of this book.

19. Hebbring Wood, "Origin of Public Bison Herds in the United States," 158; and Judi Hebbring Wood, comments at the screening of *American Buffalo: Spirit of a Nation* at the Bison Conference 2000, 8 April 2000, University of Nebraska, Lincoln.

20. "Tatanka Studies 2nd Annual Summer Institute," *Buffalo Tracks*, June 2000, 6; Cheryl Hill, "An Indigenous Overview of the *Pte Oyate*," *Buffalo Tracks*, July 2001, 6–7; and Trudy Ecoffey and Jim Garrett, "A Tribal College Perspective on Bison Education," presentation at the Bison Conference, 7 April 2000, University of Nebraska, Lincoln. See also Garrett, *Cheyenne River Tribal College Tatanka Management Program*, 44. Garrett's thesis on the Cheyenne River Tribal College program is the most comprehensive source on the tribal college bison programs. He helped design the program at Cheyenne River and has been active in the Tatanka Institutes. For information on the NPBEN, see www.united-tribestech.com/orgs/npbec/npbison.asp. One of the tribal colleges that participated in NPBEN is United Tribes Technical, which serves as the tribal college for five tribes that include Three Affiliated Tribes of Ft. Berthold, Spirit Lake Tribe, Standing Rock Sioux Tribe, Sisseton-Wahpeton Tribe, and Turtle Mountain Band of the Chippewa.

21. Louis LaRose, luncheon address, Bison Conference 2000, University of Nebraska, 7 April 2000; Louis LaRose (Winnebago), e-mail correspondence with author, 20 January 2003; and Garrett, *Cheyenne River Tribal College Tatanka Management Program*, vi, viii–ix.

22. John Williams, "Field Visit to the Ute Indian Tribe," *Buffalo Tracks*, June 2000, 10.

23. Susan Ricci, "Spokane Tribe of Indians Welcomes ITBC," *Buffalo Tracks*, June 2000, 9; Lloyd Finley (Kalispel), interview by author, 21 June 2000, Usk, Washington; Monty Ford (Spokane), interview by author, 20 June 2000, Wellpinit, Washington; and Hames interview, 16 January 2003.

24. Mike Faith (Standing Rock Sioux), telephone interview by author, 22 January 2003; Ford interview, 20 June 2000; Ricci, "Montana Tribes Demonstrate the Meaning of Cooperation," 2;

Lamont Laird (Eastern Shawnee), survey correspondence with author, 20 July 2000; Dustin Olds (Miami), telephone interview by author, 16 January 2003; James Holt (Nez Perce), telephone interview by author, 21 January 2003; Mike Durglo (Salish-Kootenai), e-mail correspondence with author, 19 June 2000; Mike Durglo (Salish-Kootenai), e-mail correspondence with author, 17 January 2003; Robert Nygard (Sault Ste. Marie Tribe of Chippewa), survey correspondence with author, 12 July 2000; and Gary Moquino, (Tesuque), telephone interview by author, 16 January 2003.

25. Mike Mithlo (Comanche), telephone interview by author, 21 January 2003; *American Buffalo: Spirit of a Nation* (video); and Garrett, *Cheyenne River Tribal College Tatanka Management Program*, 44. See also the appendix to this book.

26. Phil Follis (Modoc), telephone interview by author, 21 January 2003; Tony Willman, e-mail correspondence with author, 31 January 2003; and Follis interview, 21 January 2003. See also the appendix to this book.

27. *Bison: A Living Story* (CD-ROM); Kade Ferris (Turtle Mountain Band of Chippewa), telephone interview by author, 10 January 2003; Curley Youpee (Fort Peck, Assiniboine/ Sioux), telephone interview by author, 16 January 2003; *American Buffalo: Spirit of a Nation* (video); and Azure interview, 19 August 1999. Also see the appendix.

28. Kay Humphrey, "Buffalo Processing Industry Booming in Indian Country," *Indian Country Today*, 23–30 June 1997; Hoyt-Goldsmith, *Buffalo Days*, 18; Finley interview, 21 June 2000; and Garrett, "A Case Study of an American Indian Economic Development Project," 8. The use of a Eurasian model for preserving an indigenous large mammal-based industry in at least a semi-wild state in North America is not without precedent. For works describing the attempt to create a reindeer-raising society in Alaska, see Olson, *Alaska Reindeer Herdsmen*. The program ultimately failed in its attempted transformation of an indigenous lifestyle for Native Alaskans. Nonetheless, the program planners imported both Native Siberian Chukchi reindeer herders and Sami herders to teach their practices to Native Alaskans. See also VanStone, "Hunters, Herders, Trappers, and Fishermen."

29. Garrett, "A Case Study of an American Indian Economic Development Project," 8–9; Garrett, *Cheyenne River Tribal College Tatanka Management Program*, 53; Tim Pickner, telephone interview by author, 17 January 2003; Danz, *Of Bison and Man*, 200; and Goodstein, "Buffalo Comeback," 4.

30. Garrett, "A Case Study of an American Indian Economic Development Project," 8–10.

31. Garrett, *Cheyenne River Tribal College Tatanka Management Program*, 53; and Roy Lemmon, interview by author, 16 August 1994, LaPlant, South Dakota.

32. Fred DuBray (Lakota), interview by author, 19 August 2004, Rapid City, South Dakota.

33. Trudy Ecoffey, "Conference Puts Spotlight on Healthy Lifestyles," *Buffalo Tracks*, September 2000, 1, 3; Ricci, *Great Kinship between Native Americans and the Buffalo Nation*, 16, 20; and LaRose, luncheon address, Bison Conference 2000, University of Nebraska, 7 April 2000.

34. LaRose, luncheon address; McCarthy, "The Buffalo Is Back," A25; Louis LaRose to Jennifer Larson (Director, NHS Diabetes Center, University of Nebraska Medical

Center), correspondence, 15 January 2003, LaRose's personal papers; and *Return of the Native* (video).

35. *Fate of the Plains* (video); DuBray, comments at the screening of *American Buffalo: Spirit of a Nation*, Bison Conference 2000, 8 April 2000; Pat Cornelius (Oneida), interview by author, 22 September 1999, Polson, Montana; and Phil Follis (Modoc), telephone interview by author, 7 February 2003.

36. *Return of the Native* (video).

37. *Return of the Native* (video); Tsosie, comments at the ITBC Second Annual Conference, 21 September 1999; and LeRoy Lovato (Sandia), telephone interview by author, 10 January 2003.

38. For works on Native American cattle ranching, see Iverson, *When Indians Became Cowboys*; Iverson, "When Indians Became Cowboys"; Dyck, "Does Rodeo Have Roots in Ancient Indian Traditions?"; and Lewis, "Native Americans and the Environment," 425. Also see the appendix.

39. Douglas Broyles (Caddo), telephone interview by author, 16 January 2003; Finley interview, 21 June 2000; Ford interview, 20 June 2000; Hames interview, 16 January 2003; Meagher, Glen Jackson interview notes, 28 September 1972; Meagher to Grandy, 5 January 1973; Rudner, *Chorus of Buffalo*, 100–101; Ted Wynecoop, interview by author, 4 January 2003, Spokane, Washington; and DuBray interview, 19 August 2004. For the bison stewards who emerged from the ranks of cattle ranchers, see appendix for interviews. For a journalistic description of the conflict between ranchers and bison stewards, see Rudner, *Chorus of Buffalo*, 35–50.

40. Ford interview, 20 June 2000; Rudner, *Chorus of Buffalo*, 35–50; and *Bison: A Living Story* (CD-ROM). For a study emphasizing the communalism of reservations, see Frantz, *Indian Reservations in the United States*.

41. DuBray interview, 19 August 2004.

42. Callenbach, *Bring Back the Buffalo!*, 73; Ricci, *Great Kinship between Native Americans and the Buffalo Nation*, 16; and Associated Press, "Indians Work to Restore Buffalo to Tribal Lands." Protagonists for ecological cattle ranching argue that stock owners can manage their livestock in a manner that prevents such range damage. The key lies in the intensive management required to ensure less range degradation, which is less of a consideration with bison. For such arguments, see Savory, *Holistic Resource Management*.

43. McCarthy, "The Buffalo Is Back," A25; Tony Willman, "Keep the Beauty of Bison . . . No Genetic Tinkering," *Buffalo Tracks*, winter/spring 1999, 6; and Hebbring Wood, "Origin of Public Bison Herds in the United States," 155.

44. Johnson, "Fort Belknap Looks to Tourists"; and Rudner, *Chorus of Buffalo*, 99. Rudner's work offers a solid journalistic account of the bison program at Fort Belknap.

45. Rudner, *Chorus of Buffalo*, 108–15, 104, 96, 100, 106, 114; and Azure interview, 19 August 1999.

46. Rudner, *Chorus of Buffalo*, 104–5; *Return of the Native* (video); and Azure interview, 19 August 1999.

47. Chadwick, "Fresh Try for Ferrets"; Johnson, "Fort Belknap Looks to Tourists," 18; and Azure interview, 19 August 1999; and Susan Ricci, "Babbitt, Belknap, and Buffalo," *Buffalo Tracks* (winter/spring 1999), 4.

48. Goodstein, "Buffalo Comeback," 4; and Azure interview, 19 August 1999.

49. Azure interview, 19 August 1999.

50. Azure interview, 19 August 1999.

51. Members of the Comanche, Cheyenne River Lakota, Rosebud Lakota, Shoshone-Bannock, Southern Ute, Standing Rock Lakota, and Yakama tribes possess herds of bison. See source list in appendix for these tribes.

52. Azure interview, 19 August 1999.

5. The Yellowstone Crisis

1. *Crisis* here means a critical turning point in Yellowstone bison history, which this incident became due to the scrutiny of and publicity from the events that surrounded the herd in 1996–1997. Meagher's *Bison of Yellowstone National Park* stands as the best monograph on Yellowstone's bison. For a more general overview by Meagher, see Meagher and Houston, *Yellowstone and the Biology of Time*, 242. For a general history of the park, see Haines, *The Yellowstone Story*, and the folksy monograph by Beal, *The Story of Man in Yellowstone*. For a contemporary journalistic account of the winter's events, see Todd Wilkinson, "No Home on the Range," *High Country News*, 17 February 1997, and Scott McMillion, "For Bison, It's *Déjà Vu* All over Again," *High Country News*, 17 February 1997. The event certainly made the press. A Yellowstone National Park exhibit on the subject contained a collage of more than two hundred articles from various newspapers and other news media ("Where the Buffalo Roam: The Exhibition"). For a detailed layperson's view, see Peacock, "The Yellowstone Massacre." For an excellent academic view of the larger political and legal issues precipitating the crisis of 1996–1997, see Keiter and Froehlicher, "Bison, Brucellosis, and the Law in the Greater Yellowstone Ecosystem."

2. Wilkinson, "No Home on the Range"; Mary Meagher, e-mail correspondence with author, 3 March 2003; Associated Press, "Yellowstone's Buffalo Population May Be on the Verge of Collapse," *Lewiston Morning Tribune*, 20 January 1997; "Where the Buffalo Roam: The Exhibition"; and Wuerthner, "The Battle over Bison." See also *American Bison: Spirit of a Nation* (video); Meagher, e-mail correspondence, 3 March 2003; and *War on the Range* (video). For an explanation of the role of the Department of Agriculture and the Animal and Plant Health Inspection Service (APHIS) in causing the slaughter policy, see Pritchard, "Slaughter in the Sanctuary," and "Yellowstone Buffalo Slaughtered in Record Numbers," *National Parks*.

3. Associated Press, "Latest Bison Count Lower than Fall Number," *Lewiston Morning Tribune*, 20 March 1997. For an introduction to the controversy over management policy on the northern range and leading opponents on the issue, see Robbins, "The Elk of Yellowstone," and Budiansky, "Yellowstone's Unraveling." For a monograph focused on the history of management in Yellowstone National Park, see Pritchard, *Preserving*

Yellowstone's Natural Conditions. For more journalistic approaches, see Robbins, *Last Refuge,* and Schullery, *Searching for Yellowstone.* For more scientific assessments of Yellowstone policies, see Despain, *Plants and their Environments;* Despain et al., *Wildlife in Transition;* Keiter and Boyce, *The Greater Yellowstone Ecosystem;* and Singer, *Effects of Grazing by Wild Ungulates in Yellowstone National Park.*

The acceptance of predators proved crucial in developing the natural regulation paradigm. See Leopold, Cain, Cottam, Gabrielson, and Kimball, *Wildlife Management in the National Parks.* For a general study of the evolution of wildlife management in the national parks, see Wright, *Wildlife Research and Management in the National Parks.*

Manipulation of the park's bison herd began with the import of captive bison in 1902 to augment the beleaguered existing wild population, which had suffered from poaching. For the history of the herd from the establishment of the park in 1872 through the mixing of the wild and domesticated herds around 1920, see Barsness, *Heads, Hides and Horns,* 152–57; Coder, *National Movement to Preserve the American Buffalo,* 63–81; Dary, *Buffalo Book,* 129–44; Geist, *Buffalo Nation,* 94, 111, 114; Haines, *Yellowstone Story,* 2:54–77; Pritchard, *Preserving Yellowstone's Natural Conditions,* 11–12; Schullery, "Buffalo Jones and the Bison Herd in Yellowstone"; and Schullery, "Yellowstone's Ecological Holocaust." For works addressing the Yellowstone herd later in the twentieth century, see Danz, *Of Bison and Man,* 178–80; Isenberg, *Destruction of the Bison,* 189–92; and Pritchard, *Preserving Yellowstone's Natural Conditions,* xiv–xviii.

4. *War on the Range* (video); Geist, *Buffalo Nation,* 124; and see Despain et al., *Wildlife in Transition,* 112, 115. Mary Meagher and Douglas Houston address the problems associated with the term *natural* in *Yellowstone and the Biology of Time.* They define *natural* as the full expression of a system's processes without major change or disruption by modern humans (251, 272).

5. Wilkinson, "No Home on the Range"; Wuerthner, "The Battle over Bison," 39, 38; Meagher, e-mail, 3 March 2003; Meagher and Meyer, "On the Origin of Brucellosis in Bison of Yellowstone National Park," 650, 649; Todd Wilkinson, "To the South, Bison and Cattle Can Coexist," *High Country News,* 17 February 1997; Richard Archuleta (Taos), interview by author, 18 January 1999, Taos, New Mexico; and Norman Cheville, "Brucellosis in Bison: Its Effects and Approaches for Disease Control," presentation at the ITBC Second Annual Conference, 21 September 1999, Polson, Montana. See also Whittlesey, "Cows All over the Place"; Thorne, Meagher, and Hillman, "Brucellosis in Free-Ranging Bison"; and Geist, *Buffalo Nation,* 130–31. For other works about diseases introduced to bison, see Koucky, "Buffalo Disaster of 1882," 23–30; Owens and Owens, "Montana Commentary—Buffalo and Bacteria," 65–67; and Flores, "Bison Ecology and Bison Diplomacy," 481, 484.

6. Wuerthner, "The Battle over Bison," 40, 39; and Wilkinson, "To the South, Bison and Cattle Coexist." See also *War on the Range* (video).

7. Judith Kohler (AP), "Pact Allows Bison to Be Relocated," *Lewiston Morning Tribune,* 23 January 1997.

8. Kohler, "Pact Allows Bison to Be Relocated"; and K. Marie Porterfield, "Winter Bison Kill Begins," *Indian Country Today,* 16–23 February 1998.

9. Robbins, "In the West, A Matter of the Spirit"; Associated Press, "Yellowstone's Bison Population May Be on the Verge of Collapse"; and "Yellowstone Bison to Be Slaughtered," *National Parks*. See also David Melmer, "Buffalo Slaughter Not Necessary," *Indian Country Today*, 3–10 February 1997; David Melmer, "Bison Die in Sacrilegious Slaughter," *Indian Country Today*, 24 February–3 March 1997; and Porterfield, "Winter Bison Kill Begins."

For academic works on Yellowstone bison movements, see Meagher, "Evaluation of Boundary Control for Bison of Yellowstone National Park"; Meagher, "Range Expansion by Bison of Yellowstone National Park"; and Mary Meagher, M. L. Taper, and C. L. Jerde, "Recent Changes in Population Distribution: The Pelican Bison and the Domino Effect," presentation at the Yellowstone National Park Science Proceedings, October 2001, Yellowstone National Park. See also the interview of Dr. James Halfpenny in Ruth Yellowhawk, "Unusual Conditions Threaten the Buffalo in Yellowstone," *Indian Country Today*, 24 February–3 March 1997.

10. Robbins, "In the West, A Matter of the Spirit"; and Peacock, "The Yellowstone Massacre," 108. For native concerns about slaughter methods, see also Melmer, "Bison Die in Sacrilegious Slaughter"; and Angus M. Thuermer Jr., "Tribes Welcome Refuge Bison Hunt," *Jackson Hole News*, 15 April 1998.

11. Van Putten, "Restoring an Important Part of America's Heritage."

12. Kohler, "Pact Allows Bison to Be Relocated"; Robbins, "In the West, A Matter of the Spirit";

Meagher, "Evolutionary Pathways and Relationships" (unpublished paper), 6; Steve Torbit (NWF veterinarian), comments at the screening of *American Buffalo: Spirit of a Nation*, Bison Conference 2000, 8 April 2000, University of Nebraska, Lincoln; and Melmer, "Buffalo Slaughter Not Necessary."

13. H. Josef Hebert, "Babbitt to Montana: Hold Your Fire on Wayward Buffalo," *Lewiston Morning Tribune*, 13 March 1997; Wilkinson, "No Home on the Range"; and Robbins, "In the West, A Matter of Spirit."

14. "Shields Addresses Montana Legislature," *Indian Country Today*, 24 February–3 March 1997.

15. Haines, *Yellowstone Story*, 1:15–20; Janetski, *The Indians of Yellowstone National Park*, 14–15; Meagher and Houston, *Yellowstone and the Biology of Time*, 248–49; Meagher, *Bison of Yellowstone National Park*, 13–14; Cannon, "Paleoindian Use of Obsidian in the Greater Yellowstone Area"; Cannon, "Blood Residue Analyses of Ancient Stone Tools Reveal Clues to Prehistoric Subsistence Patterns in Yellowstone," 248–49; Brown, "The Buffalo Drive"; and Davis and Zeier, "Multi-Phase Late Period Bison Procurement at the Antonsen Site." See also, Janetski, *Indians of Yellowstone National Park*, 20–23.

16. Haines, *Yellowstone Story*, 1:20–30; Janetski, *Indians of Yellowstone National Park*, 28–29; Meagher and Houston, *Yellowstone and the Biology of Time*, 248–49; and Affiliated American Indian Tribes of Yellowstone National Park (map).

17. Janetski, *Indians of Yellowstone National Park*, 54–55. For a more detailed work examining this process in Yellowstone National Park and elsewhere, see Spence, *Dispossessing*

the Wilderness. For works devoting far less attention to Yellowstone but dealing with the marginalization of Native Americans from national parks, see Burnham, *Indian Country, God's Country*; and Keller and Turek, *American Indians and National Parks*.

18. Isenberg, *Destruction of the Bison*, 189; Bison Shipments File, Yellowstone National Park Archives; Memorandum, 7 April 1948, YNP Superintendent to Region 2 Director, 1948 Annual Bison Report, Annual Bison Reports File, 1931–1950, Yellowstone National Park Archives; Memorandum, 28 March 1950, YNP Superintendent to Region 2 Director, 1950 Annual Bison Report, Annual Bison Reports File, 1931–1950, Yellowstone National Park Archives; and Mary Meagher, e-mail correspondence with author, 12 August 2002.

19. Melmer, "Buffalo Slaughter Not Necessary"; Melmer, "Bison Die in Sacrilegious Slaughter"; and Porterfield, "Winter Bison Kill Begins"; Carla Rae Brings Plenty, quoted in Porterfield, "Winter Bison Kill Begins"; Winona LaDuke, quoted in *War on the Range* (video); and Mary Meagher, interview by author, 26 June 1999, Mammoth Hot Springs, Yellowstone National Park.

20. "Shields addresses Montana Legislature."

21. *War on the Range* (video); Hope Sieck (Greater Yellowstone Coalition), interview by author, 22 September 1999, Polson, Montana; Porterfield, "Winter Bison Kill Begins"; Rosalie Little Thunder, comments at the ITBC Second Annual Conference, 21 September 1999, Polson MT. Little Thunder's activism includes being a founding member of the Buffalo Field Campaign, chairwoman of the Seventh Generation Fund, and member of Honor the Earth. See www.wildrockies.org/bison, www.7genfund.org, www.honortheearth.com.

22. Louis LaRose and Steve Torbit, "Wildlife and Cultural Restoration: The Opportunity Provided by the Partnership between the National Wildlife Federation and the Intertribal Bison Cooperative," presentation at the Bison Conference 2000, 8 April 2000, University of Nebraska, Lincoln; and *War on the Range* (video). See also LaDuke's chapter on bison, "Buffalo Nations, Buffalo Peoples," in her book *All Our Relations*, 139–66. LaDuke's tribal affiliation is Anishinabe.

23. Little Thunder, comments at the ITBC Second Annual Conference, 21 September 1999; Carrie McCleary, "Advocate for Bison Arrested While at Prayer," *Indian Country Today*, 17–24 March 1997; David Melmer and Sharon Harjo, "A Prayer Day Held for Buffalo," *Indian Country Today*, 17–24 March 1997; *War on the Range* (video); and Peacock, "The Yellowstone Massacre," 109.

24. McCleary, "Advocate for Bison Arrested." Another remarkable story of Native activism from 1997 is the effort of Lakota Larry Hand Boy, who made a 3,400–mile pilgrimage throughout Indian country as part of a personal Yellowstone bison tribute and awareness campaign. See K. Marie Porterfield, "Runner Crier for the Spirit of the Buffalo," *Indian Country Today*, 23–30 June 1997.

25. Associated Press, "Court Refuses to Stop Buffalo Slaughter Outside of Yellowstone National Park," *News Review* (Roseburg, Oregon), 7 May 1999; Jim Robbins, "An Old Rite Is Invoked to Protect the Park Bison," *New York Times* (L), 2 March 1999; and *War on the Range* (video).

26. *War on the Range* (video); Louis LaRose, "Yellowstone Issue Overview," presentation at the ITBC Second Annual Conference, 21 September 1999, Polson MT.

27. Tim Wapato, "Yellowstone: The ITBC Alternative," presentation at the ITBC Second Annual Conference, 22 September 1999, Polson MT. See also Wapato, "Executive Director's Corner," 2–3; K. Marie Porterfield, "Bison Activists Get Prepared for Slaughter," *Indian Country Today*, 15–22 December 1998; and Fred DuBray and Louis LaRose, comments at the Bison Conference 2000, 8 April 2000, University of Nebraska, Lincoln.

28. Greater Yellowstone Coalition, *The Citizen's Plan to Save Yellowstone Buffalo*; and *Yellowstone Buffalo Wild and Free*, 1.

29. Angus M. Thuermer Jr., "Tribes Welcome Bison Refuge Hunt," *Jackson Hole News*, 15 April 1998; Associated Press, "Wyoming Bison Hunt Is Called Off by Federal Judge," *Arizona Daily Star*, 1 November 1998; *Yellowstone Buffalo Wild and Free*, 2; Barbara Sutteer, comments during "Yellowstone Issue Overview," ITBC Second Annual Conference, 21 September 1999, Polson MT; Wapato, "Executive Director's Corner," 2; and Little Thunder, memorandum to tribal councils.

30. Curly Bear Wagner (Blackfeet), interview by author, 9 August 1999, Browning, Montana; Tim Wapato, comments at the ITBC Second Annual Conference, 21 September 1999, Polson MT; LaRose, ITBC Second Annual Conference, 21 September 1999; Rosalie Little Thunder, comments at the ITBC Second Annual Conference, 21 September 1999; Little Thunder, memorandum to tribal councils; and LaRose, "Yellowstone Issue Overview."

31. Steve Torbit and Louis LaRose, "Wildlife & Cultural Restoration: The Opportunity Provided by the Partnership between the NWF and ITBC," presentation at the Bison Conference 2000, 8 April 2000; and *Yellowstone Buffalo Wild and Free*.

32. Mary Meagher, e-mail correspondence to author, 28 February 2003; Associated Press, "The Road Ahead for Yellowstone's Bison," *News Review* (Roseburg, Oregon), 3 March 2002; Associated Press, "Montana Expands Killing of Bison that Leave Yellowstone," *Wenatchee World* (Wenatchee, Washington), 5 May 2002; and Katherine Q. Seelye (*New York Times*), "Bison Rebound in Yellowstone: New Risks Loom," *Seattle Times*, 26 January 2003.

33. Geist, *Buffalo Nation*, 123, 126.

34. Seelye, "Bison Rebound in Yellowstone"; and Scott McMillion, "Bison Abound," *Bozeman Daily Chronicle*, 27 February 2000.

35. Arvol Looking Horse, quoted in Peacock, "Yellowstone Massacre," 109; Wagner interview, 9 August 1999; and Curly Bear Wagner (Blackfeet), telephone interview by author, 4 March 2003.

6. A Perspective on Canada's Restoration of the Bison

1. Burns, "Bison: Back from the Brink," 22; and Dunn, "Bison Ranching in Canada," 154–58.

For overviews of public bison herds in Canada, see Geist, *Buffalo Nation*, 121–22; and Harvey Payne and Karen Stock, "The Re-Establishment of Endangered Wood Bison in

Manitoba, Canada," unpublished paper, presented at the Bison Conference 2000, 7 April 2000, University of Nebraska, 8–10. The paramount public Canadian herds roam Wood Buffalo National Park, the Mackenzie Bison Sanctuary, Elk Island National Park, and the Nissling River area of the Yukon. Other herds exist in parks and refuges from Manitoba to British Columbia and north into the Northwest Territories. Native in this chapter refers to a distinct ethnic classification in Canada consisting of First Nations (Native American/Canadian) and Métis people.

2. Roe, North American Buffalo, 283–333; Payne and Stock, "Re-Establishment of Endangered Wood Bison in Manitoba," 4; Soper, "History, Range, and Home Life," 362; and Geist, Buffalo Nation, 122. Geist refers to the "Wood Bison" as a "phantom subspecies." Soper considered northern bison as a subspecies; see Soper, "History, Range, and Home Life," 355–57. See also van Zyll de Jong, "A Systematic Study of Recent Bison." The article by Soper set the baseline for studies of northern bison, much as the work Bison of Yellowstone Park by Mary Meagher did for bison in the United States.

3. Gates, Chowns, and Reynolds, "Wood Buffalo at the Crossroads." For a description of the evolution of the arguments over subspeciation, see Geist, Buffalo Nation. Also, Mary Meagher, who like Geist, originally thought that a subspecies existed, now believes that subspeciation is not warranted (Meagher interview, 26 June 1999). Federal officials in Canada at various times have plotted to slaughter herds of Plains Bison or mixed Plains and Wood Bison, viewing these animals as expendable so as to preserve either agricultural interests or animals perceived as genetically pure "Wood Bison." Such differential treatment hinges on distinguishing subspecies. Geist opposes such plans as based on "inadequate science." See Geist, "Agriculture versus Bison in Canada's Wood Buffalo National Park." See also Wobeser, "Disease in Northern Bison."

4. Gates, Chowns, and Reynolds, "Wood Buffalo at the Crossroads, 145–46. See also Barsness, Heads, Hides and Horns, 188–89; Dary, Buffalo Book, 50–51; and Kitto, "The Survival of the American Bison in Canada."

5. Coder, National Movement to Preserve the American Buffalo, 5–7, 228–29, 311; Hebbring Wood, "Origins of Public Bison Herds," 168; and "Pablo's Montana Buffalo Formed Nucleus for Huge Canadian Herd of Bison," Montana Standard, 15 October 1933, 1.

6. Coder, National Movement to Preserve the American Buffalo, 311; Gates, Chowns, and Reynolds, "Wood Buffalo at the Crossroads," 146–48; Geist, Buffalo Nation, 119–21; and McHugh, Time of the Buffalo, 304–6, 231. See also The Great Buffalo Saga (video). For a work focusing on predation of bison by wolves in Canada, see Carbyn, "Wolves and Bison." In contrast to the situation in Yellowstone National Park where reintroduced wolf predation has been fairly negligible (see Smith et al., "Wolf-Bison Interactions in Yellowstone National Park"), Carbyn concludes about wolf predation in northern Canada: "All the studies have shown that wolves regularly and successfully prey on bison" (170).

7. Coder, National Movement to Preserve the American Buffalo, 312; Great Buffalo Saga (video); Hebbring Wood, "Origin of Public Bison Herds in the United States," 181; and Geist, Buffalo Nation, 119–23.

8. For a general work on Canadian conservation, see Foster, Working for Wildlife.

9. See Surtees, "Canadian Indian Policies"; and Surtees, "Canadian Indian Treaties."

10. Ferguson and Burke, "Aboriginal Communities and the Northern Buffalo Controversy," 191.

11. Burns, "Bison: Back from the Brink," 18.

12. Kelly, "United States Indian Policies, 1900–1980," 78–80; Ferguson and Burke, "Aboriginal Communities and the Northern Buffalo Controversy," 192; and Doug Stewart (Northwest Territories Resources, Wildlife and Economic Development, Director of Wildlife and Fisheries) to Mike Carpenter (United States Fish and Wildlife Service), 10 August 1999, 5, Correspondence File, Alberta Environmental Protection Natural Resources Service, High Level Alberta.

13. Stewart to Carpenter, 10 August 1999, 2; and Payne and Stock, "The Re-Establishment of Endangered Wood Bison in Manitoba," 7–8.

14. Payne and Stock, "The Re-Establishment of Endangered Wood Bison in Manitoba," 2–3; and Morton (Alberta Environmental Protection Natural Resources Service wildlife biologist), "Wood Bison Re-Introduction."

15. Morton, "Wood Bison Re-Introduction," 1–3; Gates, Chowns, and Reynolds, "Wood Buffalo at the Crossroads," 152; and Great Buffalo Saga (video).

16. Gates, Chowns, and Reynolds, "Wood Buffalo at the Crossroads"; Morton, "Wood Bison Re-Introduction," 3–4, 5, 10; and Kim Morton, interview by author, 12 August 1999, High Level, Alberta.

17. Gates, Chowns, and Reynolds, "Wood Buffalo at the Crossroads," 153.

18. Ron LaFramboise, interview by author, 16 August 1999, John D'or Prairie, Alberta; and Peter Lamb (Field Superintendent of Southwest Northwestern Territories), "Welcome to Wood Buffalo National Park." For Native harvesting around Wood Buffalo National Park, see Gates, Chowns, and Reynolds, "Wood Buffalo at the Crossroads," 157. Collaboration between various government agencies and First Nations extended beyond field management and into park and museum oversight. For examples, see Fagan, "Bison Hunters of the Northern Plains"; Brink, "Blackfoot and Buffalo Jumps"; and Leo Pard, Peigan (Piikani), interview by author, 10 August 1999, Head-Smashed-In Buffalo Jump, Alberta.

19. Ferguson and Burke, "Aboriginal Communities and the Northern Buffalo Controversy," 202, 189–92.

20. Ferguson and Burke, "Aboriginal Communities and the Northern Buffalo Controversy," 189–90, 195–96, 194, 192, 198–99.

21. Ferguson and Burke, "Aboriginal Communities and the Northern Buffalo Controversy," 204; Gates, Chowns, and Reynolds, "Wood Buffalo at the Crossroads," 160; and George Kurszewski, personal communication with Theresa Ferguson, 18 July 1991, quoted in Ferguson and Burke, "Aboriginal Communities and the Northern Buffalo Controversy," 204.

22. "RAC Who's Who"; "Integrated Traditional and Scientific Knowledge," Bison Research and Containment Program Newsletter; and "Containment Program," Bison Research and Containment Program Newsletter.

23. "Hook Lake Recovery Project," 1–4; Karesh, "Society Page: Wood Bison Recovery Project"; and Janna Van Kessel, interview by author, 14 August 1999, Fort Resolution, Northwest Territories.

24. Darren Campbell (wildlife biologist, Integrated Resource Management Program), interview by author, 13 August 1999, Fort Providence, Northwest Territories; and Greg Nyuli (chief, Dene Got ie), interview by author, 13 August 1999, Fort Providence, Northwest Territories. For numbers on the Mackenzie bison herd, see also Gates, Chowns, and Reynolds, "Wood Buffalo at the Crossroads," 150; and Stewart to Carpenter, 2.

25. Campbell interview, 13 August 1999; and Nyuli interview, 13 August 1999.

26. Nyuli interview, 13 August 1999; and Art Look, interview by author, 13 August 1999, Fort Providence, Northwest Territories.

27. Nyuli interview, 13 August 1999; and Campbell interview, 13 August 1999.

28. Nyuli interview, 13 August 1999.

29. Nyuli interview, 13 August 1999.

30. Darrell Bellerose (Métis), interview by author, 17 August 1999, Kikino, Alberta. For a work addressing the Métis and their conservation ethic during the bison harvests of the 1800s, see Foster, "The Metis and the End of the Plains Buffalo in Alberta." Foster contends that the Métis never were a subsistence people and that "consumerism had become institutionalized in their culture" (72–74). For another work on the Métis specific to the fur trade, see Ray, "Reflections on Fur Trade Social History and Métis History in Canada." For a more general work, see Peterson and Brown, *The New Peoples.*

31. Bellerose interview, 17 August 1999, and Ron Delorme (Plains Cree), interview by author, 18 August 1999, Whitefish Lake Reserve, Alberta.

32. Darryl Steinhauer (Plains Cree), interview by author, 18 August 1999, Whitefish Lake Reserve, Alberta; and Geist, *Buffalo Nation,* 122.

33. Steinhauer interview, 18 August 1999.

34. Alvin Stonechild (Plains Cree), telephone interview by author, 27 February 2003.

35. Stonechild telephone interview, 27 February 2003; Ramona Stonechild (Iroquois), telephone interview by author, 27 February 2003; Sue Michalsky (the Nature Conservancy, Canada), e-mail correspondence with author, 3 March 2003; Harvey Payne, e-mail correspondence with author, 31 July 1999; and http://www.bisoncentral.com/nba/associations.asp?ID=23&catid=2 (accessed 16 October 2004).

36. Edwin Small Legs (Piikani [Piegan]), telephone interview by author, 27 February 2003.

37. Harley Frank (Blood), interview by author, 9 August 1999, Cardston, Alberta.

38. Frank interview, 9 August 1999; and Manning, *Grassland,* 239–44.

39. Frank interview, 9 August 1999; Lois Frank (Blood), interview by author, 9 August 1999, Cardston, Alberta; Pard interview, 10 August 1999; and Harley Frank, telephone interview by author, 28 December 2004.

Conclusion

The chapter epigraph is from Garrett, *Cheyenne River College Tatanka Management Program*, 54. See also Lewis, "Native Americans and the Environment," 423–50, and Smith, "The Issue of Compatibility between Cultural Integrity and Economic Development among Native American Tribes."

1. Pickering, *Seeing the White Buffalo*, 1–14, 2, 131, 92–93, 51–72; Murray, "Miracle, the White Buffalo"; and Diane Carroll (*Kansas City Star*), "American Indians Differ in How They See Birth of White Buffalo," *Lewiston Morning Tribune*, 18 September 1994. Pickering's monograph details the story of white buffalo both historically and in the present. Regarding Miracle's birth, his book covers four perspectives: that of the owners, cultural views of aboriginal people, biological implications, and spiritual ramifications. For a historiographic view of white buffalo, see McCracken, "The Sacred White Buffalo."

2. Carroll, "American Indians Differ in How They See Birth of White Buffalo"; Murray, "Miracle, the White Buffalo," 63; and Pickering, Seeing the White Buffalo, 74–96.

3. *Dances with Wolves* (video). For a work addressing the effect of culture on landscape restoration, see Whittey, "Ways of Seeing."

4. Geraldine Fabrikant (*New York Times*), "Turner's New Empire," *The Oregonian*, 29 November 1996; Webster, "Welcome to Turner Country," 52; Scott, "The Big Open"; Manos, "Ready for a Buffalo Commons," 1; and "A Site to See," *Nature Conservancy*, 36. In contrasting the land ownership by magnates such as Turner to the government, community, or ecological interest group, Valerius Geist poses the following question: "Would we and those that follow us not be better served by a wilderness in the center of the continent than let the land disappear into private duchies ruled over by the corporate and Hollywood nobility?" (*Buffalo Nation*, 135).

5. Standing Bear, *Land of the Spotted Eagle*, 248.

6. Fleischner, "Ecological Costs of Livestock Grazing in Western North America," 629; and Stolzenburg, "Good Cow, Bad Cow," 19. See Garrett, *Cheyenne River College Tatanka Management Program*, 9–17, 28–31; and McNaughton, "Grazing Lawns." For a work on manipulating livestock to simulate native ungulate grazing regimes, see Savory, *Holistic Resource Management*. A fine example of the banter over the ecology of bison restoration emerged from a series of articles and responses in *Conservation Biology*. See Fleischner, "Ecological Costs of Livestock Grazing in Western North America"; Fleischner, "Livestock Grazing: Replies to Brown and McDonald"; Dudley, "Paleontological and Cultural Perspectives on Livestock Grazing in Southwestern Rangelands"; and Brown and McDonald, "Historical and Cultural Perspectives on Grazing." For arguments over whether to graze bison or cattle on a specific site for conservation purposes, see Michael Mansur (Knight Ridder), "Future of Tallgrass Prairie Debated," *Lewiston Morning Tribune*, 22 February 1999. For a comparison on cattle and bison grazing, see Plumb and Dodd, "Foraging Ecology of Bison and Cattle on a Mixed Prairie," and Waggoner, "Summer and Fall Browse Utilization by an Alaskan Bison Herd." For a general work on wildlife conservation and restoration, see Morrison, "Wildlife Conservation and Restoration Ecology."

7. Callenbach, *Bring Back the Buffalo!*, 122; Dunn, "Bison Ranching in Canada," 156; LaFranco, "Bison Meisters"; Robbins, "In the West, A Matter of the Spirit"; Sam Albrecht (National Bison Association President), "Bison—Status and Future of Bison and Bison Industry," presentation at the Bison Conference 2000, 8 April 2000, University of Nebraska; and Associated Press, "Buffalo Market Volatile; 1 Million Head by 2010 Projected," *Wenatchee World*, 29 October 2000.

8. Mathews, *Where the Buffalo Roam*, 20–21; Frank Popper, "The Buffalo Commons and Its Environmental Implications," presentation at the ITBC Second Annual Conference, 21 September 1999, Polson, Montana; and Frank Popper, "Buffalo Commons," presentation at the Bison Conference 2000, 8 April 2000, University of Nebraska, Lincoln; and Popper and Popper, "The Great Plains." See Deborah Popper and Frank Popper, "The Bison Are Coming," *High Country News*, 2 February 1998. For an alternative for the plains, see Callenbach, *Bring Back the Buffalo!*, who proposes replacing cattle with bison and utilizing the wind of the plains for energy production, thereby producing a twofold sustainable economic base.

9. Barsness, *Heads, Hides and Horns*, 168–72; Coder, *National Movement to Preserve the American Buffalo*, 118–70, 322–29; Dary, *Buffalo Book*, 236–40; Garretson, *American Bison*, 205–14; and Isenberg, *Destruction of the Bison*, 168–88. For an analysis of eastern interests in bison restoration, see Coder, *National Movement to Preserve the American Buffalo*, 322–29; and Isenberg, *Destruction of the Bison*, 168–88. For a counterpoint emphasizing the primary role played by westerners, see Zontek, "Hunt, Capture, Raise, Increase."

10. Edward Valandra, "Seeking Refuge: Establishing a Native American Bison Refuge within the Bison Range Boundary Area," presentation at the Bison Conference 2000, 8 April 2000, University of Nebraska, Lincoln.

11. Valandra, "Seeking Refuge"; and Joseph Dupris, "Revitalizing the Buffalo Way of Life: Community Service and Tribal Citizenship," presentation at the Bison Conference 2000, 7 April 2000, University of Nebraska, Lincoln.

12. John Stromnes, "Proposal Would Return Native Grasslands to Tribes," *The Missoulian*, 21 September 1999.

13. Jodi Rave (Lee Newspapers), "Revival of a Heritage: Plains Indian Tribes Work Hard to Maintain Important Cultural Link," http://www.billingsgazette.com/region/980920_rego25.html, (accessed 25 March 2003); *American Buffalo: Spirit of a Nation* (Spirit of a Nation);

Rudner, *Chorus of Buffalo*, 96, 100, 106; Azure interview, 19 August 1999; *Fate of the Plains* (video); DuBray, comments at the screening of *American Buffalo: Spirit of a Nation*, Bison Conference 2000, 8 April 2000; and Harlan, " Rosebud Sioux Endorse Massive Effort to Bring Back Buffalo."

14. Harlan, " Rosebud Sioux Endorse Massive Effort to Bring Back Buffalo"; Archuleta interview, 18 January 1999; and Hughes T. R. and Hughes, Kay, "Buffalo Are Wild Animals." For the appeal of bison for a rancher concerned with conservation and switching from cattle to bison, see O'Brien, *Buffalo for the Broken Heart*. See the following websites for program overviews: http://www.nwf.org/buffalo/programHomepage.

cfm?cpId=15&CFID=25203&CFTOKEN=83404864; http://www.defenders.org/wildlife/
new/prairie/ferret.html; and http://nature.org/wherewework/northamerica/states/okla-
homa/preserves/tallgrass.html.

15. Jack Sullivan (AP), "Tribes Negotiating to Manage National Bison Range," Yakima Herald-Republic, 7 July 2003; U.S. Fish and Wildlife Service, "Congressman Denny
Rehberg"; Sullivan, "Tribes Negotiating to Manage National Bison Range"; and Salish
and Kootenai Confederated Tribes website: www.cskt.org/nr/bison.html (accessed 19
October 2004).

16. U.S. Fish and Wildlife Service, "Congressman Denny Rehberg."

17. Shaw and Meagher, "Bison," 462 (see also pages 458–59); Louis LaRose, "Yellowstone: The ITBC Alternative," presentation at the ITBC Second Annual Conference,
22 September 1999, Polson MT; and Geist, Buffalo Nation, 133. For a description of the
negative effects on wildlife caused by game ranching, see Geist, "Game Ranching:
Threat to Wildlife Conservation in North America." For a presentation of alternative
science based on indigenous knowledge and described as "spiritual management," see
Deloria, "Prospects for Restoration on Tribal Lands." For the positive effects of land
stewardship considering indigenous knowledge in grasslands and semideserts, see
Olson, The Struggle for the Land.

18. Brings Plenty, "The 'Land of Plenty' Needs Bison."

Cheyenne River Lakota: Photo Essay

1. DuBray interview, 19 August 2004; Dennis Rousseau, interview by author, 16 August 2004, Eagle Butte, SD; and Bruchac, "Indian Renaissance," 90.

2. Zontek, "Hunt, Capture, Raise, Increase," 143–45; Jim Garrett (Lakota), interview
by author, 20 September 1999, Dupree, SD; Dupuis interview, 6 April 2000; and DuBray
interview, 19 August 2004.

3. Jim Garrett interview by author, 16 August 2004, Dupree, SD.

4. Garrett interview, 16 August 2004; and Zontek, "Hunt, Capture, Raise, Increase,"
143–45.

5. American Buffalo: Spirit of a Nation (video); and Garrett, Cheyenne River College Tatanka
Management Program, passim.

6. Lee, Scotty Philip, 231–34; Philip, "James (Scotty) Philip," 394; Robinson, West from
Fort Pierre, 126–27; and Hebbring Wood, "Origin of Public Bison Herds in the United
States," 159–66, 175–77.

7. Garrett interview, 16 August 2004; Rousseau interview, 16 August 2004; and Du-
Bray interview, 19 August 2004.

8. Garrett interview, 16 August 2004; Rousseau interview, 16 August 2004; and Du-
Bray interview, 19 August 2004; and Hebbring Wood, "Origin of Public Bison Herds in
the United States," 169–77.

9. DuBray interview, 19 August 2004; Rousseau interview, 16 August 2004; and Bruchac,
"Indian Renaissance," 90.

10. Rousseau interview, 16 August 2004; Bruchac, "Indian Renaissance," 90.

11. Roy Lemmon, telephone interview by author, 23 November 2004.

12. DuBray interview, 19 August 2004; *www.crstgfp.com/bufhunts.html* (accessed 25 October 2004).

13. *www.crstgfp.com/tours.html* (accessed 25 October 2004).

14. Garrett interview, 16 August 2004; DuBray interview, 19 August 2004; Lemmon interview, 23 November 2004; and Rousseau interview, 16 August 2004.

15. Lemmon interview, 23 November 2004.

16. DuBray interview, 19 August 2004.

17. DuBray interview, 19 August 2004.

18. Roy Lemmon, interview by author, 16 August 2004, La Plant, South Dakota.

19. Lemmon interviews, 16 August 2004 and 23 November 2004.

20. Bruchac, "Indian Renaissance," 90; and Lemmon interview, 23 November 2004.

21. Garrett interview, 16 August 2004.

List of References

Primary Sources

Annual Bison Reports File, 1931–1950. Yellowstone National Park Archives. Mammoth Hot Springs, Yellowstone National Park WY.

Barnaby, Tony. Interview by Bon I. Whealdon. "Pablo Loved His Herd," 14 October 1941. WPA Writer's Project File Number 910.037. Montana State University, Bozeman.

Bison File. Yellowstone National Park Archives. Mammoth Hot Springs, Yellowstone National Park WY.

Bison Shipments File. Yellowstone National Park Archives. Mammoth Hot Springs, Yellowstone National Park WY.

Charles Goodnight File, J. Evetts Haley Collection. Nita Stewart Haley Memorial Library, Midland TX.

Doane, Gustavus A., and F. D. Pease. *Report to the Commission of Indian Affairs, 19 February 1873*. M234, Roll 498, National Archives, Washington DC.

Dupree, Calvin. "The First Dupree into South Dakota." Dupree Family File, South Dakota State Archives. Pierre SD.

Dupuis, Frederick. "The Dupuis Letters." Dupree Family File. South Dakota State Archives. Pierre SD.

History of the Bison in Yellowstone National Park (1942–1951) File, by C. K. Skinner and W. B. Alcorn. Yellowstone National Park Archives. Mammoth Hot Springs, Yellowstone National Park WY.

McDonald, Duncan. Interview by Cora Van Deusen, N.d. "Duncan McDonald" (transcript) in the Duncan McDonald file. Montana Historical Society Collections, Helena.

———. "Legend of the Red Buffalo Leader." Compiled by Mabel Olson. 28 August 1941. WPA Writer's Project File Number 300.051. Montana State University, Bozeman.

McDonald, Joseph. Interview by Bon I. Whealdon. "Samuel's Buffalo Calves," September 1941. WPA Writer's Project File Number 910.00, Montana State University, Bozeman.

Meagher, Mary. Shipment of Live [Yellowstone National Park] Bison for Restocking

Purposes (Crow Indian Reservation) [document]. 8 September 1972. Bison Shipments File, Yellowstone National Park Archives. Mammoth Hot Springs, Yellowstone National Park, Wyoming.

Mary Meagher to John W. Grandy IV. 5 January 1973. Bison File, Yellowstone National Park Archives. Mammoth Hot Springs, Yellowstone National Park, Wyoming.

Monroe File (Jack Burton Monroe). Montana Historical Society Collections, Helena MT.

Que-que-sah. Interview by Bon I. Whealdon. "Samuel's Buffalo Calves," 7 January 1942. WPA Writer's Project File Number 910.040, 3. Bozeman, Montana State University.

Skinner, C. K., and W. B. Alcorn. History of the Bison in Yellowstone National Park (1942–1951) File. Yellowstone National Park Archives. Mammoth Hot Springs, Yellowstone National Park WY.

Stinger, Andrew. Interview by Bon I. Whealdon. "Indians Have Several Names," 14 October 1941. WPA Writer's Project File Number 910.039, 1–2. Bozeman, Montana State University.

Yatchak, Jayne. "A Population and Behavioral Study of the North American Buffalo (Bison bison)." National Bison Range files. National Bison Range, Moiese MT.

Yellowstone National Park Superintendent. Yellowstone National Park Superintendent to Region 2 Director, 7 April 1948. In 1948 Annual Bison Report. Annual Bison Reports File, 1931–1950. Yellowstone National Park Archives. Mammoth Hot Springs, Yellowstone National Park WY.

Secondary Sources

Affiliated American Indian Tribes of Yellowstone National Park [map]. Yellowstone National Park WY: Spatial Analysis Center, n.d.

Agenbroad, Larry D. "Buffalo Jump Complexes in Owyhee County, Idaho." *Plains Anthropologist* 23, no. 82, booklet 2 (November 1978): 213–21.

Albanese, Catherine. *Nature Religion in America from the Algonkian Indians to the New Age.* Chicago: University of Chicago Press, 1990.

Allen, Joel. *The American Bisons, Living and Extinct.* Cambridge: Cambridge University Press, 1876.

American Buffalo: Spirit of a Nation [video]. Directed by Judith Dawn Hallet. New York: National Wildlife Federation, Devillier Donegan Enterprises and Thirteen/WNET, 1998.

Anfinson, Scott F. "Prehistoric Subsistence-Settlement Patterns in the Prairie Lake Region." In *The Prairie: Past, Present, and Future, Proceedings of the Ninth North American Prairie Conference*, edited by Gary K. Clambey and Richard H. Pemble, 8–15. Fargo ND: Tri-College University Center for Environmental Studies, 1984.

Antoine, Lester (Dene). Interview by author, 13 August 1999, Fort Providence, Northwest Territories.

Arthur, George. *A Buffalo Round-Up: A Selected Bibliography.* Regina, Saskatchewan: University of Regina Canadian Plains Research Center, 1985.

———. *An Introduction to the Ecology of Early Historic Communal Bison Hunting among Northern Plains Indians.* Ottawa: National Museum of Canada, 1975.

Aubrey, Charles. "The Edmonton Buffalo Herd." *Forest and Stream*, 6 July 1907, 11–13.

———. "Memories of the Buffalo Range: The Last of the Plains Buffalo," *Forest and Stream*, 20 May 1905, 357, 371, 391–92.

———. "Memories of an Old Buffalo Hunter." *Forest and Stream*, vol. 71, 133–34, 173–74, 216–17.

———. "Natural History: Montana's Buffalo." *Forest and Stream*, 5 July 1902, 6.

Axtell, James. "The Ethnohistory of Native America." In *Rethinking American Indian History*, edited by Donald Fixico, 11–29. Albuquerque: University of New Mexico Press, 1997.

Bamforth, Douglas. *Ecology and Human Organization on the Great Plains.* New York: Plenum Press, 1988.

———. "Historical Documents and Bison Ecology on the Great Plains." *Plains Anthropologist* 32, no. 115 (February 1987): 1–16.

Barsness, Larry. *The Bison in Art: A Graphic Chronicle of the American Bison.* Flagstaff AZ: Northland Press, 1977.

———. "The Bison in Art and History." *American West: The Magazine of Western History*, March/April 1977, 10–21.

———. *Heads, Hides and Horns: The Complete Buffalo Book.* Fort Worth: Texas Christian University Press, 1985.

Bartlett, W. A. "The Pablo-Allard Herd." In *"I Will Be Meat for My Salish": The Montana Writers Project and the Buffalo of the Flathead Indian Reservation*, edited by Robert Bigart, 69–102. Pablo MT: Salish Kootenai College Press; Helena: Montana Historical Society Press, 2001.

Beal, Merrill D. *The Story of Man in Yellowstone.* Caldwell ID: Caxton Printers, 1949.

Belue, Ted Franklin. *The Long Hunt: Death of the Buffalo East of the Mississippi.* Mechanicsburg PA: Stackpole Books, 1996.

Berger, Joel, and Carol Cunningham. *Bison: Mating and Conservation in Small Populations.* New York: Columbia University Press, 1994.

Berry Judson, Katherine. *Myths and Legends of the Great Plains.* N.p.: A.C. McClurg, 1913.

Bierhorst, John. *The Way of the Earth: Native America and the Environment.* New York: William Morrow, 1994.

Bigart, Robert, ed. *"I Will Be Meat for My Salish: The Montana Writers Project and the Buffalo of the Flathead Indian Reservation".* Pablo MT: Salish Kootenai College Press; Helena MT: Montana Historical Society Press, 2001.

Bison Central. http://www.bisoncentral.com/nba/associations.asp?ID=23&catid=2.

Bison: A Living Story. Educational CD-ROM. Rapid City SD: ITBC, 2000.

Booth, Annie L., and Harvey M. Jacobs. "Ties that Bind: Native American Beliefs as a

Foundation for Environmental Consciousness." *Environmental Ethics* 12 (spring 1990): 27–43.

Botkin, Daniel. *Discordant Harmonies: A New Ecology for the Twenty-First Century.* Oxford: Oxford University Press, 1992.

———. *Our Natural History: The Lessons of Lewis and Clark.* New York: Berkeley Publishing, 1995.

Bowers, Alfred E., ed. "Crow's Heart Reminiscences and Personal Experiences." In *Native American Autobiography: An Anthology,* edited by Arnold Krupat, 23–30. Madison: University of Wisconsin Press, 1994.

Bozell, John. "Culture, Environment, and Bison Populations on the Late Prehistoric and Early Historic Central Plains." *Plains Anthropologist* 40, no. 152 (1995): 145–63.

Branch, Douglas E. *The Hunting of the Buffalo.* 1962. Reprint, Lincoln: University of Nebraska Press, 1997.

Braudel, Fernand. *Civilization and Capitalism: The Fifteenth through Eighteenth Centuries.* 3 vols. New York: Harper & Row, 1982–1984.

Brings Plenty, Carla Rae. "The 'Land of Plenty' Needs Bison." *Necessity: The Magazine of the Great Plains Restoration Council,* winter/spring 2001–2002, 3.

———. "Struggle to Stop Indiscriminate Slaughter of the Yellowstone Buffalo Nation." *Buffalo Tracks,* winter/spring 1999, 5.

Brink, Jack. "Blackfoot and Buffalo Jumps: Native People in the Head-Smashed-In Project." In *Buffalo,* edited by John Foster, Dick Harrison, and I. S. MacLaren, 19–43. Edmonton: University of Alberta Press, 1992.

Brown, Barnum. "The Buffalo Drive." *Natural History* 32, no. 1: 75–82.

Brown, James H., and William McDonald. "Historical and Cultural Perspectives on Grazing: Reply to Dudley." *Conservation Biology* 11, no. 1 (February 1997): 270–72.

Brown, Jennifer S. H. "Ethnohistorians: Strange Bedfellows, Kindred Spirits." *Ethnohistory* 38, no. 2 (spring 1991): 113–23.

———. "The Métis: Genesis and Rebirth." In *The Prairie West: Historical Readings,* edited by R. Douglas Francis and Howard Palmer, 105–17. 2d ed. Edmonton, Alberta: Pica Pica Press, 1992.

Brown, Joseph Epes. *Animals of the Soul: Sacred Animals of the Oglala Sioux.* Rockport MA: Element, Inc., 1992.

Bruchac, Joseph. "Indian Renaissance." *National Geographic,* September 2004, 76–95.

Bryan, Liz. *The Buffalo People: Prehistoric Archaeology on the Canadian Plains.* Edmonton: University of Alberta Press, 1991.

Bryson, Reid A. "A Perspective on Climatic Change." *Science* 184, no. 4138 (17 May 1974): 753–60.

Budiansky, Stephen. "Yellowstone's Unraveling." *U.S. News and World Report,* 16 September 1996, 80–83.

"Buffalo Market Volatile; 1 Million Head by 2010 Projected." *Wenatchee World* (Wenatchee WA), 29 October 2000.

Burlingame, Merrill G. "The Buffalo in Trade and Commerce." *North Dakota Historical Quarterly* 3, no. 4 (July 1929): 262–91.

Burnham, Philip. *Indian Country, God's Country: Native Americans and the National Parks.* Washington DC: Island Press, 2000.

Burns, Bill. "Bison: Back from the Brink." *The Beaver* 82, no. 5 (October/November 2002): 16–22.

Butler, B. Robert. "Bison Hunting in the Desert West before 1800: The Paleo-Ecological Potential and the Archeological Reality." *Plains Anthropologist* 23, no. 82, booklet 2 (November 1978): 106–12.

Butzer, Karl W. "The Americas Before and After 1492: An Introduction to Current Geographical Research." *Annals of the Association of American Geographers* 82, no. 3 (September 1992): 345–68.

Callenbach, Ernest. *Bring Back the Buffalo!: A Sustainable Future for America's Great Plains.* Washington DC: Island Press, 1996.

Callicott, J. Baird. "American Indian Land Wisdom? Sorting Out the Issues." *Journal of Forest History* 33, no. 1 (January 1989): 35–42.

Cannon, K. P. "Blood Residue Analyses of Ancient Stone Tools Reveal Clues to Prehistoric Subsistence Patterns in Yellowstone." *Cultural Resource Management* 18, no. 2: 1–7.

———. "Paleoindian Use of Obsidian in the Greater Yellowstone Area." *Yellowstone Science* 1, no. 4: 6–9.

Carbyn, L. N. "Wolves and Bison: Wood Buffalo National Park—Past, Present and Future." In *Buffalo*, edited by John Foster, Dick Harrison, and I. S. MacLaren, 167–78. Edmonton: University of Alberta Press, 1992.

Carlson, Paul H. *The Plains Indians.* College Station: Texas A&M Press, 1998.

Catlin, George. *Letters and Notes on the Manners, Customs, and Condition of the North American Indians.* 2 vols. 1841. Reprint, Minneapolis: Ross & Haines, 1965.

Chadwick, Douglas. "Fresh Try for Ferrets." *Defenders: The Conservation Magazine of Defenders of Wildlife,* winter 1997–1998, 14–17, 19–20, 25–27.

Chalfant, Stuart A. "Aboriginal Territories of the Flathead, Pend d'Oreille, and Kutenai Indians of Western Montana." In *Interior Salish and Eastern Washington Indians,* vol. 2, edited by D. A. Horr, 1–32. New York: Garland Publishing, 1974.

"Charles Aubrey," *Forest and Stream,* 5 September 1908, 371.

Cheyenne River Sioux Tribe Game, Fish, and Parks. http://www.crstgp.com/bufhunts .html and http://www.crstgp.com/tours.html.

Child, Brenda J. *Boarding School Seasons: American Indian Families, 1900–1940.* Lincoln: University of Nebraska Press, 1998.

Claiborne, Robert, ed. *The Emergence of Man: The First Americans.* New York: Time-Life Books, 1973.

Clark, Ella E. *Indian Legends of the Northern Rockies.* Norman: University of Oklahoma Press, 1966.

Clifford, E. J. "Bison Hunting." *Oregon Historical Quarterly* 52 (December 1951): 254–64.

Clow, Richmond. "Bison Ecology, Brulé and Yankton Winter Hunting and the Starving Winter of 1832–1833." *Great Plains Quarterly* 15 (fall 1995): 259–70.

Coby, Alonzo (Fort Hall, Shoshone-Bannock). Telephone interview by author, 9 January 2003.

Coder, George D. *The National Movement to Preserve the American Buffalo in the United States and Canada between 1880 and 1920.* PhD diss., Ohio State University, 1975.

Cohen, Mark N. *The Food Crisis in Prehistory: Overpopulation and the Origins of Agriculture.* New Haven: Yale University Press, 1977.

Confederated Salish and Kootenai Tribes. http://www.cskt.org/nr/bison.html.

Connell Szaz, Margaret, and Carmelita S. Ryan. "American Indian Education." In *History of Indian-White Relations,* edited by Wilcomb E. Washburn, 284–300. Vol. 4 of *Handbook of North American Indians,* edited by William C. Sturdevant. 20 vols. Washington DC: Smithsonian Institution, 1988.

"Containment Program." *Bison Research and Containment Program Newsletter* 1, no. 1 (summer 1996): 14.

Cotes, O. J., ed. *The Kalispels: People of the Pend d'Oreille.* 1980. Reprint, Usk WA: Kalispel Tribal Office, 1996.

Cox, Ross. *The Columbia River.* Edited by Edgar Stewart and Jane Stewart. 1957. Reprint, Norman: University of Oklahoma Press, 1976.

Cronon, William, and Richard White. "Ecological Change and Indian-White Relations." In *History of Indian-White Relations,* edited by Wilcomb E. Washburn, 417–29. Vol. 4 of *Handbook of North American Indians,* edited by William C. Sturdevant. 20 vols. Washington DC: Smithsonian Institution, 1988.

Crosby, Alfred W. *The Columbian Exchange: Biological and Cultural Consequences of 1492.* Westport CT: Greenwood Press, 1972.

———. *Germs, Seeds, and Animals: Studies in Ecological History.* Armonk NY: M.E. Sharpe, 1994.

"Dakota Images." *South Dakota History* 16, no. 1 (spring 1986): 89.

Dances with Wolves (video). Produced by Jim Wilson and Kevin Costner. Directed by Kevin Costner. Los Angeles: MGM Inc., 1990.

Danz, Harold. *Of Bison and Man.* Boulder: University Press of Colorado, 1997.

Dary, David. *The Buffalo Book: The Full Saga of the American Animal.* 1974. Reprint, Chicago: Swallow Press/Ohio University Press, 1989.

Davis, L. B., and C. Zeier. "Multi-Phase Late Period Bison Procurement at the Antonsen Site, Southwestern Montana." *Plains Anthropologist,* 23, no. 82, booklet 2 (November 1978): 222–34.

Death Wind on the Plains (video). Directed by David Smits and Barbara Smits. Billings MT: Big Sky Western Heritage Productions, 1997.

Defenders.org. http://www.defenders.org/wildlife/new/prairie/ferret.html.

Deland, Charles E. "Basil Clement (Claymore): The Mountain Trappers." In *South Dakota Historical Collections.* 41 vols. Vol. 2, 380–89. Pierre: Hipple Printing, 1922.

Deloria, Vine. *God Is Red.* New York: Grosset and Dunlap, 1973.

————. "Prospects for Restoration on Tribal Lands." *Restoration and Management Notes*, 10, no. 1 (summer 1992): 48–50.

DeMallie, Raymond J. "The Lakota Ghost Dance: An Ethnohistorical Account." *Pacific Historical Review* 51 (November 1982): 385–405.

DeMallie, Raymond J. and Douglas R. Parks, eds. *Sioux Indian Religion: Tradition and Innovation.* Norman: University of Oklahoma Press, 1987.

Denevan, William M. "The Pristine Myth: The Landscape of the Americas in 1492." *Annals of the Association of American Geographers* 82, no. 3 (September 1992): 369–87.

Denny, Butch (Santee Sioux). Survey correspondence with author, 27 June 2000.

Despain, Don, ed. *Plants and Their Environments: Proceedings of the First Biennial Scientific Conference on the Greater Yellowstone Ecosystem.* Technical Report: NPS/NRYELL /NRTR-93/XX. Denver: NPS, Natural Resources Publication Office, 1994.

Despain, Don, D. Houston, M. Meagher, and P. Schullery. *Wildlife in Transition: Man and Nature on Yellowstone's Northern Range.* Boulder CO: Roberts Rinehart, 1986.

"Destruction of Buffalo." *Forest and Stream*, 30 April 1874, 189.

Diamond, Jared. *Guns, Germs, and Steel: The Fates of Human Societies.* New York: W.W. Norton, 1997.

Dickinson, William R. "Changing Times: The Holocene Legacy." *Environmental History* 5, no. 4 (October 2000): 483–502.

Dillehay, Tom. "Late Quaternary Bison Population Changes on the Southern Plains." *Plains Anthropologist* 19, no. 65 (August 1974): 180–96.

Dippie, Brian, ed. *Charles M. Russell, Word Painter: Letters 1887–1926.* Fort Worth TX: Amon Carter Museum, 1993.

Dixon, Joseph. *To Establish a Permanent National Bison Range.* Senate Executive Document, No. 467. 60th Cong., 1st sess., vol. 2. Washington DC: Government Printing Office, 1908.

Dobak, William A. "Killing the Canadian Buffalo, 1821–1881." *Western Historical Quarterly* 27, no. 1 (spring 1996): 33–52.

Dobyns, Henry F. "Native American Population Collapse and Recovery." In *Scholars and the Indian Experience: Critical Reviews of Recent Writings in the Social Sciences*, edited by William R. Swagerty, 17–35. Bloomington: University of Indiana Press, 1984.

Dolph, James A., and Ivar C. Dolph. "The American Bison: His Annihilation and Preservation." *Montana: The Magazine of Western History*, summer 1975, 14–25.

Dorsey, George A., ed. *Traditions of the Skidi Pawnee.* Boston: Houghton, Mifflin, 1904. Reprint, New York: Kraus Reprint Co., 1969.

Dudley, Joseph P. "Paleontological and Cultural Perspectives on Livestock Grazing in Southwestern Rangelands: Response to Brown and McDonald." *Conservation Biology* 11, no. 1 (February 1997): 267–69.

"Duncan McDonald." *Phillips County News and the Enterprise*, Malta MT, 23 August 1908, 1.

Dunn, Doug. "Bison Ranching in Canada." *Western Horseman*, November 1993, 154–58.

Dunsmore, Roger. *Earth's Mind: Essays in Native Literature*. Albuquerque: University of New Mexico Press, 1997.

Dyck, Ian. "Does Rodeo Have Roots in Ancient Indian Traditions?" *Plains Anthropologist* 41, no. 157 (August 1996): 205–19.

Echo Hawk, Roger. "Working Together." *Nebraska History* 75, no. 1 (spring 1994): 138.

———. "Working Together—Exploring Ancient Worlds." *Society for American Archeology Bulletin* 11, no. 4: n.p.

Ecoffey, Trudy. "Conference Puts Spotlight on Healthy Lifestyles." *Buffalo Tracks*, September 2000, 1, 3.

Edmunds, R. David, ed. *The New Warriors: Native American Leaders Since 1900*. Lincoln: University of Nebraska Press, 2001.

Elrod, Morton J. *The Flathead Buffalo Range: A Report to the American Bison Society of an Inspection of the Flathead Indian Reservation MT for the Purpose of Selecting a Suitable Location for a National Buffalo Range*. Senate Executive Document, No. 467. 60th Cong., 1st sess., vol. 2. Washington DC: Government Printing Office, 1908.

Ens, Gerhard. "Dispossession or Adaptation? Migration and Persistence of the Red River Métis, 1835–1890." In *The Prairie West: Historical Readings*, edited by R. Douglas Francis and Howard Palmer, 136–62. Edmonton, Alberta: Pica Pica Press, 1992.

Epes Brown, Joseph. *Animals of the Soul: Sacred Animals of the Oglala Sioux*. Rockport MA: Element, Inc., 1992.

Epp, Henry T. "Way of the Migrant Herds: Dual Dispersion Strategy among Bison." *Plains Anthropologist* 33, no. 121 (August 1988): 309–20.

Epstein Popper, Deborah, and Frank J. Popper. "The Great Plains: From Dust to Dust." *Planning* (December 1987): 572–77.

Erdoes, Richard, and Alfonso Ortiz, eds. *American Indian Myths and Legends*. New York: Pantheon Books, 1984.

Evers, Larry, and Barre Toelken, eds. *Native American Oral Traditions: Collaboration and Interpretation*. Logan: Utah State University Press, 2001.

Ewers, John. *The Blackfeet: Raiders of the Northwestern Plains*. Norman: University of Oklahoma Press, 1958.

———. *The Horse in Blackfoot Indian Culture with Comparative Material from Other Western Tribes*. Bulletin 159, Bureau of American Ethnology. Washington DC: Smithsonian Institution, 1955.

———. *Indian Life on the Upper Missouri*. Norman: University of Oklahoma Press, 1968.

———. "The Influence of the Fur Trade upon the Indians of the Northern Plains." In *Plains Indian History and Culture: Essays on Continuity and Change*, edited by John C. Ewers, 38–60. Norman: University of Oklahoma Press, 1997.

———. "The Last Bison Drives of the Blackfoot Indians." *Journal of the Washington Academy of Sciences* 39, no. 11 (November 1949): 358–61.

———. "Were the Blackfeet Rich in Horses?" *American Anthropologist* 45, no. 4 (October–December 1943): 602–10.

Fagan, Brian. "Bison Hunters of the Northern Plains." *Archaeology* (May/June 1994): 37–41.

Faith, Mike (Standing Rock Sioux). Telephone interview by author, 22 January 2003.

Faragher, John Mack, Mary Jo Buhle, Daniel Czitrom, and Susan H. Armitage. *Out of Many: A History of the American People.* 2 vols. Englewood Cliffs NJ: Prentice-Hall, 1994.

Fate of the Plains (video). Producer, Christine Lesick. Lincoln: University of Nebraska, 1995.

Ferguson, Theresa A., and Clayton Burke. "Aboriginal Communities and the Northern Buffalo Controversy." In *Buffalo,* edited by John Foster, Dick Harrison, and I. S. MacLaren, 189–206. Edmonton: University of Alberta Press, 1992.

Fisher, Floyd (Northern Cheyenne). Interview by author, 29 June 1999, Lame Deer MT.

Fixico, Donald. "Ethics and Responsibilities in Writing American Indian History." *American Indian Quarterly* 20, no. 1 (1996): 29–39.

———. "Twentieth Century Indian Policy." In *Scholars and the Indian Experience: Critical Reviews of Recent Writings in the Social Sciences,* edited by William R. Swagerty, 123–61. Bloomington: University of Indiana Press, 1984.

Fleischner, Thomas L. "Ecological Costs of Livestock Grazing in Western North America." *Conservation Biology* 8, no. 3 (September 1994): 629–44.

———. "Livestock Grazing: Replies to Brown and McDonald." *Conservation Biology* 10, no. 4 (August 1996): 927–29.

Flores, Dan. "Bison Ecology and Bison Diplomacy: The Southern Plains from 1800 to 1850." *Journal of American History* 78, no. 2 (September 1991): 465–85.

———. *Caprock Canyonlands: Journeys into the Heart of the Southern Plains.* Austin: University of Texas Press, 1990.

Forbis, R. G., L. B. Davis, O. A. Christensen, and G. Fedirchuk, eds. *Post-Pleistocene Man and His Environment.* Calgary, Alberta: The Student's Press/University of Calgary, 1969.

Foster, Janet. *Working for Wildlife: The Beginning of Preservation in Canada.* Toronto: University of Toronto Press, 1978.

Foster, John. "The Métis and the End of the Plains Buffalo in Alberta." In *Buffalo,* edited by John Foster, Dick Harrison, and I. S. MacLaren, 61–78. Edmonton: University of Alberta Press, 1992.

Foster, John, Dick Harrison, and I. S. MacLaren, eds. *Buffalo.* Edmonton: University of Alberta Press, 1992.

Fox, M. W. *Concepts in Ethology: Animal and Human Behavior.* Minneapolis: University of Minnesota Press, 1974.

Frantz, Klaus. *Indian Reservations in the United States: Territory, Sovereignty, and Socioeconomic Change.* Chicago: University of Chicago Press, 1999.

Fraser, Frances. *The Bear Who Stole the Chinook: Tales from the Blackfoot.* Vancouver, British Columbia: Douglas & MacIntyre, 1990.

Frison, George. "Animal Population Studies." *Plains Anthropologist* 23, no. 82, booklet 2 (November 1978): 44–52.

————. "Paleo-Indian Winter Subsistence Strategies on the High Plains." In *Plains Indian Studies: A Collection of Essays in Honor of John C. Ewers and Waldo R. Wedel*, edited by Douglas Ubelaker and Herman J. Viola, 193–219. Washington DC: Smithsonian Institution Press, 1982.

Frison, George, with contributions by Bruce Bradley. *Prehistoric Hunters of the High Plains*, 2d. ed. 1978. Reprint, San Diego: Academic Press, 1991.

Fryxell, F. M. "The Former Range of the Bison in the Rocky Mountains." *Journal of Mammalogy* 9 (1928): 129–39.

Gard, Wayne. *The Great Buffalo Hunt*. New York: Alfred A. Knopf, 1959.

Garretson, Martin S. *The American Bison: The Story of Its Extermination as a Wild Species and Its Restoration under Federal Protection*. New York: New York Zoological Society, 1938.

Garrett, Jim. "A Case Study of an American Indian Economic Development Project: The Cheyenne River Reservation Bison (*Bison bison*) Program." Unpublished paper in author's possession, 23 April 2000.

————. *The Cheyenne River Tribal College Tatanka (Bison bison) Management Program*. Master's thesis, Humboldt State University, 2001.

Garvin, Cecil (Ho Chunk). Survey correspondence with author, 20 June 2000.

Gates, Cormack, Tom Chowns, and Hal Reynolds. "Wood Buffalo at the Crossroads." In *Buffalo*, edited by John Foster, Dick Harrison, and I. S. MacLaren, 139–66. Edmonton: University of Alberta Press, 1992.

Geist, Valerius. "Agriculture versus Bison in Canada's Wood Buffalo National Park." *Conservation Biology* 4, no. 4 (December 1990): 345–46.

————. *The Buffalo Nation: History and Legend of the North American Bison*. Stillwater MN: Voyageur Press, 1996.

————. "Game Ranching: Threat to Wildlife Conservation in North America." *Wildlife Society Bulletin* 13 (1985): 594–98.

————. "The Relation of Social Evolution and Dispersal in Ungulates during the Pleistocene, with Emphasis on the Old World Deer and the Genus Bison." *Journal of Quaternary Research* 1 (1971): 283–315.

Giago, Tim. "Indian or Native? It's an Easy Call." *Yakima Herald Republic*, 24 November 2002, 7E.

Gibson, Arrell Morgan. *The American Indian: Prehistory to the Present*. Lexington MA: D.C. Heath, 1980.

————. "Indian Land Transfers." In *History of Indian-White Relations*, edited by Wilcomb E. Washburn, 211–29. Vol. 4 of *Handbook of North American Indians*, edited by William C. Sturdevant. 20 vols. Washington DC: Smithsonian Institution, 1988.

Gilbert, Miles. *Getting a Stand*. Union City TN: Pioneer Press, 1986.

Gill, George W. "Human Skeletal Remains on the Northwestern Plains." In *Prehistoric Hunters of the High Plains*, edited by George Frison, 431–47. 2d ed. 1978. Reprint, San Diego: Academic Press, 1991.

Gill, Sam. *Mother Earth: An American Story*. Chicago: University of Chicago Press, 1987.

Goff, John H. "The Buffalo in Georgia." *Georgia Review* 11, no. 1 (spring 1957): 19–28.

Goodnight, Charles, Emanuel Dubbs, John Hart, and T. J. Vantine. *Pioneer Days in the Southwest from 1850–1879*. Guthrie OK: State Capital Co., 1909.

Goodstein, Carol. "Buffalo Comeback." *Amicus Journal* 17, no. 1 (spring 1995): 34–38 (reprint from Proquest).

Grassel, Shaun (Lower Brule Sioux). Survey correspondence with author, 20 June 2000.

Gray, Gary G. *Wildlife and People: The Human Dimensions of Wildlife Ecology*. Urbana: University of Illinois Press, 1993.

The Great Buffalo Saga (video). Produced by Mark Zannis and Barrie Howells. Ottawa, Ontario: National Film Board of Canada and Parks Canada, 1985 (video reissue, 1994).

Greater Yellowstone Coalition, *The Citizen's Plan to Save Yellowstone Buffalo*. Bozeman MT: Greater Yellowstone Coalition, 1999.

Greeley, Horace. *An Overland Journey from New York to San Francisco in the Summer of 1859*. Edited by Charles Duncan. New York: Alfred A. Knopf, 1964.

Green, Joe, and June Allard. "The Life and Times of Joe Allard Described in His Own Words Recorded by Him in 1957 and 1958," in *Joseph Allard: His Life and Times and Family History*. Privately published, 1986.

Grinnell, George Bird. "The American Bison in 1924." In *Hunting and Conservation: The Book of the Boone and Crockett Club*, edited by George Bird Grinnell and Charles Sheldon, 393–411. New Haven: Yale University Press, 1925.

———. *Blackfeet Lodge Tales*. 1892. Reprint, Lincoln: University of Nebraska Press, 2003.

———. *The Cheyenne Indians*. 2 vols. Lincoln: University of Nebraska Press, 1972.

Gudeman, Stephen F. *Economic Anthropology: Models and Metaphors of Livelihood*. London: Routledge and Kegan Paul, 1986.

Guthrie, Dale (R. D.). "Bison Evolution and Zoogeography in North America during the Pleistocene." *Quarterly Review of Biology* 45 (March 1970): 1–15.

———. "Bison and Man in North America." *Canadian Journal of Anthropology* 1, no. 1 (June 1980): 55.

———. *Frozen Fauna of the Mammoth Steppe*. Chicago: University of Chicago Press, 1989.

———. "Mosaics, Allelochemics and Nutrients: An Ecological Theory of Late Pleistocene Megafaunal Extinctions." In *Quaternary Extinctions: A Prehistoric Revolution*, edited by Paul S. Martin and Richard G. Klein, 259–98. Tucson: University of Arizona Press, 1984.

Hagan, William T. "United States Indian Policies, 1860–1890." In *History of Indian-White Relations*, edited by Wilcomb E. Washburn, 51–65. Vol. 4 of *Handbook of North American Indians*, edited by William C. Sturdevant. 20 vols. Washington DC: Smithsonian Institution, 1988.

Haines, Aubrey L. *The Yellowstone Story: A History of Our First National Park*. 2 vols. Denver:

Yellowstone Library and Museum Association/Colorado Associated University Press, 1977.

Haines, Francis. *The Buffalo: The Story of American Bison and Their Hunters from Prehistoric Times to the Present.* 1970. Reprint, Norman: University of Oklahoma Press, 1995.

———. *Horses in America.* New York: Thomas Y. Crowell, 1971.

———. "The Northward Spread of Horses among the Plains Indians." *American Anthropologist* 40, no. 3 (July–September 1938): 429–37.

———. *The Plains Indians: Their Origins, Migrations and Cultural Development.* New York: Thomas Y. Crowell, 1976.

———. "Where Did the Plains Indians Get Their Horses?" *American Anthropologist* 40, no. 1 (January–March 1938): 112–17.

Haley, J. Evetts. *Charles Goodnight: Cowman and Plainsman.* Norman: University of Oklahoma Press, 1936.

Hamner, Laura. *The No-Gun Man of Texas: A Century of Achievement, 1835–1929.* Amarillo TX: Hamner, 1935.

Hanson, Jeffery R. "Bison Ecology in the Northern Plains and a Reconstruction of Bison Patterns for the North Dakota Region." *Plains Anthropologist* 29, no. 104 (May 1984): 93–113.

Harlan, Bill. "Rosebud Sioux Endorse Massive Effort to Bring Back Buffalo," Associated Press, 26 August 2001. In *Necessity: The Magazine of the Great Plains Restoration Council,* winter/spring 2001–2002, 1.

Harper, Francis. "Letter to the Canadian Field Naturalist." *Canadian Field Naturalist* 39 (1925): 45.

Harrington, John A., Jr. and Jay R. Harman. "Climate and Vegetation in Central North America: Natural Patterns and Human Alterations." *Great Plains Quarterly* 11 (spring 1991).

Harrod, Howard. *The Animals Came Dancing: Native American Sacred Ecology and Animal Kinship.* Tucson: University of Arizona Press, 2000.

———. *Becoming and Remaining a People: Native American Religions on the Northern Plains.* Tucson: University of Arizona Press, 1995.

———. *Renewing the World: Plains Indian Religion and Morality.* Tucson: University of Arizona Press, 1987.

Hasselstrom, Linda. *Bison: Monarch of the Plains.* Portland OR: Graphic Arts Center Publishing, 1998.

Hebbring Wood, Judith. "The Origin of Public Bison Herds in the United States." *Wicazo Sa Review* 15, no. 1 (spring 2000): 157–82.

Hebert, H. Josef. "Babbitt to Montana: Hold Your Fire on Wayward Buffalo." *Lewiston Morning Tribune,* 13 March 1997, 3C.

Henderson, John. "The Former Range of the Buffalo." *American Naturalist* 6 (1872): 80.

Hill, Cheryl. "An Indigenous Overview of the *Pte Oyate.*" *Buffalo Tracks,* July 2001, 6–7.

"History of Buffalo Legislation." *Forest and Stream,* 6 April 1882, 1, 890.

Hodgson, Bryan. "Buffalo: Back Home on the Range." *National Geographic* 185, no. 5 (November 1994): 64–89.

Holder, Preston. *The Hoe and the Horse on the Plains*. Lincoln: University of Nebraska Press, 1970.

Holterman, Jack. *Pablo of the Buffalo: Historical Monographs*. West Glacier MT: Glacier Natural History Association, 1991.

"Hook Lake Recovery Project: Progress Report." Unpublished paper in author's possession, winter 1997–1998.

Honor the Earth. http://www.honortheearth.com.

Hornaday, William T. "Discovery, Life, History, and Extermination of the American Bison." In *Report of the National Museum, 1887*. Washington DC: Government Printing Office, 1889.

———. *Thirty Years War for Wild Life*. 1930. Reprint, New York: Arno/New York Times, 1970.

Hough, Emerson. "A Buffalo Hunt Indeed." *Forest and Stream*, 14 October 1887, 337.

Hough, Walter. "The Bison as a Factor in Ancient American Culture History." *Scientific Monthly* 30 (January–June 1930): 315–19.

Howard, Helen Addison. "The Men Who Saved the Buffalo." *Journal of the West*, July 1975, 122–29.

Hoxie, Frederick E. "The Curious Story of Reformers and the American Indians." In *Indians in American History*, edited by Frederick Hoxie, 205–30. Arlington Heights IL: Harlan Davidson, 1988.

———. "Ethnohistory for a Tribal World." *Ethnohistory* 44, no. 4 (fall 1997): 595–615.

Hoyt-Goldsmith, Diane. *Buffalo Days*. New York: Holiday House, presented by the Intertribal Bison Cooperative, 1997.

Huebner, Jeffrey. "Late Prehistoric Bison Populations in Central and Southern Texas." *Plains Anthropologist* 36, no. 137 (1991): 343–57.

Hughes, Donald J. *American Indian Ecology*. El Paso: Texas Western Press, 1983.

Hughes, Kay, and T. R. Hughes. "Buffalo Are Wild Animals—and Why They Need to Remain So." *The Great Plains Buffalo Association Newsletter* 4, no. 1 (January–March 2000): 1–2.

Hultkrantz, Åke. *Belief and Worship in Native North America*. Syracuse NY: Syracuse University Press, 1981.

———. "Water Sprites: The Elders of Fish in Aboriginal North America." *American Indian Quarterly* 7, no. 3 (summer 1983): 1–22.

Humphrey, Kay. "Buffalo Processing Industry Booming in Indian Country," *Indian Country Today*, 23–30 June 1997, A1–A2.

Hunter, John D. *Manners and Customs of Indian Tribes*. Philadelphia, 1832.

Inman, Henry, ed. *Buffalo Jones' Adventures on the Plains*. Lincoln: University of Nebraska Press, 1970.

"Integrated Traditional and Scientific Knowledge." *Bison Research and Containment Program Newsletter* 1, no. 1 (summer 1996): 13.

Intertribal Bison. http://www.intertribalbison.org.

Intertribal Bison Cooperative. *Gifts of the Buffalo Nation*. Rapid City SD: ITBC, 1998.

———. *1998 Annual Report*. Rapid City SD: ITBC, 1998.

———. *Intertribal Bison Cooperative*. Rapid City: ITBC, 1999.

Isenberg, Andrew. *The Destruction of the Bison: An Environmental History, 1750–1920*. Cambridge: Cambridge University Press, 2000.

Iverson, Peter. *When Indians Became Cowboys: Native Peoples and Cattle Ranching in the American West*. Norman: University of Oklahoma Press, 1994.

———. "When Indians Became Cowboys," *Montana: The Magazine of Western History*, winter 1995, 16–31.

Jackson, Donald, and Mary Lee Spence, eds. *The Expeditions of John Charles Fremont, Vol. 1: Travels from 1838 to 1844*. Urbana: University of Illinois Press, 1970.

Jackson Penney, Grace. *Tales of the Cheyennes*. Boston: Houghton Mifflin, 1953.

Jacobs, Wilbur. *The Fatal Confrontation: Historical Studies of American Indians, Environment and Historians*. Albuquerque: University of New Mexico Press, 1996.

Janetski, Joel. *The Indians of Yellowstone National Park*. Salt Lake City: Bonneville Books/University of Utah Press, 1987.

Johnson, Minette. "Fort Belknap Looks to Tourists." *Defenders: The Conservation Magazine of Defenders of Wildlife*, winter 1997–1998, 18.

Johnson, Sandy. *The Book of Elders: The Life Stories and Wisdom of Great American Indians as Told to Sandy Johnson*. San Bruno CA: Audio Literature, 1996.

Johnston, A. "Man's Utilization of the Flora of the Northwest Plains." In *Post-Pleistocene Man and His Environment on the Northern Plains*, edited by R. G. Forbis, L. B. Davis, O. A. Christensen, and G. Fedirchuk, 109–77. Calgary, Alberta: The Student's Press/University of Calgary, 1969.

Jones, Tom. *The Last of the Buffalo*. Cincinnati: Scenic Souvenirs, 1909.

Kardulias, P. Nick. "Fur Production as a Specialized Activity in a World System: Indians in the North American Fur Trade." *American Indian Culture and Research Journal* 14, no. 1 (1990): 25–60.

Karesh, William. "Society Page: Wood Bison Recovery Project." *Wildlife Conservation* 101, no. 6 (November/December 1998): 8.

Kay, Charles. "Aboriginal Overkill and Native Burning: Implications for Modern Ecosystem Management." *Western Journal of Applied Forestry* 10, no. 4 (October 1995): 121–26.

———. "Aboriginal Overkill: The Role of Native Americans in Structuring Western Ecosystems." *Human Nature* 5, no. 4: 359–98.

Keeler, Kathleen. "Grasslands: An Introduction." *Great Plains Quarterly* 15, no. 3 (summer 1995): 163–68.

Keiter, R., and M. Boyce, eds. *The Greater Yellowstone Ecosystem: Redefining America's Wilderness Heritage*. New Haven: Yale University Press, 1991.

Keiter, Robert, and Peter Froehlicher. "Bison, Brucellosis, and the Law in the Greater Yellowstone Ecosystem." *Land and Water Law Review* 28, no. 1 (1993): 1–75.

Keller, Robert, and Michael F. Turek. *American Indians and National Parks*. Tucson: University of Arizona Press, 1998.

Kellert, Stephen R., and Edward O. Wilson. *The Biophilia Hypothesis*. New York: Shearwater Books, 1993.

Kelly, Lawrence C. "United States Indian Policies, 1900–1980." In *History of Indian-White Relations*, edited by Wilcomb E. Washburn, 66–80. Vol. 4 of *Handbook of North American Indians*, edited by William C. Sturdevant. 20 vols. Washington DC: Smithsonian Institution, 1988.

Keyser, James D., and George C. Knight. "The Rock Art of Western Montana." *Plains Anthropologist* 21, no. 171 (February 1976): 1–10.

Kingston, C. S. "Buffalo in the Pacific Northwest." *Washington Historical Quarterly* 23, no. 3 (July 1932): 163–72.

Kitto, F. H. "The Survival of the American Bison in Canada." *The Geographical Journal* 58 (January–June 1924): 431–37.

Knoblock, Frieda. *The Culture of Wilderness: Agriculture as Colonization in the American West*. Chapel Hill: University of North Carolina Press, 1996.

Koucky, Rudolph W. "The Buffalo Disaster of 1882." *North Dakota History* 50 (winter 1983): 23–30.

Krantz, Robert (San Juan). Telephone interview by author, 16 January 2003.

Krech III, Shepard. *The Ecological Indian: Myth and History*. New York: W.W. Norton, 1999.

Krupat, Arnold, ed. *Native American Autobiography: An Anthology*. Madison: University of Wisconsin Press, 1994.

Kvasnicka, Robert V. "United States Indian Treaties and Agreements." In *History of Indian-White Relations*, edited by Wilcomb E. Washburn, 195–201. Vol. 4 in *Handbook of North American Indians*, edited by William C. Sturdevant. 20 vols. Washington DC: Smithsonian Institution, 1988.

LaDuke, Winona. *All Our Relations: Native Struggles for Land and Life*. Cambridge MA: Southend Press; Minneapolis: Honor the Earth, 1999.

LaFranco, Robert. "Bison Meisters." *Forbes*, 27 March 1995, 64–65.

Lagrand, James B. "Whose Voices Count? Oral Sources and Twentieth Century American Indian History." *American Indian Culture and Research Journal* 21, no. 1 (1997): 73–105.

Lake, Don. "Department of Labor Funding for Education/Training." *Buffalo Tracks*, June 2000, 1, 4.

Lamb, Peter. "Welcome to Wood Buffalo National Park." *Wood Buffalo National Park Tales* 1998, 2–3. Fort Smith, Northwest Territories: Parks Canada, 1998.

Lame Deer, John. "White Buffalo Woman." In *American Indian Myths and Legends*. Edited by Richard Erdoes and Alfonso Ortiz, 47–52. New York: Pantheon Books, 1984.

Lee, C. Wayne. *Scotty Philip: The Man Who Saved the Buffalo*. Caldwell ID: Caxton Printers, 1975.

Lehmer, Donald. "The Plains Bison Hunt—Prehistoric and Historic." *Plains Anthropologist* 8, no. 22 (November 1963): 211–17.

Leopold, Aldo Starker, S. A. Cain, C. M. Cottam, I. N. Gabrielson, and T. L. Kimball. *Wildlife Management in the National Park: Report to the Secretary of Interior.* Washington DC: Government Printing Office, 1963. Reprinted as "Wildlife Management in the National Parks," in *Transcripts of the North American Wildlife Conference,* edited by Aldo Starker Leopold, 28–45. Washington DC: Wildlife Management Institute, 1963.

Lewis, David Rich. "Native Americans and the Environment: A Survey of Twentieth Century Issues." *American Indian Quarterly* 19, no. 3 (summer 1995): 423–50.

———. *Neither Wolf Nor Dog: American Indians, Environment, and Agrarian Change.* New York: Oxford University Press, 1994.

———. "Still Native: The Significance of Native Americans in the History of the Twentieth-Century American West." *Western Historical Quarterly* (May 1993): 203–27.

Linderman, Frank B. *American: The Life Story of a Great Indian, Plenty Coups Chief of the Crows.* Yonkers-on-Hudson NY: World Book, 1930.

———, ed. "Plenty Coups, Chief of the Crows." In *Native American Autobiography: An Anthology,* edited by Arnold Krupat, 241–57. Madison: University of Wisconsin Press, 1994.

Little Thunder, Rosalie. Memorandum to tribal councils, 7 May 1999. www.honor theeearth.com/buffalo/consult (accessed 23 July 2000).

Lopez, Barry. *Of Wolves and Men.* New York: Charles Scribner's, 1978.

Lott, Dale. *American Bison: A Natural History.* Berkeley: University of California Press, 2002.

Lundwickson, John. "Historic Indian Tribes: Ethnohistory and Archeology." *Nebraska History* 75, no. 1 (spring 1994): 140–41.

Lupo, Karen D. "The Historical Occurrence and Demise of Bison in Northern Utah." *Utah Historical Quarterly* 64, no. 2 (spring 1996): 168–81.

MacLeish, William H. *The Day before America.* Boston: Houghton Mifflin, 1994.

Malin, James. *The Grassland of North America: Prolegomena to Its History with Addenda.* Lawrence KS: James Malin, 1947.

Manning, Richard. *Grassland: The History, Biology, Politics, and Promise of the American Prairie.* New York: Viking Press, 1995.

Manos, Jarid. "Ready for a Buffalo Commons—Getting the Hard Work Done." *Necessity: The Magazine of Great Plains Restoration Council,* summer 2001, 1.

Martin, Paul S., ed. *Pleistocene Extinctions: The Search for a Cause.* New Haven CT: Yale University Press, 1967.

Martin, Paul S. and Richard G. Klein, eds. *Quaternary Extinctions: A Prehistoric Revolution.* Tucson: University of Arizona Press, 1984

Martin, Paul S. and Christine R. Szuter. "War Zones and Game Sinks in Lewis and Clark's West." *Conservation Biology* 13, no. 1 (February 1999): 36–45.

Mathews, Anne. *Where the Buffalo Roam: The Storm over the Revolutionary Plan to Restore America's Great Plains.* New York: Grove Weidenfeld, Grove Press, 1992.

Mathiessen, Peter. *Indian Country.* New York: Penguin Books, 1979.

McCarthy Ferguson, Mary. *The Honorable James McKay of Deer Lodge*. Winnipeg, Saskatchewan: Privately printed, 1972.

McCracken, Harold. "The Sacred White Buffalo." *Natural History* (September 1946): 304–9, 341.

McDonald, Jerry. *North American Bison: Their Classification and Evolution*. Berkeley: University of California Press, 1981.

———. "The Reordered North American Selection Regime and Late Quaternary Megafaunal Extinctions." In *Quaternary Extinctions: A Prehistoric Revolution*, edited by Paul S. Martin and Richard G. Klein, 404–39. Tucson: University of Arizona Press, 1984.

McHugh, Tom. *The Time of the Buffalo*. 1972. Reprint, Lincoln: University of Nebraska Press, 1979.

McNaughton, Sam. "Grazing Lawns: Animals in Herds, Plant Form, and Co-evolution." *American Naturalist* 6: 863–83.

———. *Review of Wildlife Policies in the U.S. National Parks*. Edited by Fred Wagner, Ronald Foresta, R. Bruce Gill, Dale R. McCullough, Michael R. Pelton, William F. Porter, and Hal Salwasser. *Journal of Wildlife Management* 60, no. 3: 685–87.

McWhorter, L. V., ed. "Yellow Wolf: His Own Story." In *Native American Autobiography: An Anthology*, edited by Arnold Krupat, 186–202. Madison: University of Wisconsin Press, 1994.

Meagher, Mary. *The Bison of Yellowstone National Park*. Washington DC: Government Printing Office, 1973.

———. "Evaluation of Boundary Control for Bison of Yellowstone National Park." *Wildlife Society Bulletin* 17 (1989): 15–19.

———. "Evolutionary Pathways and Relationships." Unpublished paper in author's possession, dated 1 July 2001.

———. "Evolutionary Pathways and Relationships." Unpublished draft of book chapter in author's possession, July, 2001.

———. "Range Expansion by Bison of Yellowstone National Park." *Journal of Mammalogy* 70, no. 3: 670–75.

Meagher, Mary, and Douglas B. Houston. *Yellowstone and the Biology of Time: Photographs Across a Century*. Norman: University of Oklahoma Press, 1999.

Meagher, Mary, and Margaret Meyer. "On the Origin of Brucellosis in Bison of Yellowstone National Park: A Review." *Conservation Biology* 8, no. 3 (September 1994): 645–53.

Medicine Crow, Joe. "Notes on Crow Indian Buffalo Jump Traditions." *Plains Anthropologist* 23, no. 82, booklet 2 (November 1978): 249.

Meinig, D. W. "The Beholding Eye: Ten Versions of the Same Scene." In *The Interpretation of Ordinary Landscapes: Geographical Essays*, edited by D. W. Meinig, 33–50. New York: Oxford University Press, 1979.

Merriam, H. G., ed. *Frontier Woman: The Story of Mary Ronan as Told to Margaret Ronan*. Missoula: University of Montana Press, 1973.

Mihesuah, Devon. *So You Want to Write about American Indians?*. Lincoln: University of Nebraska Press, 2005.

———. "Voices, Interpretations, and the 'New Indian History': Comment on the *American Indian Quarterly's* Special Issue on Writing about American Indians." *American Indian Quarterly* 20, no. 1 (1996): 91–108.

Mitchell, Joseph D. "The American Indian: A Fire Ecologist." *American Indian Culture and Research Journal* 2, no. 2 (1978): 26–31.

Momaday, N. Scott. "Native American Attitudes toward the Environment." In *Seeing with a Native Eye*, edited by Walter H. Capps, 80–97. New York: Harper and Row, 1976.

Mooney, James. *The Ghost Dance Religion and the Sioux Outbreak of 1890*. Chicago: University of Chicago Press, 1965. Reprinted from *Fourteenth Annual Report of the Bureau of Ethnology to the Secretary of the Smithsonian Institution, 1892–1893*, part 2. Washington DC: Government Printing Office, 1896.

"Montana Buffalo Preserve." *Forest and Stream*, 25 April 1908, 697.

Morey, Mark. "Yakima Bison Herd Still Growing," *Wenatchee World* (Wenatchee WA), 3 February 2002, C7.

Morrison, Michael L. "Wildlife Conservation and Restoration Ecology." *Restoration & Management Notes* 13, no. 2 (winter 1995): 203–8.

Morton, Kim. "Wood Bison Re-Introduction: Hay/Zama Herd Progress Report—April 1999." Unpublished paper in author's possession.

Mountain Tree Community School (Potsdam, New York). *The Gift of the Great American Bison*. Potsdam NY: Mountain Tree Community School, 1998.

Murphy, John Mortimer. *Sporting Adventures in the Far West*. London: Sampson, Low, Marston, Searle and Rivington, 1879.

Murray, Louann W. "Miracle, the White Buffalo." *Persimmon Hill* 24, no. 2 (summer 1996): 62–63.

Muscoda Bison Herd (Ho Chunk). http://www.muscodabison.com (accessed 26 January 2003).

National Wildlife Federation. http://www.nwf.org/buffalo/programHomepage.cfm?cpld=15&CFID=25203&CFTOKEN=83404864

Nature.org. http://nature.org/wherewework/northamerica/states/oklahoma/preserves/tallgrass.html

O'Brien, Dan. *Buffalo for the Broken Heart: Restoring Life to a Black Hills Ranch*. New York: Random House, 2002.

Olguin, Chris (Southern Ute). Telephone interview by author, 16 January 2003.

Olson, Dean F. *Alaska Reindeer Herdsmen: A Study of Native Management in Transition*. Fairbanks: Institute of Social, Economic and Government Research, University of Alaska, 1969.

Olson, Paul A., ed. *The Struggle for the Land: Indigenous Insight and Industrial Empire in the Semi-Arid World*. Lincoln: University of Nebraska Press, 1990.

Ortiz, Alfonso. "Some Concerns Central to the Writing of 'Indian' History." *The Indian Historian* (winter 1977): 17–22.

Osborn, Alan J. "Ecological Aspect of Equestrian Adaptations in Aboriginal North America." *American Anthropologist* 85 (1983): 563–91.

Ostler, Jeffrey. "They Regard Their Passing as Wakan." *Western Historical Quarterly* 30, no. 4 (winter 1999): 475–97.

Owens, Kenneth, and Sally Owens. "Montana Commentary—Buffalo and Bacteria." *Montana: The Magazine of Western History,* spring 1987, 65–67.

"The Outlaw Buffalo." *Forest and Stream,* 12 November 1910, 778.

"Pablo Buffalo Sale." *Forest and Stream,* 8 June 1907, 893.

Pahmahmie, Alan (Prairie Band of the Potawatomi). Telephone interview by author, 16 January 2003.

Palladino, Lawrence. *Indian and White in the Northwest: A History of Catholicity in Montana, 1831–1891.* 2d ed. Lancaster PA: Wickersham Publishing, 1922.

Parker, Valentine (Omaha). Telephone interview by author, 10 January 2003.

Pate, Jack (Choctaw). Survey correspondence with author, 19 June 2000.

Peacock, Doug. "The Yellowstone Massacre." *Audubon: Magazine of the National Audubon Society,* May–June 1997, 4–49, 102–3, 106–10.

Peterson, Jacqueline, and Scott Anfinson. "The Indian and the Fur Trade." In *Scholars and the Indian Experience: Critical Reviews of Recent Writing in the Social Sciences,* edited by W. R. Swagerty, 223–58. Bloomington: Indiana University Press, 1984.

Peterson, Jacqueline, and Jennifer S. H. Brown. *The New Peoples: Being and Becoming Métis in North America.* Winnipeg: University of Manitoba Press, 1985.

Philip, George. *James (Scotty) Philip.* Vol. 20 of *South Dakota Historical Collections.* Pierre SD: Hipple Printing, 1940.

Philip, Kenneth R. *Termination Revisited: American Indians on the Trail to Self-Determination.* Lincoln: University of Nebraska Press, 1999.

Pickering, Robert. "Natural History and Human Interaction." *Bison World* 25, no. 1 (January–March 2000), 14–15.

———. *Seeing the White Buffalo.* Denver: Denver Museum of Natural History, 1997.

Pielou, E. C. *After the Ice Age: The Return of Life to Glaciated North America.* Chicago: University of Chicago Press, 1991.

"Plains or Wood Bison." In *Elk Island National Park 1999 Visitors' Guide,* 13. Ottawa, Ontario: Parks Canada, 1999.

Plumb, Glenn E., and Jerrold L Dodd. "Foraging Ecology of Bison and Cattle on a Mixed Prairie: Implications for Natural Area Management." *Ecological Applications* 3, no. 4 (1993): 631–43.

Popper, Deborah E., and Frank J. Popper. "The Buffalo Commons: A Bioregional Vision of the Great Plains." *Landscape Architecture* (April 1994): 144.

Popper, Frank J., and Deborah Popper. "The Great Plains: From Dust to Dust." *Planning* (December 1987): 572–77.

Pringle, Heather. *In Search of Ancient North America: An Archaeological Journey to Forgotten Cultures.* New York: John Wiley & Sons, 1996.

Pritchard, James A. *Preserving Yellowstone's Natural Conditions: Science and the Perception of Nature*. Lincoln: University of Nebraska Press, 1999.

Pritchard, Paul. "Slaughter in the Sanctuary." *National Parks: The Magazine of the National Parks and Conservation Association*, March/April 1997, 4.

"Progress Report." *Hook Lake Recovery Project Newsletter*, winter 1997–1998, 1–4.

Prucha, Francis Paul. "United States Indian Policies, 1815–1860." In *History of Indian-White Relations*, edited by Wilcomb E. Washburn, 40–50. Vol. 4 of *Handbook of North American Indians*, edited by William C. Sturdevant. 20 vols. Washington DC: Smithsonian Institution, 1988.

Quigg, J. Michael. "Winter Bison Procurement in Southwestern Alberta." *Plains Anthropologist* 23, no. 82, booklet 2 (November 1978): 53–58.

"RAC Who's Who." *Bison Research and Containment Program Newsletter* 1, no. 1 (summer 1996): 9.

Ray, Arthur J. "Reflections on Fur Trade Social History and Métis History in Canada." *American Indian Culture and Research Journal* 6: 91–107.

Reeves, Brian. "Communal Bison Hunters of the Northern Plains." In *Hunters of the Recent Past*, edited by Leslie Davis and Brian Reeves, 173–91. London: Unwin Hyman, 1990.

———. "The Southern Alberta Paleo-Cultural—Paleo-Environmental Sequence." In *Post-Pleistocene Man and His Environment on the Northern Plains*, edited by R. G. Forbis, L. B. Davis, O. A. Christensen, and G. Fedirchuk, 6–46. Calgary, Alberta: The Student's Press/University of Calgary, 1969.

Reher, Charles A. "Buffalo Population and Other Deterministic Factors in a Model of Adaptive Process on the Shortgrass Plains." *Plains Anthropologist* 23, no. 82, booklet 2 (November 1978): 23–39.

Reiger, John F. *American Sportsmen and the Origins of Conservation*. Rev. ed. Lincoln: University of Nebraska Press, 1986.

Return of the Native. Written and produced by Sam Hurst. Rapid City SD: Intertribal Bison Cooperative, 1995.

Ricci, Susan. "Babbitt, Belknap, and Buffalo." *Buffalo Tracks*, winter/spring 1999, 4.

———. *The Great Kinship between Native Americans and the Buffalo Nation*. Rapid City SD: ITBC and NPS Historic Preservation Fund, 2001.

———. "ITBC Takes Buffalo Restoration Movement to DC." *Buffalo Tracks*, winter/spring 1999, 1–2.

———. "Montana Tribes Demonstrate the Meaning of Cooperation." *Buffalo Tracks*, March 2001, 2.

———. "Spokane Tribe of Indians Welcomes ITBC." *Buffalo Tracks*, June 2000, 9.

Ricklis, Robert A. "The Spread of a Late Prehistoric Bison Hunting Complex: Evidence from the South-Central Coastal Prairie of Texas." *Plains Anthropologist* 37, no. 140 (1992): 261–74.

Riggs, Reverend Thomas L., as told to Margaret Kellogg Howard. "Sunset to Sunset: A Lifetime with My Brothers, the Dakotas." *South Dakota Historical Collections*. Vol. 29. Stickney SD: Argus Printers, 1958.

Riney, Scott. *The Rapid City Indian School, 1898–1933.* Norman: University of Oklahoma Press, 1999.

Robbins, Jim. "The Elk of Yellowstone." *Wildlife Conservation*, March/April 1998, 36–45.

———. "Historians Revisit Slaughter on the Plains." *New York Times*, 16 November 1999.

———. *Last Refuge: The Environmental Showdown in Yellowstone and the American West.* New York: William Morrow and Company, 1993.

Robinson, Charles M., III. *The Buffalo Hunters.* Austin TX: State House Press, 1995.

Robinson, James M. *West from Fort Pierre: The Wild World of James (Scotty) Philip.* Los Angeles: Westernlore Press, 1974.

Roe, Frank Gilbert. *The Indian and the Horse.* Norman: University of Oklahoma Press, 1955.

———. *The North American Buffalo: A Critical Study of the Species in Its Wild State.* 2d ed. Toronto: University of Toronto Press, 1970. First published 1951.

Ronan, Peter. "Annual Report to the Commissioner of Indian Affairs, 1888." *Annual Report of the Commissioner of Indian Affairs to the Secretary for the Year, 1888.* Washington DC: Government Printing Office, 1888.

Rorabacher, J. Albert. *The American Buffalo in Transition: A Historical and Economic Survey of the Bison in America.* St. Cloud MN: North Star Press, 1970.

Rudner, Ruth. *Chorus of Buffalo.* Short Hills NJ: Burford Books, 2000.

Rylatt, R. M. *Surveying the Canadian Pacific: Memoir of a Railroad Pioneer.* Salt Lake City: University of Utah Press, 1991.

Sample, Michael. *Bison: Symbol of the American West.* Billings MT: Falcon Press, 1987.

Sandoz, Mari. *The Buffalo Hunters: The Story of the Hide Men.* New York: Hastings House Publishers, 1954.

Sauer, Carl O. "A Geographic Sketch of Early Man in America." *Geographic Review* 34, no. 4 (1944): 529–73.

Savory, Allan. *Holistic Resource Management.* Washington DC: Island Press, 1988.

Schama, Simon. *Landscape and Memory.* New York: Alfred A. Knopf, 1995.

Scott, Bob. "The Big Open." *Restoration & Management Notes* 10, no. 1 (summer 1992): 51–52.

Schilz, Thomas F., and Jodye L. D. Schilz. "Beads, Bangles, and Buffalo Robes: The Rise and Fall of the Indian Fur Trade along the Missouri and Des Moines Rivers, 1700–1820." *The Annals of Iowa* 49, nos. 1–2 (summer/fall 1987): 5–25.

Schullery, Paul. "Buffalo Jones and the Bison Herd in Yellowstone: Another Look." *Montana: The Magazine of Western History*, summer 1979, 40–51.

———. *Searching for Yellowstone: The Ecology and Wonder of the Last Wilderness.* New York: Houghton Mifflin, 1997.

———. "Yellowstone's Ecological Holocaust." *Montana: The Magazine of Western History*, autumn 1997, 16–33.

7genfund.org. http://www.7genfund.org.

Seton, Ernest Thompson. "The American Bison or Buffalo Bison Americanus (Gamelin, 1788)." Scribner's Magazine 40, no. 4 (October 1906), 384–405.

Shaw, James H. "How Many Bison Originally Populated Western Rangelands?" Rangelands 17, no. 5 (October 1995): 148–50.

Shaw, James H. and Mary Meagher. "Bison." In Ecology and Management of Large Mammals in North America, edited by S. Damarais and P. R. Krausman, 447–66. Newark NJ: Prentice-Hall, 1999.

Shay, C. Thomas. "Late Prehistoric Bison and Deer Use in the Eastern Prairie-Forest Border." Plains Anthropologist 23, no. 82, booklet 2 (November 1978): 194–212.

Sherow, James E. "Workings of the Geodialectic: High Plains Indians and their Horses in the Region of the Arkansas River Valley, 1800–1870." Environmental History Review 16, no. 2 (summer 1992): 61–84.

Shoemaker, Nancy. American Indian Population Recovery in the Twentieth Century. Albuquerque: University of New Mexico Press, 1999.

Singer, Francis J., ed. Effects of Grazing by Wild Ungulates in Yellowstone National Park. Technical Report: NPS/NRYELL/NRTR96–01. Denver: NPS, Natural Resource Information Division, 1996.

"A Site to See." Nature Conservancy, July/August 2000, 36.

Skinner, Morris F., and Ove C. Kaisen. "The Fossil Bison of Alaska and Preliminary Revision of the Genus." Bulletin of the American Museum of Natural History 89, no. 3 (1947): 131–242.

Smith, Dean Howard. "The Issue of Compatibility between Cultural Integrity and Economic Development Among Native American Tribes." American Indian Culture and Research Journal 18, no. 2 (1994): 177–205.

Smith, Douglas L., David Mech, Mary Meagher, and Wendy Clark. "Wolf-Bison Interactions in Yellowstone National Park." Journal of Mammalogy 81, no. 4 (November 2000): 1128–35.

Smith, Vic. "Roping Buffalo Calves." Recreation (May 1896): 365–66.

Smits, David D. "The Frontier Army and the Destruction of the Buffalo: 1865–1883." Western Historical Quarterly (autumn 1994): 312–38.

Soper, Dewey J. "History, Range, and Home Life of the Northern Bison." Ecological Monographs 11, no. 4 (October 1941): 349–412.

Speer, Roberta. "Bison Remains from the Rex Rodgers Site." Plains Anthropologist 23, no. 82, booklet 2 (November 1978): 113–27.

Spence, Mark David. Dispossessing the Wilderness: Indian Removal and the Making of the National Parks. New York: Oxford University Press, 1999.

Speth, John D. Bison Kills and Bone Counts: Decision Making by Ancient Hunters. Chicago: University of Chicago Press, 1983.

Spielmann, Katherine A. "Late Prehistoric Exchange between the Southwest and Southern Plains." Plains Anthropologist 28, no. 102, booklet 1 (November 1983): 257–72.

Standing Bear, Luther. Land of the Spotted Eagle. Boston: Houghton Mifflin, 1933.

Stanford, Dennis. "Bison Kill by Ice Age Hunters." National Geographic, January 1979, 114–22.

Stolzenburg, William. "Good Cow, Bad Cow: A Two-Headed Question over Cattle on the Range." *Nature Conservancy* (July/August 2000): 12–19.

Strong, W. D. "The Plains Culture in Light of Archaeology." *American Anthropologist* 35, no. 2 (April–June 1933), 271–87.

Surtees, Robert J. "Canadian Indian Policies." In *History of Indian-White Relations*, edited by Wilcomb E. Washburn, 81–95. Vol. 4 of *Handbook of North American Indians*, edited by William C. Sturdevant. 20 vols. Washington DC: Smithsonian Institution, 1988.

———. "Canadian Indian Treaties." In *History of Indian-White Relations*, edited by Wilcomb E. Washburn, 202–10. Vol. 4 of *Handbook of North American Indians*, edited by William C. Sturdevant. 20 vols. Washington DC: Smithsonian Institution, 1988.

Szaz, Margaret Connell, and Carmelita S. Ryan. "American Indian Education." In *History of Indian-White Relations*, edited by Wilcomb E. Washburn, 284–300. Vol. 4 of *Handbook of North American Indians*, edited by William C. Sturdevant. 20 vols. Washington DC: Smithsonian Institution, 1988.

"Tatanka Studies 2nd Annual Summer Institute." *Buffalo Tracks*, June 2000, 6.

"The Buffalo: The Waste of Animal Life on the Plains and How to Correct It." *Forest and Stream*, 22 January 1874, 376.

Thomas, David Hurst. *Exploring Ancient America: An Archaeological Guide*. New York: Routledge, 1999.

Thompson, Larry (Yankton Sioux). Survey correspondence with the author, 19 June 2000.

Thorne, E. Tom, Mary Meagher, and Robert Hillman. "Brucellosis in Free-Ranging Bison: Three Perspectives." In *The Greater Yellowstone Ecosystem: Redefining America's Wilderness*, 275–87. New Haven: Yale University Press, 1991.

Thwaites, Reuben Gold, ed. *The Original Journals of the Lewis and Clark Expedition*. Vol. 4. New York: Dodd and Mead, 1904.

To Establish a Permanent National Bison Range. Senate Executive Document, No. 467. 60th Congress, 1st sess., vol. 2. Washington DC: Government Printing Office, 1908.

Tough, Frank. "Indian Economic Behavior Exchange and Profits in Northern Manitoba during the Decline of the Monopoly, 1870–1930." *Journal of Historical Geography* 16, no. 4 (1990): 385–401.

Tuan, Yi-Fu. "Thought and Landscape: The Eye and the Mind's Eye." In *The Interpretation of Ordinary Landscapes: Geographical Essays*, edited by D. W. Meinig, 89–102. New York: Oxford University Press, 1979.

Two Eagle, Leonard (Rosebud Sioux). Telephone interview by author, 21 January 2003.

U.S. Fish and Wildlife Service, "Congressman Denny Rehberg, U.S. Fish and Wildlife Service, and the Confederated Salish and Kootenai Tribes Announce Reopening of Public Comment Period for National Bison Range Complex Draft Annual

Funding Agreement" (news release), 13 October 2004, http://mountain-prairie
.fws.gov/cskt-fws-negotiation/

Utley, Robert M. *The Indian Frontier of the American West 1846–1890*. 1984. Reprint, Albuquerque: University of New Mexico Press, 1993.

———. "Indian-United States Military Situation, 1848–1891." In *History of Indian-White
Relations*, edited by Wilcomb E. Washburn, 163–82. Vol. 4 of *Handbook of North
American Indians*, edited by William C. Sturdevant. 20 vols. Washington DC:
Smithsonian Institution, 1988.

Valandra, Edward. *Lakota Buffalo Theology: Implications for Buffalo Reintroduction into the Great
Plains*. Unpublished master's thesis, University of Colorado, Boulder, 1993.

Van Putten, Mark. "Restoring an Important Part of America's Heritage." *National Wildlife*, April/May 1997, 19.

VanStone, James W. "Hunters, Herders, Trappers, and Fishermen." In *Crossroads of Con-
tinents: Cultures of Siberia and Alaska*, edited by William W. Fitzugh and Aron
Crowell, 173–83. Washington DC: Smithsonian Institution Press, 1988.

Van Vuren, Dirk. "Bison West of the Rocky Mountains: An Alternative Explanation."
Northwest Science 61, no. 12 (1987): 65–69.

Van Zyll de Jong, C. G. "A Systematic Study of Recent Bison, with Particular Consideration of the Wood Bison (*Bison bison athabascae* Rhoads 1898)." In *Publications
in Natural Sciences, No. 6*, 1–57. Ottawa, Ontario: National Museum of Natural
Science/National Museums of Canada, 1986.

Vecsey, Christopher, and Robert W. Venables, eds. *American Indian Environments: Ecological Issues in Native American History*. Syracuse NY: Syracuse University Press,
1980.

Voorhies, Michael. "Hooves and Horns: The Coming of the Bison." *Nebraska History* 75,
no. 1 (spring 1994): 75–79.

Waggoner, Van, and Mike Hinkes. "Summer and Fall Browse Utilization by an Alaskan
Bison Herd." *Journal of Wildlife Management* 50, no. 2 (1986): 322–24.

Wagner, Fred, Ronald Foresta, R. Bruce Gill, Dale R. McCullough, Michael R. Pelton,
William F. Porter, and Hal Salwasser. *Wildlife Policies in the U.S. National Parks*.
Washington DC: Island Press, 1995.

Walker, E. "The Seasonal Nature of Post-Altithermal Communal Bison Procurement
on the Northwestern Plains." *Na'pao: A Saskatchewan Anthropology Journal* 4,
no. 2 (April 1974): 1–6.

Waller, David. "Friendly Fire: When Environmentalists Dehumanize American Indians."
American Indian Culture and Research Journal 20, no. 2 (1996): 107–26.

Wallerstein, Immanuel. *The Modern World System*. 3 vols. New York: Academic Press,
1974–1989.

Wapato, Tim. "Executive Director's Corner." *Buffalo Tracks*, October 1999, 2–3.

"War on the Range" (video). *A & E Investigative Reports*. Produced by Bill Curtis. New
York: Arts & Entertainment Television Network, 2000.

Warren, Edward R. "Altitudinal Limits of Bison." *Journal of Mammalogy* 8, no. 1:
60–61.

Webster, Donovan. "Welcome to Turner Country." *Audubon: Magazine of the National Audubon Society*, January–February 1999, 48–56.

Wedel, Waldo. *Central Plains Prehistory: Holocene Environments and Culture Change in the Republican River Basin*. Lincoln: University of Nebraska Press, 1986.

———. *Prehistoric Man on the Great Plains*. Norman: University of Oklahoma Press, 1961.

"Welcome." In *Wood Buffalo National Park Tales 1999*, 2. Ottawa, Ontario: Parks Canada, 1999.

West, Elliott. *The Contested Plains: Indians, Goldseekers, and the Rush to Colorado*. Lawrence: University Press of Kansas, 1998.

———. *The Way to the West: Essays on the Central Plains*. Albuquerque: University of New Mexico Press, 1995.

Westerly, Suzanne. "Thoughts of Bison Roaming and Free over the Land." *Canku Ota (Many Paths)*, online newsletter. http://www.turtletrack.org/Issues02/C002232002/CO_02232002_Bison (accessed 21 November 2002).

Wheat, Joe Ben. "A Paleo-Indian Bison Kill." *Scientific American*, January 1967, 44–52.

Whelan, Mary K. "Dakota Indian Economics and the Nineteenth Century Fur Trade." *Ethnohistory* 40, no. 2 (spring 1993): 247.

"Where the Buffalo Roam: The Exhibition." Collaborative historical display of Yellowstone National Park and the Buffalo Bill Historical Center. Viewed by author, 26 June 1999. Canyon Village, Yellowstone National Park, Wyoming.

White, Richard. "American Indians and the Environment." *Environmental Review* 9, no. 2 (summer 1985): 101–3.

———. "Indian Peoples and the Natural World: Asking the Right Questions." In *Rethinking American Indian History*, edited by Donald Fixico, 87–100. Albuquerque: University of New Mexico Press, 1997.

———. *"It's Your Misfortune and None of My Own": A History of the American West*. Norman: University of Oklahoma Press, 1991.

———. "Native Americans and the Environment." In *Scholars and the Indian Experience: Critical Reviews of Recent Writing in the Social Sciences*, edited by W. R. Swagerty, 179–204. Bloomington: Indiana University Press, 1984.

———. *The Roots of Dependency: Subsistence, Environment, and Social Change among the Choctaws, Pawnees, and Navajos*. Lincoln: University of Nebraska Press, 1983.

Whittey, Annie. "Ways of Seeing: Restoration and the Perception of Landscape." *Restoration & Management Notes* 15, no. 1 (summer 1997): 67–73.

Whittlesey, Lee H. "Cows All over the Place: The Historic Setting for the Transmission of Brucellosis to Yellowstone Bison by Domestic Cattle." *Wyoming Annals* 66, no. 4 (winter 1994–1995): 42–57.

Wildrockies.org. http://www.wildrockies.organization/bison.

Williams, John. "Field Visit to the Ute Indian Tribe." *Buffalo Tracks*, June 2000, 10.

Willman, Tony. "Funding Proposal Deadline Draws Near." *Buffalo Tracks*, June 2000, 11.

————. "Surplus Bison Proposals for ITBC Member Tribes." *Buffalo Tracks*, June 2000, 11.

Wilson, Angela Cavendar. "American Indian History or Non-Indian Perceptions of American Indian History?." *American Indian Quarterly* 20, no. 1 (winter 1996): 3–5.

————. "Power of the Spoken Word: Native Oral Traditions in American Indian History." In *Rethinking American Indian History*, edited by Donald Fixico, 101–16. Albuquerque: University of New Mexico Press, 1997.

Wilson, Elijah Nicholas. *The White Indian Boy; The Story of Uncle Nick Among the Shoshones*, revised and edited by Howard R. Driggs. Yonkers-on-Hudson NY: World Book, 1919.

Wilson, Michael. "Archaeological Kill Site Populations and the Holocene Evolution of the Genus Bison." *Plains Anthropologist* 23, no. 82, booklet 2 (November 1978): 9–22.

————. "Bison in Alberta: Paleontology, Evolution, and Relationships with Humans." In *Buffalo*, edited by John Foster, Dick Harrison, and I. S. MacLaren, 1–18. Edmonton: University of Alberta Press, 1992.

————. "Problems in the Speciation of American Fossil Bison." In *Post-Pleistocene Man and His Environment*, edited by R. G. Forbis, L. B. Davis, O. A. Christensen, and G. Fedirchuk, 178–99. Calgary, Alberta: Student's Press/University of Calgary, 1969.

Wissler, Clark. "The Influence of the Horse in the Development of Plains Culture." *American Anthropologist* 16, no. 1 (January–March 1914): 1–25.

Wobeser, Gary. "Disease in Northern Bison: What to Do?: A Personal Perspective." In *Buffalo*, edited by John Foster, Dick Harrison, and I. S. MacLaren, 179–88. Edmonton: University of Alberta Press, 1992.

Wright, R. Gerald. *Wildlife Research and Management in the National Parks*. Urbana: University of Illinois Press, 1992.

Wuerthner, George. "The Battle over Bison." *National Parks: The Magazine of the National Parks and Conservation Association*, November/December 1995, 39.

"Yellowstone Bison to Be Slaughtered," *National Parks: The Magazine of the National Parks and Conservation Association*, November/December 1996, 16, 18.

"Yellowstone Buffalo Slaughtered in Record Numbers." *National Parks: The Magazine of the National Parks and Conservation Association*, March/April 1997, 12, 14, 16.

Yellowstone Buffalo Wild and Free. Boulder CO: NWF; Rapid City SD: ITBC, 1999.

Yochim, Michael J. "Aboriginal Overkill Overstated: Errors in Charles Kay's Hypothesis." *Human Nature* 12, no. 2: 141–67.

Zontek, Ken. "Hunt, Capture, Raise, and Increase: The People Who Saved the Bison." *Great Plains Quarterly* 15, no. 2 (spring 1995): 133–49.

————. *Sacred Symbiosis: The Native American Effort to Restore the Buffalo Nation*. PhD diss., University of Idaho, 2003.

————. *Saving the Bison: The Story of Samuel Walking Coyote*. Master's thesis, New Mexico State University, 1993.

Index